D1832016

PUBLIC POLICY AND ADMINISTRATION

B. Venkatappiah 1907-1997

PUBLIC POLICY AND ADMINISTRATION

Formulation, Implementation and Evaluation

Editors

Ramesh Kumar Tiwari
Aasha Kapur Mehta

INDIAN INSTITUTE OF PUBLIC ADMINISTRATION

GYAN

Public Policy and Administration : Formulation, Implementation and Evaluation

© Indian Institute of Public Administration, New Delhi

ISBN : 978-81-212-1149-9

All rights reserved. No part of this book may be reproduced in any manner without written permission

Published in 2012 in India by
Gyan Publishing House
23, Main Ansari Road, Daryaganj,
New Delhi - 110002
Phones : 23282060, 23261060
Fax : (011) 23285914
E-mail: books@gyanbooks.com
website: gyanbooks.com

Laser Type Setting : Rajender Vashist, Delhi
Printed at : Chawla Offset Press, Delhi

This book is dedicated with gratitude
to the memory of
Shri B. Venkatappiah
1907-1997
Member, Planning Commission
1967-1971
Chairman, Standing Committee
Indian Institute of Public Administration
1974-1989

Contents

PART II
Some Selected Writings of B. Venkatappiah

Foreword

Policy advice has always been an important aspect of Indian thinking in administration and governance. Kautilya's *Arthasastra* is acknowledged as a manual of statecraft designed to guide the ruler of a state along with those engaged in the governance of its people. *Arthasastra* gives detailed instructions on the control of the state, the organization of the economy, and the conduct of foreign policy. In contemporary India, the Directive Principles of State Policy are fundamental in the governance of the country. It is true that these provisions are not enforceable in a court of law. But it is the duty of the State to direct its policy towards securing of a more humane society. Increasing public awareness and judicial activism have provided considerable push in that direction.

The definition of public policy, simply put, is to choose a course of action. This depends to a large extent on the understanding of the problem. It is in this context, since the thirties, an effort has been made to integrate knowledge in social sciences. This has been essential because of the complexity of the problem(s) as well as the fact that the solution of a problem is not restricted to a particular academic discipline. It was this kind of orientation which led to the emergence of public policy not only as an approach, but also as a subject in the social sciences.

Since the Second World War, in the west, many quantitative techniques like cost benefit analysis, operations research, systems analysis, etc. helped in solving complex industrial and military problems. However, it was realized that these quantitative techniques are not readily applicable to the complex societal situations. In human affairs, not only are these problems complex but also not very well defined. As a consequence, over a period of past more than 50 years there has been a constant endeavour to provide an approach to solve such complex problems as defy mechanistic solutions. The effort primarily made by Harold Lasswell and Yehezkel Dror as well as many others led to the emergence of policy sciences or policy analysis for its wider application in the social and economic field. Besides, policy analysis approach also provides and gives due attention to the problem of values in policy making.

We faced acute shortage of foodgrains in the mid sixties of the last century. Agricultural policy enunciated by the Government of India to increase food production is an example of the formulation of a successful policy. Shri C. Subramaniam who was Union Food and Agriculture Minister, has provided a graphic account of policy making in the agriculture sector of this period in his book *Hand of Destiny: The Green Revolution* (Vol. II). As analysed in this book, the Green Revolution was the result of a policy involving the introduction of new high yielding varieties, improved methods of cultivation, the use of chemical fertilizers and pesticides, provision of a guaranteed floor price, creation of foodgrain marketing organization - production of hybrid seeds, re-organization of agricultural research and educational programs and other factors. This book has also provided the processes involved in the formulation of the policy: defined the problem, prepared a framework of possible solutions, consultation with concerned ministries including the Planning Commission and its approval by the Cabinet. However, choosing the course of action was not as straight forward as there was conflict of interests and honest differing view points amongst ministries. The resolution of these conflicts has brought to surface the problems of inter-ministerial relationship in public policy making. The book also brought into the focus the role of the leadership in matters of larger social and economic considerations. The initiatives taken in the proposed agricultural policy needed moving away from the *status quo* and making some radical changes. As a result, there was as usual resistance to change.

In India, during the last three or four decades, a number of memoirs dealing with high policy questions have become available. The analysis of this literature not only will provide us problems and complexities relating to choosing a course of action, but also bring out realities of important decisions made at the high level.

In some developed countries, public policy as a discipline is growing at a very fast pace. This growth is a result of the application of public policy approach to problems in a large number of areas like: transport, health urbanization, defence, education, etc. This subject has a lot of potential on the one hand as well as on the other there is need of professionals who are capable of analyzing complex problems. This is possible when we have professionals who are capable of looking into the problems from the perspective of effectiveness, feasibility and efficiency taking into account the resources constraint. In India, for long it has been felt that there is a need to introduce teaching in public policy in the University system.

I am indeed happy that the Indian Institute of Public Administration (IIPA) is bringing as part of the Golden Jubilee series a publication devoted to public policy. It has been the endeavour in these publications to give emphasis to the frontier areas of public administration. This collection provides a number of useful articles published in the *Indian Journal of Public Administration* during 1955-2008. It combines not only theoretical aspects of public policy, but also policy evaluation and implementation, as well as policies covering preventive detention, wildlife conservation and population. I think this volume will serve a long-felt need. I congratulate Professor Ramesh Kumar Tiwari and Professor Aasha Kapur Mehta for providing an incisive overview of the public policy approach as well as summing up the basic themes of these essays. This volume is dedicated to the memory of Dr. B. Venkatappiah, who for long, in different capacities and manner, guided the IIPA. He would often draw attention to the importance of different aspects of the study of policy making and policy analysis.

T.N. Chaturvedi

Chairman, Indian Institute of Public Administration
Former Governor of Karnataka and Kerala

Preface

During the celebrations of the Silver Jubilee of the Indian Institute of Public Administration (IIPA) in 1980, a number of publications dealing with various facets of public administration were brought out. These publications had covered issues like district administration, union-state relations, panchayati raj, administrative theory, comparative public administration, local institutions, urban development, police administration, planning and its implementation, public enterprises, administrative reforms, development administration, and local government. Publications on Public Policy, and on Organizational and Procedural Issues in Government were planned, but could not be brought out. Shri T.N. Chaturvedi, Chairman, Indian Institute of Public Administration who was earlier the Series Editor of the IIPA Silver Jubilee volumes subsequently suggested to bring these publications at the time when we were commemorating IIPA's Golden Jubilee. Somehow the book got delayed and is only seeing the light of day now. Like the earlier publications, this volume is also a collection of articles originally published in the *Indian Journal of Public Administration* covering different facets of public policy and combining theoretical aspects along with some issues of public policy in the Indian context.

To my mind Public Policy involves decisions to determine certain goals of government regarding some sector or sub sector or the polity-society as a whole, reviewing and selecting alternative strategies and measures or policy instruments to achieve the stated policy goals or objectives, formally announcing the policy- its goals and proposed measures to achieve them, and taking steps to implement the policy, followed by evaluating policy impacts to determine whether modifications are required in the said policy. The papers included in this book look at policy making, policy evaluation, policy implementation, policy failure etc. on the theoretical plane, and the cases of policies on preventive detention, on population, and on wild life conservation in the Indian context are examples of policies in practice. Also examined is the evolution of Policy Sciences.

This book is dedicated to the memory of Shri Burra Venkatappiah, former Chairman, Standing Committee, IIPA (1974-1989). It is a fitting tribute to Shri Venkatappiah as in his professional career he dealt with numerous policy questions. We are indeed grateful to Shri T.N. Chaturvedi, Chairman, IIPA for contributing a tribute to the memory of Shri Burra Venkatappiah. As part of the tribute we have also included three articles written by Shri Venkatappiah.

We are thankful to Professors Ramesh Kumar Tiwari and Aasha Kapur Mehta for putting together this compilation.

Dr. Rakesh Hooja
Director,
Indian Institute of Public Administration

Acknowledgements

Our thanks to Dr. Dolly Chakrabarty, formerly Executive Director, Rural Electrification Corporation Ltd., New Delhi for providing us information on Shri Venkatappiah. We are also thankful to Gurmeet Kaur, Librarian, Council for Social Development, New Delhi, who brought to our notice some of the studies conducted by Shri Venkatappiah. Our thanks to Sunita Gulati and Narendra Kumar of IIPA's Library for providing necessary information and references on this volume. Our thanks to Sunil Dutt, Assistant Editor and other members of IIPA's Publication Section for their effort in ensuring the quality of this publication. We are also thankful to Gulshan Arora, Senior Personal Secretary to the Director IIPA for providing some important information regarding this volume.

We are grateful to Ajay Singh Verma who handled matters relating to this publication, with lot of efficiency. We are also thankful to Taruna Rani, Sanjay Pratap and Sonia Bajaj for providing all necessary support in the library and computer related work.

Ramesh Kumar Tiwari
Aasha Kapur Mehta

Shri B. Venkatappiah : A Tribute

T.N. CHATURVEDI*

Shri Burra Venkatappiah during the course of his public service career in the I.C.S. and subsequently occupied important positions in the field of public finance: Finance Secretary, Government of Bombay, Deputy Governor, Reserve Bank of India and Chairman, State Bank of India. He was a Member of the Planning Commission, 1967-1971 and Chairman, Rural Electrification Corporation, 1969-1979. He was closely associated as a Member with a number of committees: All India Rural Credit Survey Committee, Taxation Enquiry Committee, Foodgrains Policy Committee, etc. He had also served as Chairman: Fertilizer Credit Committee, All India Rural Credit Review Committee, Central Excise Review Committee and the First Administrative Reforms Commission (ARC), Study Team on Financial Administration, etc. Throughout his public service career, rural development and the development of the small farmers, marginal farmers and landless labourers and cooperatives remained as areas of interest to him.

As a member of the All India Rural Credit Survey (1954), Shri Venkatappiah was to a large extent responsible for developing an integrated scheme of rural credit and setting up of institutions such as the Central Warehousing Corporation, State Warehousing Corporations, and the National Cooperative Development Corporation and Warehousing Board (now known as National Cooperative Development Corporation). Shri Venkatappiah, as Chairman of the All India Rural Credit Review Committee (1969), made some important recommendations of far reaching importance and significance: the Rural Electrification Corporation, Agricultural Credit Board (in the Reserve Bank of India) and Small Farmers Development Agency and Marginal Farmers Development Agency.

*Chairman, Indian Institute of Public Administration, Former Governor of Karnataka and Kerala

This report also provided a policy frame within which rural credit can be delivered effectively and efficiently. As a member of the Planning Commission, he was responsible for the inclusion of these recommendations in the Fourth Five Year Plan.

As Chairman, Rural Electrification Corporation 1969-1979, he outlined a development approach comprising of the objectives and priorities, methodologies regarding formulation and implementation, adaptability of concepts, financial viability, efficiency of administration, levels of decision-making; and machinery of coordination, etc. This approach played a significant role in making the Rural Electrification Corporation as one of the successful enterprises contributing to rural prosperity.

Besides, he particularly emphasized the need of coordination in the small farmers' and marginal farmers' agencies. He was of the view that the existing level of coordination is not enough. He was in favour of more detailed coordination and effort to ensure optimum results. He was also of the view that the success of rural projects, need systemized data, prompt feed back and periodic evaluation. He advocated close monitoring and efficient inspection of all on-going development programmes.

He was particularly keen for the proper study of development projects to get feedback and periodic evaluation. For this purpose, he was of the view that both management and the management institutes can be of much help. He always felt that research studies can contribute a better perspective on the problems. He himself conducted few studies dealing with the feasibility of forming small rural electric cooperatives in Andhra Pradesh.

As Chairman of the ARC Study Team on Financial Administration, he advocated the need to "readjust and re-model financial procedures, institutions and concepts" with the changing requirements of the federal set-up. The report suggested a re-organization of the Finance Commission and the establishment of a National Development Bank. He was of the view that re-organized Finance Commission should be entrusted with the total task of having a view of both plan and non-plan expenditure both of Union and the states and making the requisite allocation to the states; devise criteria for allocating un-tied plan assistance among various states; review the achievements of each state etc. The key objective of the National Development Bank was to provide central loans to states for financing identifiable projects in fields like power, transport, irrigation and manufacture etc.

Wit and humour was an integral part of his personality. Most of his observations or even criticism on sensitive issues he always conveyed the truth coupled with his usual sense of humour. While the lesson would be driven home there would not be any hurt feelings. In the context of poverty, he observed "Rural poverty throughout one millennium is bad enough; but rural poverty over two or more millennia seems to be national carelessness – if not callousness – on a stupendous scale." Similarly, while paying a tribute to the genius of the Indian cultivator he pointed out that though "For, over the years, he has adapted himself competently to the defaults of the monsoon, but not yet completely to the delays of Government."

Shri Venkatappiah was closely associated with a number of academic institutions. He was Executive Chairman of the Council for Social Development, New Delhi. It is his sagacious guidance which enabled the Council of Social Development to undertake many unexplored areas in the field for research and action. He was Chairman, Standing Committee of the IIPA, 1974-1989 and its Vice President, 1977-1990 and 1991-1995. In this association of more than twenty years, he was instrumental in facilitating many vital decisions to be taken up like setting up of specialized centres of study, Advanced Professional Programme in Public Administration, etc. which have proved to be important for the growth and development of the Institute.

The Chairmen of the IIPA like Shri Jagjivan Ram and later on Shri S.B. Chavan greatly depended on him during the deliberations of the Executive Council for his views or advice before taking any decision. His views were always constructive. In view of his wide and varied experience in public life, he could find a solution to any difficulty. He was very persuasive and would convince others by his logical presentation of his views. He would have very effective interaction, with members of the faculty and the staff. He had a fund of anecdotes with which he would regale, enlighten or win over anybody who had any doubt in any matter. Even a brief discussion with him was a learning experience. I worked with him closely and for long. I remember fondly his wise counsel, support and sagacious guidance. I take this opportunity to pay my respectful tribute to the memory of Dr. B. Venkatappiah.

Introduction

RAMESH KUMAR TIWARI AND AASHA KAPUR MEHTA

The origin of public policy and policy advice can be traced to the beginning of civilization. However, the development of contemporary policy sciences as a distinct field of study basically occurred just over half a century ago. What is public policy? The term public policy "comprises political decisions for implementing programs to achieve societal goals" that represent a "consensus of values."[1] It comprises a "plan of action" in which the objectives tell us what we want to achieve through policy and who will be affected by it. Since resources are limited, choices need to be made and the objectives reflect these choices. Public policy "plans or programs outline the process or the necessary steps to achieve the policy objectives."[2]

Public policy is necessarily about the people who are to be served by the nation. It must therefore be based on an understanding and analysis of their existing situation and that of groups and sub-groups within the aggregate (whether based on gender or caste or tribe or class) so that existing deviations and anomalies can be addressed and gaps between the optimal or desirable and actual are bridged.

The term 'Policy Sciences' is primarily associated with Harold Lasswell and Yehezkel Dror, who are considered major figures in this field. Lerner and Lasswell's book entitled "The Policy Sciences: Recent Developments in Scope and Method"[3] is considered the first systematic effort towards a field of inquiry dealing with problems related to policy making. In his lead chapter entitled "The Policy Orientation" Lasswell defines "the focus of policy science as an amalgamation of law, political science, sociology and psychology into one overarching discipline dealing with the general subject of public choice and decision making."[4] He draws attention to the fact that "A policy orientation has been developing that cuts across the existing specializations. The orientation is two fold. In part it is directed toward the policy process, and in part toward the intelligence needs of policy."[5] He argues that policy sciences include methods by which the policy process is investigated, the results of the study of policy as well as findings of the disciplines making the most important contributions to the intelligence needs of the time. The basic emphasis of the policy approach is "upon the fundamental problems of man in society."[6] This approach also calls for clarification of the value goals involved in policy. Lasswell placed considerable emphasis in policy sciences on the "development of knowledge pertinent to the fuller realization of human dignity."[7] He referred to this aspect as the evolution of the "policy sciences of democracy".

The growth and development of operations research and systems analysis had an important bearing on the development of policy sciences/policy analysis. The main object of inquiry of operations research was on the tactical problems faced during the Second World War, followed by the strategic problems investigated by the defence analysts during the 1950s and 1960s. Further developments in the framework of operations research through the inclusion of decision theory and micro-economic logic of choice extended its scope and areas of application and the refined framework is now called systems analysis. This is a systematic attempt to provide decision-makers with a full, accurate, and meaningful summary of the information relevant to clearly defined issues and alternatives. This systematic attempt brings to bear on the problem, many relevant disciplines and does it in an integrated manner. The list includes planning, economics, political science, and other social sciences, applied mathematics and the physical sciences. Systems analysis has been applied to the following categories of problems: management of operations; choice of tactical alternatives; design and development of weapon systems; and determination of major policy alternatives.

While systems analysis is one of the foundations of policy sciences, contemporary systems analysis is unable to analyse complex social issues, due to the following reasons:

- It focuses on proposing preferable policies, neglecting the institutional context and does not take into account political needs.
- It has difficulties in dealing with "irrational" phenomena and situations of primary uncertainty cannot be handled by it.
- It does not take into account the basic value issue.
- Invention of radically new alternatives is beyond the scope of systems analysis.

- It requires significant quantification of the main relevant variables.[8]

Hence, so as to overcome these inabilities, Yehezkel Dror, in his book "Public Policy Making Re-examined,"[9] advocated the study of policy making as a major topic of social sciences. To this end, he evaluated contemporary public policy making as well as identified its weaknesses. He suggested that a separate field of study is essential for the development of policy knowledge, and advocated that the central theme of policy sciences will be public policy making which will include knowledge on both policy issues and policy making itself. It will be an inter-disciplinary field and the methodologies of policy sciences must be adjusted to its particular needs. He also pointed out that value and fact would be inter-related in policy sciences.

A few years later, Yehezkel Dror propounded a new analytical approach, "policy analysis"[10] which adds the following components to the basic framework of systems analysis:

- Investigation into underlying values and assumptions
- Political variables including political feasibility analysis
- Consideration of broader and more complex issues.
- Emphasis on policy alternative innovation.[11]

As a result of these developments, the term policy analysis is viewed as a process of producing knowledge of policy processes, "Policy analysis is an applied social science discipline, which uses multiple methods of inquiry to generate policy relevant information and argument which can assist policy makers in solving policy problems".[12] The objectives of policy analysis extend beyond the production of "facts". Policy analysis seeks to produce information about values and preferable courses of action and also includes policy evaluation as well as policy recommendations.

There were related developments in the field of public policy through the inclusion of topics of implementation and evaluation in the broad framework of policy analysis. As a result, the scope of public policy has expanded. Policy and programme evaluation became very important in developmental programmes, as they provide information about performance. In India, with the commencement of planning, evaluation of developmental programmes became an important activity in the overall context of the planning process and a separate unit called Programme Evaluation Organization (PEO) was created in the Planning Commission to carry out evaluation studies. However, the evaluation of development programmes was not confined only to the PEO but was also conducted by academics at research institutions as well as in the universities. It is also important to emphasize that programme evaluation research in India made important contributions to public policy making.

Since, the early 1960s the failure to implement plans became a subject of major concern in the developing countries. "We in the Planning Commission and others concerned have grown more experienced and more expert in planning. I fear we are not quite so expert at implementation as at planning...."[13] The problem of implementation of the plans of the developing countries has been analyzed by Waterston who observed: "The gradual awakening to the realization that plans do not implement themselves, and that specific measures must be adopted if plans are to be converted from expressions of aspiration to programme of action, has led to considerable discussion about what role the planner should play in implementation."[14] Concern was also voiced elsewhere. Simultaneously in the United States in the late 1960s impetus to the study of policy implementation came from the failures of the programmes established during the 'war on poverty' period. This resulted in a number of in-depth case studies focusing on implementation of policies in the area of education, urban planning, civil rights, environmental quality and health services. As a result of the research on policy implementation, attention was also directed to conceptualize the implementation process. It was asserted that: "The problems of implementation are profound in Western and non-Western nations alike: they are generic to complex organizations."[15]

Since the early 1970s, there has been rapid growth of public policy education in the United States. Institutions imparting education in public policy were set-up in almost all the universities in the United States. However, the same thrust was not given in a large number of developed and developing countries. But of late, in a number of developed and in some developing countries, public policy programmes have been established as a part of the university system, both for teaching and training of civil servants. The latest example is the London School of Economics and the University of Singapore, which gives Master's degree in public policy to the civil servants as well as freshers.

The contemporary trends in the teaching of public policy have been standardized in almost all the major and well-known teaching programmes. Firstly, this programme consists of a core curriculum, which includes quantitative analysis, the political, legal and institutional environment of policy formulation and implementation, economic theory with special reference to microeconomics, behavioural and non-behavioural decision making and implementation strategies. There has also been an emphasis on ethics and values. There is an integrated approach to problem analysis with a focus on inter-disciplinary learning. In a Symposium on the Future of the Policy Sciences, organized by the Journal of the Society for the Policy Sciences, it was advocated that "the policy sciences must become institutionalized along the lines of a conventional discipline."[16]

The Indian Context

In the Indian context, the Report of the Administrative Reforms Commission on the 'Machinery of the Government of India and its Procedures of Work' in the late 1960s recommended the setting up of a "Policy Advisory Committee" to consider all the important issues of long-term policy and to inject thinking from different areas of specialization into problem-solving. However, nothing much was done in this direction. In the planning process, D.R. Gadgil in the mid 1960's observed that "The outstanding feature of the 'planned' Indian economy has also been the total absence of a policy frame."[17] Besides, there has been inability "to undertake sustained analysis of policy at different levels."[18] As a consequence, there was very little policy analysis, as the term is understood, in the literature on public policy. It has also been noticed that there is a good deal of regulatory framework in the system, based not on economic analysis, but on legal issues.

For the civil servants, short-term training programmes on public policy were organized at the Indian Institute of Public Administration, New Delhi since the early 1970s. A module on public policy, has also been a part of the Advanced Professional Programme in Public Administration, since its inception in 1974. The Government of India, also sponsored a one-week compulsory training programme in public policy for the IAS officers in a number of training institutions, during 1985 to 1988. The Indian Institute of Management, Bangalore, and Management Development Institute, Gurgaon have been organizing a post-graduate programme in public policy and management for the middle level civil servants over last few years. The focus of the programme is to equip the civil servants with the concepts, skills and techniques in public policy formulation and the strategic management of public systems. The emphasis of the programme is inter-disciplinary learning and competence in a specific area of public policy.

This manuscript brings together some selected significant and influential articles that have been published in the Indian Journal of Public Administration on a range of facets of public policy. The salient observations in these selected contributions to the literature on public policy are briefly outlined below.

In "Dynamics of Public Policy", S.N. Sadasivan tells us that a policy is a "public need that assumes importance" or "the mirror that reflects the working of the mind of the government on the question for which it is enunciated." It is "an accommodation of wants and demands of many social groups" based on a "variety of circumstances, constraints and compulsions." He provides an overview of policy making under different systems of government. He gives a detailed outline of the policy-making system prevailing in the United States and that of Britain. He discusses the meaning of public policy within the broad framework of the democratic context and tells us that in a democracy, the mandate for a policy is always obtained from the legislature. He explains the making of public policy in the context of both political competence and organizational capability including the role of pressure groups. He points out that while pressure groups operate in all systems of government, in democracy they "often act in tandem with political parties to bend the course of public policies to their ends" and this is especially evident at the time of Budget formulation. Public opinion plays a critical role in the "making and execution of public policy" and can even unseat a government. Outlining the critical role of political adequacy and effective control, he draws attention to the persistent propaganda by vested interests against large ministries and more ministers in one department and the resultant disappearance of political adequacy. He argues that political adequacy must be accompanied by political competence and based on education, training and organizational ability for it to be effective.

In public policy making information system plays a very critical role. This is more important due to the technological development. He stresses the importance of participation and discussion at all executive and managerial tiers and consultation on a contemplated policy with eminent public men and leading members of the academic community capable of upholding independent views, and having courage to express their dissent. There is also a need for social analysis in the overall context of public policy.

The specialization of civil servants in public policy analysis is highly desirable. He has pleaded for a professional service as is available in the west to undertake in-depth studies to enlighten political leaders about the problems and the possible solutions. To enrich the quality of analysis and policy making, he suggested the inclusion of specialists in the government at the highest level. In India, there is a need not only for policy analysis, but also close monitoring, implementation and evaluation of programmes.

In his seminal paper entitled "The Fact-value Distinction as an Analytical Tool", V. Subramaniam draws attention to the element of choice in decision-making and the obligation to choose one thing to the exclusion of other things. While decision makers rarely make conscious use of the fact-value distinction, he argues that it can be used effectively by academics and examines its use as an analytical tool by relating it to probability and utility; the peculiar difficulties that blur the fact-value distinction in public administration; the specialist-administrator conflict and dialogue; and the use of management tools in decision-making. With reference to probability and utility, the author observes that they directly connect the fact-value pair to the process of choice.

Referring to the complications in decision-making in a democratic system, he points out that "probabilities about other people's values remain basically incalculable" and it is difficult for "any one body to decide about other people's values." As a consequence, even bodies like "Parliament or even cabinets, prove less and less adequate to cope up with the fast-increasing number of occasions for such decisions." Because of these factors, "the image of the average decision differs from society to society and organization to organization in the same society." Similarly, the fact-value distinction also helps to throw new light on the specialist - administrator controversy. Societies that place a premium on value-sensitivity rather than fact collection tend to favour the general administrator rather than the specialist. The generalist tends to dominate any administrative situation "where values are not assumed as settled and open", while the specialist dominates in the opposite case.

The fact-value distinction also plays an important role in organization theory. In this connection, earlier the network analysis, operations research, linear programming and computer simulation were treated as mere techniques, however, now these are regarded as important aids to decision-making. Besides, these concepts perform different functions in terms of providing policy alternatives; computer simulation formulates alternatives; linear programming helps evaluate several alternatives and network analysis helps in carrying out a decision effectively. It is rare for the majority of human decision-makers to make conscious use of fact-value distinction but academics can use it effectively as an analytical tool in decision-making.

V. Subramaniam's article "Dror on Policy Making" seeks to review and introduce the Indian reader to Dror's book 'Public Policy Making: Re-examined", which he describes as "the most important book on public policy making published in this century." To this end, he provides both an outline of the book, Dror's approach to analyzing, evaluating and improving public policy making as well as appreciation and criticism. He observes that the existing decision theory is narrow, sectoral and specialized and as a consequence does not help in the study of policy making.

Dror stresses the "low quality of public policy making in all countries and its continuous deterioration." Since knowledge is growing rapidly and policy makers are aware of only a small part of it and use an even smaller segment of this, there is "a wide gap between actual policy and policy possible in terms of available knowledge, and a still wider gap *vis-à-vis* the best policy in terms of existing knowledge; and the latter widens alarmingly fast as knowledge accumulates faster." Dror makes what Subramanian describes as alarmingly true criticisms, which include the use of case studies that are "unstructured, unanalytical, unoriented and not related to any theoretical or conceptual framework" that form the base of public policy making. Further, "theories of decision-making are highly developed in a narrow way, less developed in regard to collective organizational decisions and refuse to come to grips with the complex policy making process."

Subramaniam gives a comprehensive account of the most original contribution of Dror by providing a detailed account of the optimal model of public policy making. This model consists of three major stages: meta-policy making, policy making, and post policy making (each of which is sub-divided into several phases).

Meta-policy making, that is, policy making about policy making includes processing values, reality, problems, surveying, processing and developing resources, designing, evaluating and redesigning the policy-making system and determining policy making strategy. The (middle) stage of policy making itself involves sub-allocating resources to the various phases; establishing operational goals with some order of priority; establishing a set of other significant values; preparing a set of major alternative policies; preparing reliable predictions of the significant benefits and costs of the various alternatives; comparing the predicted benefits and costs of the various alternatives and identifying the best ones; and evaluating the benefits and costs of the 'best' alternatives and deciding whether they are good or not.

The post-policy making state is essentially one of execution, evaluation and feedback and consists of four stages, namely, motivating the implementation of the policy; executing the policy; evaluating policy making after the policy has been executed; and communication and feedback channels, connecting all phases. All three stages of meta-policy making, policy making and post-policy making are closely inter-connected by communication and feedback channels.

The major characteristics of the optimal model are: it is qualitative, not quantitative; it has both rational and extra-rational components.

In order to overcome the existing limitations against policy improvements, Dror suggests the need for "aggregation" of all the relevant material from different fields; encouragement of inter-disciplinary policy-oriented studies at a high level as well as establishment and pursuit of a definite "policy science." Dror also stresses the need for educating politicians into policy knowledge and also training civil servants in a rigorous manner in public policy making. He specifically advocates establishment of independent policy analysis organizations for this purpose.

In his paper on "The Paradox of Policy Science", Stephen Brooks presents an overview of the status of policy science up to the 1980s. More specifically Brooks discusses the usefulness of policy science as a method for grappling with social problems; reviews the argument that social science analysis is of very limited value as an approach to social problem solving; and that the policy science movement represents an attempt to escape from 'messy' politics; and examines the beginnings of an alternative approach to policy-making. Brooks provides a detailed account of the developments in policy science and the idea of policy science as a guide to public policy making. However, this idea has not gone unchallenged and a number of alternative roles have been suggested. Though sometimes based on legitimation through past precedent or ideology or conceptualization, "policy science can have an influence upon the political agenda through sensitising both decision-makers and the general population."

Brooks points out that it is difficult to make a choice in any problem without carefully going into the advantages and disadvantages of each course of action. It is true that policy analysis provides new approaches and insights, which enable policy makers to make better-informed choices. However, the analytical approach is only one, and not always the most appropriate, of the means of solving social problems. Among the many arguments presented by Lindblom and Cohen against the use of the policy analysis approach is its unacknowledged dependence on what they call "ordinary knowledge." They therefore suggest that the use of analytical and interactive approaches to social problem solving is more appropriate. On the other hand, Cohen and Weiss, argue that intensive research of a policy problem generally produces a picture of greater complexity rather than clarity. And Brooks demonstrates that policy science is only "the most recent manifestation of a long-standing tradition in American social science, *viz.,* the flight from 'messy' confrontational politics." Quoting Tribe, he notes that the analytical approach "structures in certain concerns while structuring out others."

Brooks provides an overview of the substantial body of criticism by Hughes, Scott, Shore, Lindblom, Cohen, Tribe and Horowitz that analytical approach to policy making has limitations of method and language. Besides, it is very difficult to resolve the question of value through analysis. As a result of these limitations of the policy approach Vickers and Jantsch suggested social regulation through cultural design while Lindblom and Cohen advocated interactive problem solving and gave much needed recognition to the 'art' of policy making. This essay by Brooks is an attempt "to establish an appropriate balance between the art and science of public policy making."

Implementation has not been accorded the importance that it deserves and S.R. Maheshwari's article on "Politics of Implementation: The Achilles' Heel of Public Administration" points out that the "evaluation of plans and programmes disclosed recurring weakness in implementation" and easily constitutes "a critical policy need across all levels of business of government." Stressing that "the field holds the key to successful implementation" he draws attention to the fact that while a policy or programme may be made in the secretariat, it is necessarily implemented in the field. Hence, the implementation process necessarily gets tied up with the dynamics of relationship between the headquarters and the field as well as between different agencies in the field.

In order to achieve effective and efficient implementation, a well-designed integrated plan of reform of headquarters – field relation is necessary. There is a need for a full appreciation of a particular field situation so as to help in making appropriate decisions. The field officers must be given adequate powers, tenure system needs to be strengthened, informal visits by officers from headquarters help to build rapport, training and conferences should be organized to build capacity, etc.

In the Indian context, to improve implementation, attention has to be given to the framework of policies and procedures as well as to the question whether the formulation of plans themselves need a major of re-orientation to narrow the gap between promise and performance. Implementers confront a large number of complex problems from the locally entrenched vested interests. Effective implementation depends to a large extent on the sustained political and administrative commitment and support. Some of the important factors of implementation failures are: paucity of staff, financial and infrastructural constraints, unrealistic targets; shortage of time; passive attitude of implementers; poor design of development programmes, etc. Administrative reform, in the broad sense of the term, must be carried out urgently to improve policy making and its implementation.

Arie Halachmi in his article on "The Use of Policy Evaluation in Public Making" discusses in detail the importance of evaluation in generating policy-related knowledge. He also describes the theoretical aspects of policy evaluation by stating that in policy evaluation organizational settings, procedures and the impact of programmes are linked in an empirically demonstrable manner. In the larger context, policy evaluation provides the benefits of learning from the past experience.

Halachmi also emphasizes that policy evaluation involves identification of indicators that will be used to determine what has been attained. From this perspective, policy evaluation is different from other modes of policy analysis. Policy evaluation is carried out after a decision is made and implemented, while other methods of policy analysis such as cost benefit analysis, etc. are used mostly before the decision is made to identify and help in the initial choice. Halachmi also points out that policy evaluation has become an integral part of all the phases of the policy making process. By and large, policy evaluation provides the policy maker with a direct reference to the substantive impact of a policy. Policy evaluation seeks to examine the advocacy of the impact and the way it was brought about. As such, it is intimately concerned with effectiveness. To prove effectiveness, the evaluation attempts to establish whether the policy is capable of bringing about the desired results; the alleged results are products of the specific characteristics of the policy; the policy is feasible for a given policy maker and his political environment etc. It has also been pointed out by Halachmi that policy evaluation is not a value free analysis.

"Analyses of Policy Failure: A Three Dimensional Framework" by Thomas B. Smith discusses the elements of success and failure of public policies. In doing so, he first examines the concept of policy success and policy failure. Smith has devised three major categories for policy success or failure. The first category is policy design. This criterion includes appropriate perspective based upon ideology and acceptable values. This dimension often leads to the clashes of values and interests thereby needing consensus and agreement. It has been advocated, that public policies, are also judged with regard to how they were formulated and how they fared during the implementation phase. The second aspect of policy failure deals with policy process. Examining the policy process can provide answers about the effort put into making the policy and it can also serve to explain policy achievement. Economic analysis with efficiency as the key criterion can be used to judge the failure of the policy. Besides, failure to achieve objectives can be an important cause of policy failure. A large number of factors are responsible for this failure such as the lack of capacity of implementing organizations; lack of direction, leadership or shortages of skilled personnel, discretionary behaviour of lower ranked implementers as well as deliberate distortions of the policy goals by the subordinates. Further, there are many policy failures if success is judged in terms of its stated objectives. He also observes that policies and policy processes are not static entities in an unchanging environment and to this extent any consideration of success and failure must take this into account.

In "Organization for Public Policy in Government", Ishwar Dayal examines the organizational demands of effective policy formulation in public administration. He reviews the processes involved in decision-making and public policy making. He explains that policy formulation is concerned with the objectives and determining the choice of action, while decision making refers to the process by which policy is determined. From this perspective both policy and decision-making are parts of administration. He explains Herbert Simon's suggestion of decision-making process, and the role of intelligence activity, the decision activity and the choice activity in the decision process. Some unique characteristics of the Government system that impinge upon the decision processes are: environment of the decision situation; the political system and the distance between the decision-maker and the people. The intelligence and design activities require innovation, analysis of data and the evaluation of alternatives while the choice activity requires experience, maturity and administrative judgment. To conduct these activities, there is a need for support system in an organization. The support system must provide data analysis, interpretation and innovative solutions both to recurring and new issues.

After examining activities involved in decision-making, Ishwar Dayal examines the nature of supportive systems required for policy-making functions of the Government. He observes that policy level tasks consist of three related areas: review of effectiveness of policy; design activity for new policy decisions; and anticipatory policy. All major decisions are Cabinet decisions and taken collectively by the Government as a whole. The Ministry and the Cabinet must have an organization to design decision-choice. In public administration, there is emphasis on creating differentiated systems and de-emphasis on integrated systems. The Cabinet Secretary, by virtue of his position as Secretary to the Cabinet and its committees, performs the integrating role. The supportive system, at the top level, must have the capability of building the base for relevant data analysis and design activities in decision-making.

The article on "Administrative Culture Desiderata" by Yehezkel Dror deals with the requirements needed to change administrative culture in the Indian context. Dror discusses nine main components, needed to bring out administrative cultural transformation in the higher level of Indian public administration. These components are: total devotion to tasks; a strong sense of commitment; tactical handling of issues; professionalism; costs consciousness; science and technology friendly; open mind; i.e. "active search for new inputs and readiness to change one's mind"; innovativeness and public entrepreneurship and policy sophistication.

Policy sophistication according to Dror is the most important necessity of administrative culture. Dror identifies "tolerance of uncertainty, risk-taking readiness, willingness to subordinate; misleading intuitions to disciplined decision protocols and many other features of "uncertainty sophistication as a main facet of policy sophistication." He also observes that in a country like India, it is necessary to have a wider perspective on the problems. This involves deeper knowledge of history and society; "careful consideration of appropriate policy scales"; generate alternative development strategies, etc. He recommends subject policy R&D organizations for this purpose. He pleads that to develop policy sophistication, it is necessary to be receptive to "such ways of policy thinking".

In his article on "The policy of Preventive Detention" David H. Bayley seeks to examine the experience of modern India with preventive detention from 1950 to 1963. The legislation of preventive detention was passed originally just after one month of India's Constitution. The Preventive Detention Act provides that upon order of the central and the state governments persons may be detained for periods ranging up to one year if the Government is satisfied that they are likely to engage in behaviour which would be "pre-judicial to any of the following interests: the defence of India, the relations of India with foreign powers, the security of India, the security of the state, the maintenance of public order, or the maintenance of supplies and services essential to the community." However, the author points out that the phrases are in general vague.

Preventive Detention is important because it sets aside many elements in ordinary judicial procedure. This Act provides some safeguards: a person detained under the Act must be informed of the grounds for his detention within five days; the detention order must be notified as well as it may be; and detention order must be notified by their own subordinate officers within 12 days of the date of the detention; and lastly, all detention orders must be examined by a quasi-judicial body known as Advisory Board, within 30 days to 10 weeks of the date of detention. Advisory Boards are appointed by both the central and state governments, and must be composed of three members who are qualified to be appointed as judges of a High Court. The Advisory Board procedure provides to the Act trained legal minds, while retaining the informality and speed of an administrative tribunal.

The operation of Preventive Detention Act has shown that the Advisory Boards have not been unwilling to challenge the judgment of Government as to the potential threat posed by the activities of detenus. The Advisory Board provides the only opportunity of *ex-parte* judgment to be brought to bear upon the reasoning of the executive authority. Bayley observes that in the working of the Preventive Detention Act during 1950-1963, the working of Advisory Boards despite all the information provided, the critical questions still remain un-answered, namely how independent of executive persuasion are the Advisory Boards? The author concludes that the Act has been administered in a generally careful and circumspect manner, by both central and state governments. In conclusion Bayley points out that there is every likelihood of the Preventive Detention Act of 1950 becoming a permanent part "of the legal arsenal of Government for controlling incipient threats to law and order".

Uday C. Desai's article on "Professional Policy Making: The Case of Indian Population Policy" examines the process of population policy making in India. This paper addresses the following questions: how has the population problem been defined and by whom; how and why has the definition changed over the years; underlying assumptions and self-interests; the problem of implementation etc. The author has given a historical account of the perception of the population policy by the Congress party, before independence and delineated how the problem was viewed in the Five Year Plans. Within this broad perspective, a solution to the population problem was implicitly assumed to be found through health care. As a matter of fact, the population problem was transformed into a family planning problem. There was little public debate on the issue and the policy response was basically in tune with the moralistic and traditional thinking. In this effort, some international agencies and American foundations became very active. In the second half of the 1960s the pattern of policy making continued with some shifts in emphasis. During this period, Department of Family Planning at the Union Government level was established and a new Cabinet Committee was set up to provide policy guidance. The policy process remained dominated by the professional experts and bureaucrats mostly in health and demography. The top level leadership had no clear idea as to what policy responses are needed to solve it. There was little or no participation on the part of public or local institutions in this policy. There was a considerable amount of political apathy, bureaucratic competition and meddling of foreign experts. The author advocates the need for more detailed and extensive empirical studies of the policy making process in India in general and the population policy process in particular.

W.A. Rodgers's paper on "Policy Issues in Wildlife Conservation" begins by providing reasons that wildlife is the most complex of natural resources. He is of the view that management of any resource cannot take place in a vacuum. The very act of management suggests the need for a goal. However, in the context of wildlife conservation the overall goals are not stated, or if they are stated, they are vague, non-definable and highly generalized. As a consequence, there is always a handicap in integrating wildlife into other resource management strategies.

The major management issues in wildlife conservation arise mostly because of human – animal protected area conflict. We have not been able to develop strategies to cope up with this problem. In these conflict situations, administration needs more explicit policy guidelines. This conflict arises due to the shortage of land for people and for forest and wildlife. Most of our national parks and sanctuaries have villages within their boundaries. As a result of this, most wildlife populations are in the proximity of villages. This conflict will grow as human population increases. There is also conflict between the resource managers and the administration, and the resource users, and environmentalists. Many of these conflicts reflect gaps in land-use policies. There is a need to coordinate such issues for effective national level, land use planning for wildlife and a long-term pragmatic wildlife conservation policy, which ensures, a network of protected areas covering the full range of India's bio-diversity. These areas have to be large. Besides, planning must be a rational compromise between biological needs and people's requirements. For people living near wildlife areas, he suggests eco-development, which includes micro-dams, agro-forestry, tree farming, improved husbandry, sericulture, poultry and cottage industry as components of economic development.

Notes

1. Cochran, Charles L. and Malone, Eloise F. 2007, Public Policy: Perspectives and Choices, Viva Books, New Delhi. p. 5-6.
2. *ibid*, p. 6.
3. Lerner Daniel and Lasswell, Harold D. 1951, *The Policy Sciences – Recent Developments in Scope and Method,* Stanford University Press, Stanford, California.
4. Rodney Muth, Rodney, Finley, Mary M. and Muth, Marcia F.1990, (ed.) *Harold D. Lasswell: An Annotated Bibliography*, New Haven Press, New Haven New York. p. 21.
5. Lerner and Lasswell, op.cit., p. 3.
6. *ibid*, p.8.
7. *ibid*, p. 10.
8. Majone, G. 1981. Systems Analysis: A Generic Approach, in *Handbook of Systems Analysis: Overview of Uses, Procedures, Applications and Practices*, edited by Hugh J. Miser & Edward S. Quade, John Wiley & Sons, New York, p. 49.

9. Yehezkel, Dror, 1968, *Public Policymaking Reexamined*, Chandler Publishing Company, Pennsylvania.
10. Yehezkel, Dror, 1971, Design for Policy Sciences, American Elsevier, New York, pp. 55-62.
11. *ibid*, pp. 56-57.
12. William N. Dunn, 1981, Public Policy Analysis: An Introduction, Prentice Hall, New Jersey, p. 36.
13. Quoted in *Jawaharlal Nehru and Public Administration*, Indian Institute of Public Administration, New Delhi, 1975, pp. 97-98.
14. Waterston, A, 1965, *Development Planning: Lessons of Experience*, John Hopkins, Baltimore, p. 375.
15. Van Meter D.S. and Van Horn, C.E, 1975, The Policy Implementation Process: A Conceptual Framework, *Administration and Society*, Vol. 13, No. 4, p. 452.
16. Pielke Jr. Roger A, 2004, What Future for the Policy Sciences? *Policy Sciences*, Vol. 37, No. 3 and 4, p. 222.
17. Gadgil, D.R, 1967, Planning Without a Policy Frame, *Economic and Political Weekly*, Vol. 2, No.1, p. 253.
18. Mozoomdar, Ajit, 1996, The Rise and Decline of Development Planning in India, In *Development Policy and Administration*, edited by Kuldeep Mathur, Sage Publications, New Delhi, p. 55.

List of Contributors

Arie Halachmi, Faculty of Social Sciences, Tel-Aviv University, Israel.

David Bayley, Senior Research Fellow, American Institute of Indian Studies.

Ishwar Dayal, Formerly Director, Indian Institute of Public Administration, New Delhi.

S.N. Sadasivan, Formerly Professor of Public Administration, Indian Institute of Public Administration, New Delhi.

S.R. Maheshwari, Formerly Professor of Political Science and Public Administration, Indian Institute of Public Administration, New Delhi.

Stephen Brooks, Department of Political Science, Carleton University, Ottawa, Canada.

Thomas B.N. Smith, Senior Lecturer, Department of Political Science, The National University of Singapore, Singapore.

Uday C. Desai, Member of the Faculty, Administrative Staff College of India, Hyderabad.

V. Subramanian, Professor of Public Administration, University of Zambia, Lusaka.

W.A. Rodgers, Wildlife Expert, FAO Project, Wildlife Institute of India, Dehradun.

Yehezjek Dror, Professor of Policy Analysis (on leave from Hebrew University of Jerusalem), European Institute of Public Administration, Maastricht, The Netherlands.

PART I

Some Selected Articles on Public Policy and Administration from Indian Journal of Public Administration

1

Dynamics of Public Policy*

S.N. SADASIVAN

An administrative sphere where bureaucratic flamboyance seeks its fabulous expression and to establish fantastic claims is that of policy. It is normally set apart as an exclusive preserve, where pretensions and predilections seek their fusion to make impressions and images for its relatively stagnant but privileged occupants. The function of policy formulation is often over emphasised, intelligibly enough to add to bureaucratic self-importance and indispensability.

Policy as a rule is the product of extensive study and intensive analysis of available data and information and therefore, it is apparently believed to be a superior function confined to the top echelons of administration. The execution of policy demands at times greater imagination, resourcefulness, alertness, perseverance, diligence and sagacity than its formulation. By force of tradition and administrative practice, the making of policy however continues to remain in a separate province and the skill and knowledge necessary for it are still believed to be a distinct or superior quality.

Policy under Different Systems of Government

Different systems of government have different ways of formulation of policy. In the USA, the political process and the operation of the theory of separation of powers locate the seat of policy formulation in the legislature but in the United Kingdom policy by and large originates in individual ministries under the collective guardianship of the cabinet. Between the presidential system of government and the parliamentary form, there is an obvious divergence in its making. In institutional arrangements, alignment of personnel and procedure, policy formulation under the presidential system has its own singularity.

The democratic pattern of administration with which the presidential system is identified from the beginning, relies on specialisation for shaping policies and the advisers to the president are generally experts in their respective fields. On the other hand, policy-making in the parliamentary system which is the specimen of the aristocratic model of administration, is mainly handled by the generalist administrator or professional civil servant, whose stock is the experience that he has accumulated over a period of time.

As the leader of the nation and the head of the executive the president has the right to make his own administrative policies but they should converge on those of the legislature to forge mutual accord on the relevant national issues. More pointedly, than in the presidential system, the election manifesto which is largely a transcription of the programme of the political party that has come to power, is the basic source of policies in the parliamentary government. A party competing in election, on its securing power, converts its programme into specific public policies and seeks to implement them using mainly the governmental machinery and resources. In other words, it is in the mill of the government, the party programme is processed into public policies.

The programme of the party is the product of its ideology and policy which in reality is born out of the party manifesto, is political in character and content but administrative in its form or make-up. Although not all policies have to draw their substance from the election programme, policy formulation in the parliamentary system is the exclusive function of the political leadership at the helm of the government and the role of the civil servant in it is limited to that of a chief adviser.

In the USA due to the ideological proximity and almost identical approaches to national issues between the two national parties, the Democrats and the Republicans, alteration of power hardly leads to any material alteration in major policies the continuation or re-formulation of which has become basically the business of a body of professional experts. Irrespective of his party affiliation, the president at times will have to limit his choice of a policy to the alternatives developed by them. However, a president with a strong personality, conceptual skill and an impressive ideational image may be successful in effecting modifications or changes in a policy, or fixing the time for its implementation or finally abandoning it. Despite the supremacy of the president as their chief architect, policies are largely the impersonal creations of working groups of various specialisations, under the cover of his official authority.

A minister in the parliamentary system has more time and less pressure of work to get directly and actively involved in the making of policies in the area of his portfolio, ofcourse with due regard to the manifesto of his party. The cabinet as a whole is an ideal discussion forum to make the policy of each minister more rational or realistic.

What is Policy?

From the political perspective, a policy is a public need assuming importance and as far as possible, appropriately assessed for its actual fulfillment. It involves an identified and definite public problem and the preparation of the state to meet it in a particular style. It conceives a line of action to achieve a certain result, negative or positive, or discloses a resolve to refrain from acting on a specific issue or matter. The want of a comprehensive definition does not act as an inhibition to identify policy as an instrument that reveals or the mirror that reflects the working of the mind of the government on the question for which it is enunciated. It is a coordination of ideas, views and opinions, an accommodation or wants and demands of many social groups and a reconciliation of plurality of interests. An intricate and sophisticated function, policy-making has to take into consideration a variety of circumstances, constraints and compulsions. Policy is essentially a fabricated contrivance adopting a course of action to achieve some socially significant ends.

Continuing Policy

The first ever public policy has been the establishment of order the meaning and means of which might have been varying for various states. Once the social order is realized, public order or public peace or tranquility has gained ascendancy as a basic and continuing policy and no state can exist without its firm implementation. Every policy takes the form of legislation and the policy of public order has been under constant re-examination and expansion covering grounds or bringing within new spheres which were outside its original purview.

The industrial and technological revolution and faster economic growth it brought about, have made society complex and its working more intricate and impersonal than before, and the state has to add to its legal armoury more laws to meet situations which it did not contemplate in the past. A continuing policy for its own effectiveness, should be subject to periodic examination especially in the light of new developments. Once a policy of permanent or long-term nature has taken its deep roots, there may be scope for its modification, but it will be too arduous a job to change it completely unless ideologically the government assumes an entirely new complexion. Even, so, a fundamental departure from such a policy will be normally impossible as it is *mutatis mutandis* essential for the survival of the state.

Mandate

In a democracy, the mandate to a policy is always obtained from the legislature and from the people described as the political or popular sovereign. It is also determined and legitimised to a large extent by the environment. Besides vindicating the need of policy, the ecological setting exerts a great influence on its making. It is the environment in the light of the adopted ideology of the state that influences the making of the upliftment of the down-trodden or the abolition of untouchability as a social policy. Similarly, environment contributes to the effectiveness of policy and equally provokes resistance against it.

Public Opinion

An integral part of the environmental test is public opinion which should be kept in favour of public policy. Public opinion is an amorphous mass and it has to be properly educated, articulated and directed to the specific objects of policy. The importance of the institution of public opinion to the making and execution of public policy is indeed enormous. A strong and sensitive public opinion over a controversial policy can at times be adequate to **unseat** a government in the parliamentary system.

Personal Philosophy and Propaganda

In democracy, parties are the principal extra-constitutional instrumentalities to inform public opinion of their ideological goals and secure the support of the people to realise them. Inside the government, party ideology undergoes a subtle transformation to be the personal philosophy of the minister to convince the professional administrators advising him of the social and national significance and purposefulness of his policies. In the realm of policy, propaganda and publicity should be judiciously and objectively employed upto a point without exploiting the elements of indoctrination and regimentation inherent in them. Public feelings and sentiments on matters of policy may be given the respect they deserve or the considerations they merit.

Although a minister may make claim for credit for a policy exclusively to himself, it is in fact the creation of a number of persons from the lowest rung to the highest of the hierarchy whose knowledge, attitude, skills, efforts, creative talents and influence contribute in a large measure to its quality and practicability.

Political Sense of Civil Servant

As policy is political, the civil servant engaged in designing it, should have a fair, if not complete, understanding of the political forces, the sources of their ideological inspirations and their activities so that he may have a realistic perspective and ability for sound judgement. A professional administrator who lacks adequate political sense is likely to be a victim of ambivalence, bereft of tact, strategy and resilience indispensable for negotiations and dealings, and perhaps, even a trader in troubles. His political sense however should not be stretched as to divorce his promise from performance even though there may at times be a yawning gap between the two, due to reasons inexplicable or force of circumstances.

Political Adequacy

The most important factor, or the sine qua non of policy is political adequacy and political competency. Government departments not only multiplied over the years, but also considerably expanded in territorial jurisdiction, activities and personnel, and they cannot be individually controlled by a single minister. If rationalisation of a sprawling department to the extent of reconstituting it into a few new ones is not feasible, it must be reorganised without impairing organisational unity into distinct sub systems, each under a minister.

Unless the political authority percolates deep into each department, neither the Minster can exercise effective control over it, nor can he be made fully responsible for its overall management nor would he find himself comfortably placed to give directions to it for definite social objectives. The practice of a single minister heading the department for complying with the principle of unity of command should necessarily yield to the idea of collective political management in obedience to the doctrine of unity. The vested interests have been carrying on persistent propaganda and adroitly offering hidden resistance against large ministries and more ministers in one department which have to some extent seriously affected the cause of democracy and forced the issue of political adequacy to disappear into the welter of oblivion.

The concept of political adequacy demands that there should be enough number of ministers in a department so that democratic counsel and direction will be available to the bureaucratic managers at all levels, greater ministerial presence may serve as a check against monopolising and misusing the government machinery by a few bureaucratic masterminds, political vigilance will be effective against manoeuvres and intrigues of officials that lend scope for widespread corruption. It will be impossible for a single minister heading a huge department to perceive its numerous ways of behaviour or apply political correctives against bureaucratic deviations, departures and high handedness which are invariably resented by the people.

If the minister as a representative of the people, answerable to the cabinet and responsible to the legislature, does not exercise political supervision over his department and adopt promptly appropriate steps to regulate the bureaucratic ways, he may lose his raison d'etre in relation to his foremost function, the making of policy. In fact, his authority for policy is a significant portion of his authority for overall management of his department which is derived from the mandate of the people.

Political Competency

The concept of political adequacy is efficacious only when it is a concomitant of political competency which is found in a political personality when his innate qualities are enriched by education, training and other techniques of self improvement. Policy leadership should have refreshingly new ideas, democratic temperament, progressive outlook, ideological faith, environmental circumspection, insight into problems, zeal for reform, critical thinking, intellectual strength, respect for dissent and literary flair. These attributes in a policy leader are bound to win for him the respect and confidence of the bureaucratic community which especially in the developing countries has no little concealed contempt for the tribe of politicians. To him will be intelligible, the strange, misleading, deceptive or clandestine behaviour of the more ingenious bureaucrats in varying organisational contexts. His courage and resolve to keep the bureaucratic functioning within the bounds of law and the framework of administrative discipline are the gifts of his social power which he built by dedicated and selfless service to society.

Organisational Capability

As political adequacy, so organisational sufficiency too is important to policy-making. Planning of policy without examining the organisational capabilities for its execution, will be a grevious error. Both general and particular organisational capacities are relevant to policy-making. The determination of organisatonal adequacy in terms of policy, takes into consideration the nature and structure of the organisation, its objectives, its personnel and their expertise, resources, its ability for future growth and expansion and a host of similar associate factors. The move to carry out overambitious policies particularly in the fields of defence, international relations and economy has proved to be disastrous for not a few countries. In the Arab states the rapid and massive inflow of foreign money has impelled to evolve glamorous expenditure policies that welcome a profound and tremendous thrust of high technology consumer civilisation devoid of its creative base and sustaining wherewithal.

Pressure Groups

Of the forces of policy environment, the most prominent are the pressure groups. Active in many spheres particularly social and economic, pressure groups compete with one another in their own chosen styles, to influence the making of policy in order to promote their interests. Organised pressure groups operate in all systems of government but in democracy they have already assumed the form of an institution and they often act in tandem with political parties to bend the course of public policies to their ends.

Modern democratic state committed to a new socio-economic order, in its monolithic style resorts to raising taxes and spending in astronomical figures and therefore, a governmental zone where the pressure groups concentrate to press their claims, is that of the budget. Budget is indeed the core and pivot of government policies and every citizen of means has to make his contributions to it with the expectation that he would in turn be benefited by it. As clientele, pressure groups equally seek to impress upon their views and wants on the respective departments either to get them accommodated in relevant policies or to get the policies suitably modified. As pressure groups vie with one another for favour from the government, the administrator at the policy-making level has to reconcile their differences, adjudicating upon their claims with patience, tact, sound arguments and understanding. Most pressure groups are amenable to reason and they are capable of articulating the amorphous and scattered public need into precise and presentable demands. Almost every policy that emerges from the executive precincts is obviously influenced by pressure groups and the policy personnel should learn to live and deal with them in a democracy.

Legislative Role

While in the presidential system national policies are generally outlined by the legislature, in the cabinet form of government, parliament in practice is the national forum that by discussion and debate probes into the strength and weakness of the policy of an individual minister. As the minister belongs to the party that commands the majority in parliament, it is not normally difficult for him to obtain legislative approval for his policy. Very rarely he may have to carry out modifications to it in the light of the inhouse discussion and debate. Nevertheless, its structure will remain by and large the same until it proves to be highly unpopular at the level of its implementation.

Subordinate Policy

A policy is a decision selected as usual from a range of alternatives and requires several sub policies or sequential decisions at the descending levels for its execution. Every administrator may have to follow a subordinate policy conducive to his environment or compatible with the conditions obtaining in the field for the success of the main policy. A policy planned or adopted by the legislature has to be again moulded in the administration to make it structurally sound from the perspective of its implementation. Each sub-policy or administrative decision meant to facilitate its success may contain one or more programmes.

Every policy decision should be taken after a careful study of the likely reactions of the public affected by it. The conditions prevailing in the field are known better to the officials there than those who occupy the vertex of the hierarchy in the far away capital, and the art of decentralisation will be the ideal or highly desirable step to be relied upon in making subordinate policies. Nevertheless, the ancillary policy should not be allowed to affect the character of and should at any time be clearly distinguishable from the principal policy. If elimination of illiteracy or poverty is adopted as a national policy, the vastness and diversity of the country necessitate a number of regional and local policies for achieving its ends. The main policy is largely composite and cannot properly be structured unless adequate information and data and data-based conclusions are available.

Participation

The making and implementation of policy tend to aver that it is not confined to a selected few at the top but a dynamic business into which all levels of a department are drawn in. Participation is one of the prime methods of rationalising the process of policy formulation. Discussion and deliberation on a policy at each executive or managerial tier will be an ideal exercise to enrich its content, sharpen its focus, make its objective more socially significant and enhance the feasibility of its execution. Involvement of every level will serve as an efficacious device to bring forth the obfuscated sources of energies, shy or unobstrusive talents and neglected skills for the purposes of policy.

Departmental Interdependence

As the government is a unity, none of its departments can plan a policy independently and without due regard to the position and objectives of other departments. For a viable and workable defence policy, the concerned department has to be in constant consultation with other departments such as the finance, external affairs, home and industry. The organisational context of policy formulation presupposes departmental conflicts may pose hindrances to the function of policy-making and a bold, enterprising and imaginative leadership should endeavour to resolve them into mutual cooperation and harmonious interaction. Policy in government is relative and not exclusive and the organisational context necessary for its making is invariably collective.

Role of Intellectuals

In administration where statesmanship is considered to be an essential asset. Profound learning, dialectical skill, analytical ability, ideational strength and foresight can immeasurably contribute to improve the quality of policy in content, structure and results. Association of intellectuals in the evolution of public policy is not followed as a consciously adopted step in all democracies but in the USA they make some indirect contribution to its making.

Discussion on public policies which was widely held in India especially by political parties in the British days, is hardly now considered a worthwhile proposition in universities, colleges and other academic institutions where intellectual standards have already fallen to intrigues, invading politics and maladministration. The industrious middle classes who have taken keen interest in public policy in the past, in the new economic prosperity and the snobbish style of living, have become victims of smugness and complacency bordering on passivity as far as debate on public policy is concerned.

Except perhaps of the extreme of left orientation, political parties in general do not find public policy a stimulating topic nor its analysis appealing to the people unless it is of controversial nature. They fail to appreciate that analysis or criticism of a complex topic such as policy, even if it is not controversial, serves the cause of apprising and educating the public in one of the cardinal functions of the government. The weaknesses or lacunae of public policy can easily be overcome, if public leaders are encouraged to make searching investigation into it with a view to make critical evaluations of its merits and demerits.

The exclusion of the intellectual from the precincts of policy is largely attributable to the dislike of him traditionally nurtured by the bureaucrat. The English East India Company triumphed over the three other rival European concerns because it had the obvious advantage of having outstanding intellectuals among its managers both for evolving superior policies and their masterly execution. In the absence of the intellectual element and element of imagination, a policy is bound to suffer from inflexibility and may tend to be unreal, and deny itself the popular appeal or support which otherwise it should have.

Consultation on a contemplated policy with eminent public men and leading members of the academic community capable of upholding independent views, and having courage to express their dissent, may provide a new cultural setting for policy-making. If a member of the Indian Administrative Service who has never before been acquainted with the working of the complex economic system of the country, is fit to hold the position of finance secretary or whose knowledge of the elaborate and increasingly complex defence organisation is not more than that of an average journalist, has the competence to hold the reins of its control, an intellectual can make the mark of distinction not only as a consultant on policy but as its formulator.

Information System

The backbone of policy planning is a well-equipped and up-to-date information system, prompt and efficient in service. The type of information system an organisation should possess, will depend upon the nature and purpose of its policy. If the defence department of a developing country has to follow a procurement policy, it should have at its disposal full information pertaining to the parallel ranges of sophisticated weaponry manufactured and made available for sale by advanced countries, their actual cost, relative operational efficiency and a host of other technical details. It also requires information and data on a wide variety of internal matters such as its economic base, scientific and technological advancement and domestic and indigenous expertise and capabilities available.

With the progress of cybernetics, information storage has assumed vast dimensions. There is however no purpose in accumulating information unless it is put to use for specific objectives especially policies. Extensive storage of information should be matched or justified by extensive use, and essential information should be immediately and easily available. The Government of Kerala found itself in an inexplicable predicament when it had no essential information at its disposal in the fifties and even in the early sixties over such a vital issue as the diversion of its waters to Tamil Nadu resorted to by the British under the mysterious concept of paramountcy.

A policy-making office cannot afford to sit idle or be complacent or over-confident as far as collection of information is concerned but should be constantly on the move to build up its information stock which should be periodically reviewed to determine its sufficiency. A costly, elaborate and high technology-oriented information system may be necessary for a complex and extraordinarily large and fast growing organisation engaged in manufacturing sophisticated technological products but its requirement seems to be doubtful for a developing country which has not fully mastered the art of manually operated information system. Each government should evolve an information system that suits its objectives, drafting talents and skills within its reach. The first essential however is a scientifically designed filing system with distinct classification, direct cross links, and quick reference indicators. All round simplicity is the hallmark of an efficient information system the character of which will be determined by the type of organisation which it has to serve.

Social Analysis

As policy is directed to social ends, the formulating department should have a complete understanding of society, its various facets and its strange ways. A formidably heterogeneous and bewilderingly caste-ridden society as India, has hardly been subjected to a searching analysis, primarily because intellectual poverty and academic dishonesty have combined to conceal its real nature in order that its stagnancy could continue to be advantageous to traditionalist and orthodox elements.

The Marxian tools of analysis which might have been efficacious to expose the capitalist society at a particular stage of its development, are highly inadequate to unravel the true characteristics of the caste society. An extremely complex and rigid feudal order that has proved to be viable through the ages, caste is a subtle fusion of the four main spheres of human life—social, economic, political and religious, in their hierarchic forms. Each hierarchic phase extends justification to the other and all together dexterously fuse themselves into a solid pyramidal structure determining the position and place of its every member in every sector of human activity on the basis for his birth and avocation arbitrarily assigned to some members of the social group in which he is forcibly included. All efforts so far made to change society by half-hearted economic measures have been unsuccessful and the expectation that economic changes in themselves would be sufficient to effect progressive transformation of society is totally belied.

The maker of a public policy aimed at social change should have at his disposal a variety of intensive social analyses, so that he could achieve its ends by realistically planning its content and course. To a government committed to the creation of a new society through radical or progressive policies, social analysis is of immeasurable importance.

Case Study

An instrument that is of substantial assistance in the area of policy is case study which is now used sparingly for training purposes. A case study conforming to its norms, explains a real life administrative situation involving a course of sequential events which in their cumulative effect have attained some finality in fulfilling or relevant to certain objectives. It is a store of experiences of persons, procedures and tangles of red-tape and it enables to locate administrative bottlenecks and to understand bureaucratic behaviour and people's reactions under parallel or similar circumstances. The past policies reduced into case studies, will easily serve as models, guides or lessons for the future framing and implementation of policies on comparable questions of sociopolitical importance. However, no department has made an earnest endeavour towards building up a rich stock of cases which is a valuable asset for the formation of policies.

Special Agency: Specialisation of Civil Servant

The quality or merit in general of a policy is by and large a contribution of the personnel engaged in its formulation. Every department should have a specialized agency entrusted with the task of planning its policies. A generalist administrator should be allowed to devote the last ten years of his career to acquire the expertise necessary for handling policy jobs. The practice of shifting, particularly at the state level, senior civil servants from post to post with every change of minister or ministry or to suit political convenience hardly enables them to gain the requisite knowledge and experience relevant to the purposes of policy. Very few however among them have the will, aptitude and studiousness to equip them with the specialisation by self-educating process as they in general tend to mystify themselves by equating power with knowledge or mistake their positions and trappings as the infallible sources of the ingredients of policies.

As a career administrator ascends in the hierarchy, inhibition to imbibe ideas particularly from theoretical provenances increases and consequently his capacity for conceptualising his experience or specific administrative ends dwindles or undergoes a constant erosion. The political leadership should inspire the civil servant to take in a well provided atmosphere to the course of continuous specialisation conducive to policy-making.

Expertise of Political Leaders

In the west almost every political party has regularly recruited and trained personnel constituting a permanent service to undertake research and study on every leading national issue in order to apprise and advise its top leaders who are the products of well-known seats of knowledge and have already achieved a fair measure of expertise in one field or another.

On the other hand, in India even national parties have no well constituted professional service to undertake indepth studies with the object of enlightening their leaders most of whom however have little academic distinction or intellectual contribution to claim. The mind of an average Indian political leader is largely influenced by his empirical knowledge, caste loyalty and ideological fancies and it has hardly undergone any training to perceive administrative realities or acquire superior conceptual skills.

The political executive responsible for the function of policy should have definite intellectual and scholastic attainment over that of the civil servants in immediate advisory position. The frequent dialogue between the policy adviser and the policy maker is likely to create a mutual understanding or a common perspective on the question of the values that should go into the making of policies and the priorities they must be accorded. While the civil servants proffering advice should have full knowledge of the organisational capabilities, the minister must have a clear vision into society to identify the differing social forces in order to bring them to agreement.

Limits of Civil Servant

In the parliamentary system, administrative traditions and constitutional norms unequivocally uphold that as far as the function of policy is concerned the civil servant should confine himself to and be satisfied with the advisory role. As democracy was implanted into India, some intransigent administrators especially in the states had developed a derisive attitude to lesser political leaders and a cavalierly tendency to outshine or overreach the ministers who lacked a high level of westernised education or were taken as novices in administration. The tussle which demarcated an area of mutual distrust and vilification continued for some years till political authority established its definite supremacy to the discomfiture of the supercilious and swaggering bureaucrats.

Lateral Entry

In a world fast changing on account of the rapid and many sided expansion of knowledge, no minister or no service can be the repository of all learning that is required for the purposes of policy which has ostensibly become a multi-disciplinary venture. A civil servant who is a victim of recurring transfers at ridiculously short intervals, cannot claim to possess an experience that enables him to develop superior abilities which are not found in a serious student of government.

The political leadership should not therefore hesitate to bring in its policy enclave lateral entrants having suitable specialisation and managerial abilities.

Scope of Discussion

Policy should always be the outcome of team work, and discussion for reconciling the differing views is an indispensable aid for its rationalisation. As policy is a choice from a range of varying alternatives, only dialectical initiative can make such a choice free from error. In India the command culture prevailing over the entire process of administration of the armed forces, has facilitated the supersession of collective wisdom and diversity of views by one dimensional vision which in its singularity has to be taken often by the defence ministry for structuring its policy. A regular interaction between high ranking service officers, top civilians and experts will provide in all probability a durable base for working out a consensus useful enough to evolve policies of high professional merit. Discussion has little scope even in other departments where ad hocism has been the rule for decision-making and whose heads are resigned to stand by the doctrine of obedience and the infallibility of seniority.

The recurring instability in the states for reasons disowned by political theory, and the capricious reshuffle of cabinet at the Centre begun from the close of the sixties, have denied ministers a tenure necessary to acquire or demonstrate the competence as policy makers with regard to their specific portfolios. Nonetheless, the Communist Party of India (Marxist) has been an exception, and due to its mass base that enables it to capture power in West Bengal and Kerala, it could keep the same portfolios for the same leaders which assured some continuity in favour of stable policies. The personality of the individual ministers assessed in terms of their strength within the party, individual following, regional base and equation with the prime minister and personal philosophy, is noticeably waned since the close of the sixties and departmental policies virtually ceased to have their distinct imprints.

Policy Study

Public policy in brief is how and when a government should do what in or for society which it is responsible to control, and consequently, policy study involves evolution, execution and analysis of policy. Policy study is the organised and systematic investigation into the making of policy and policy execution with a view to make a scientific analysis of both. The analysis should be so cogent as to determine their strength and weaknesses, deficiencies and excesses. Every public policy is a government decision aimed at solving a problem of society and it calls for a collective approach to its planning and implementation. Policy analysis is aimed at improving the quality of policy and enhancing its implementability and it encompasses a wide range of studies and research activities. It shifts and blends various items of information and fuses them with the findings of research taking into account several organisational situations, to form a proper design of policy.

Analysis is to make the policy as a course of action as real and rational as possible and not alone intended to predict its consequences but also to predicate the circumstances which it has to envisage. It cannot exhaustively deal with all ecological factors but will indicate in a given environment how opportunities and resources should be organised and efforts directed by the officials entrusted with the policy to realise its ends either in groups or as individuals.

Policy conceives certain specific goals, and the line of action it contemplates is purpose oriented. The first stage of policy formulation is to identify a problem which should become the subject of the policy and in the second, alternatives to deal with the problem are developed. A specific and more suitable alternative is adopted in the third stage and is made into an enactment or resolution. In the fourth stage the content of the policy is carried out and its success or failure or its total effect or impact may be evaluated in the fifth stage.

Policy Analysis

A policy may be the product of an analysis or formed without resorting to analytical process in the conventional bureaucratic style in which case its success will be determined by its implementation and the method of implementation. A policy adopted after analysis reduces the risks and chances of error, examines the various constraints in needed detail and seeks ways and means to eliminate obstructions and enlists the cooperation of the people. A post-implementation analysis of a public policy evolved in the traditional manner, makes available valuable lessons and valid experiences for future.

Policy analysis applies itself to reveal the structure of a problem, to monitoring and forecasting, to the necessary evaluations and to the making of recommendations and assessing the perceptible influences. Without active cooperation from all levels of bureaucracy, the affected citizens, public opinion agencies, political parties and clientele of the concerned departments, public policy analysis will be a difficult task to perform.

Limitations/Shortcomings

Originated in the USA in the sixties, policy analysis is not invariably adopted as an unfaltering or ideal tool to make political choices and in recent years, it has been on several occasions bypassed in that country itself. Adopted under the pressures of the economic discipline, policy analysis largely engages the normative research methodology, more so its empirical components and in spite of its occasional claims of success, it has been unsuccessful in convincing the politicians in power of the need of their adhering to it. Political pragmatism and intuition and bureaucratic predilections and predisposition often undermine its validity and relevance. In every society there are conflicts and contradictions which policy analysis will be unable to resolve. In the area of the application of science and technology it has its own problem of adaptability and inhibition of making itself logically sound.

Where a political ideology as social democracy plays only a superficial role in effecting social change or is held as a means to legitimise the possession of political power exclusively by a manipulating elite, policy analysis is of little use to the purpose of bringing about major socio-economic transformation. The friction between the cherished traditional values and the publicly professed principles had led to a political ambivalence that assents to the tragic execution of transcendent policies. No amount of analysis could have saved such policies as prohibition, land reform, abolition of untouchability, manumission of bonded labour and gold control from the cruel irony that conditioned their social acceptance.

Analysts themselves are not detached and impartial individuals to take dispassionate and objective view of a policy issue in which often multifarious interests are involved. The conclusions of the analysts of the manufacturers completely eclipsed the honest findings of the public health authorities that the consumption of hydrogenated vegetable oil is harmful to human health.

In Kerala the education policy of the first communist government (1957-59) in spite of its progressive nature and the comprehensive measures it contemplated to save the teaching community from manage-mental exploitation, was fanatically opposed by the Catholic Christian teachers withdrawing their unstinted earlier support to it, as a call was given to them by their church. In the struggle of interests and values, the analyst has his own angularity just as the political head of the department. The ultimate compulsion or consideration in the acceptance of a policy is not its analysis, tendentious, tame, or excelling, but the commitment of the party in power and the favourable responses it evokes from the environment.

Policy analysis cannot take into consideration all human situations and may have to ignore the imponderables and intangibles, although it may make room for unforeseen contingencies. In parliamentary system a few adverse by-elections will be an effective reminder to the existing government either to discontinue its unpopular policies or consider their modifications. Similarly, if a party tnat has mustered sufficient electoral strength to come to power, fails to convert the main promises given in its manifesto into specific policies, it may lose the confidence at least of a significant section of the voters perhaps in the next elections.

Public opinion surveys that are conducted to measure the level of popularity of policies in western democracies especially the USA, however, are no reliable instruments to gauge the people's feelings in developing countries which are victims of political backwardness and where the rule of law sometimes has to compromise itself with privileges. In a democracy, a policy which is in contravention of the provisions of the constitution is unlikely to be free from judicial probe. The 'esoteric' of successful policy-making is intellectual eminence as exemplified by a deep understanding of society and ideational strength to awaken society to the eclectic choices made for it, which are neither the gift of a service nor the acquisition of any high hierarchic position.

Note

*From *Indian Journal of Public Administration*, Vol. XXX, No. 4, 1985. pp. 1204-1220.

2

The Fact-value Distinction as an Analytical Tool*

V. SUBRAMANIAM

The concept of decision as a logical compound of fact and value propositions was first popularized by Simon in his *Administrative Behaviour* in 1945. But this part of his theory soon fell into the back-ground, mainly for two reasons. In the first place, when the distinction was criticized by several academics as reviving the old unreal politics-administration dichotomy, as obscuring values and as misleading decision-makers, Simon did not care much to answer these criticisms in detail.[1] Secondly, he shelved this element of his theory along with the means-end chain somewhat early in his discussion and rather unceremoniously in favour of concentrating straightaway on the process of choice. In doing this, Simon was instinctively right in terms of practical psychology. At the time of decision, the decision-maker is intensely aware of the element of choice – and the obligation to choose one thing to the exclusion of other things. The feeling of agony associated with choice by many[2] is partly a by-product and symptom of the obligation to exclude. This agony as such is glorified as the symbol of the basic moral commitment of human existence by the Existentialists. In the context of this agony, it is perhaps rare for the majority of human decision-makers to make conscious use of the fact-value distinction. Hence, studies of the actual decision-making process concentrate on the mechanism of choosing or problem-solving in terms of its steps, such as search and comparison, and of its criteria, such as maximizing or satisfying.

The non-use of the fact-value distinction by many decision-makers is, however, no argument against its effective use by academics as an analytical tool in regard to decision situations and decision phenomena. Our contention is that it has been neglected in that capacity for the foregoing wrong reason and can, in fact, be very illuminating when properly used. In this article, we illustrate its use as an analytical tool by relating it to :

(i) the economist's concepts of probability and utility;

(ii) the peculiar difficulties that blur the fact-value distinction in public administration;

(iii) the specialist-administrator conflict and dialogue; and

(iv) the extensive employment of management tools in decision-making.

Probability and Utility

The concepts of probability and utility are of interest to us as they directly connect the fact-value pair to the process of choice and are so used by economists widely, in teaching and practical advising on economic problems. The term probability refers to the (mathematical) probability of a particular resultant event or consequence and the term 'utility' signifies quantitatively its value or utility to the decision-maker vis-à-vis other events. The product of these two, for any resultant event is the measure of its final or net utility – and the economic decision-maker is expected to choose that (resultant) event with the highest net utility. The best example of this is betting by a scientific punter, who is expected to estimate the probability of any horse winning – say p – by studying its form and measuring its utility – say u – through the odds offered and to compare the product $p.u.$ for all horses before placing his bets.[3] It is clear that the probability-utility pair, thus, helps directly in the act of decision on the condition that both can be estimated quantitatively.

We can show that this pair is closely related to the fact-value pair. A fact statement normally relates to something which has already happened and so it is either 100 per cent true or 100 per cent false. Its "probability" is, thus, either unity or zero. The probability of the economist relates to a future happening –with a probability varying from 1 to 0. But both fact and probability belong philosophically to the same category. Moreover, the distinction between a past fact and a future probability becomes less sharp if we remember that: (a) probabilities are usually estimated by a projection of past events into the future and (b) the fact statements used by Simon are themselves "general" statements with a high probability rating rather than being particular facts.[4] Furthermore, the probabilities which are calculated from past events do not take into account the decision-maker's proposed behaviour.[5] In real life decision situations, however, the probability may be affected by such behaviour. In short, the concepts of fact and probability are pretty close to each other in a decision situation.

Value and utility are *prima facie* much closer, the latter being simply a quantitative measure of the former vis-à-vis another value. The philosopher's concept of value is usually an all or nothing affair as against their comparative measuring by the economist. In practice, again, it is often difficult to get even ordinal listings of different utilities, not to speak of cardinal measures. To sum up, the probability-utility pair is essentially an attempted quantified version of the fact-value pair to which it is closer than is indicated by verbal definition.

This very attempt at quantification helps to bring out the mutual influence of probability and utility. In an actual decision situation, the subjective probability as estimated by the decision-maker is what matters – not the objective probability as calculated by a neutral mathematician. The former, in the *very long run*, gets closer to the latter according to several studies, but in the short run it would be strongly influenced by the utility factor.[6] In common parlance, optimists tend to rate high the probability of a (favourable) event of higher utility while pessimists err in the opposite direction. This mutual influence becomes more complex when decisions are taken on behalf of many by a few as in a democratic polity – by an administrator or politician in office.

Facts About Other's Values

Thus, a decision in public administration involves two types of facts or probabilities, namely, (i) more or less, absolute facts about existing material resources, their extractability and employment under given restrictions, and (ii) estimated probabilities concerning the opinions of separate interest groups and the whole public, in a general way, as well as in regard to the specific problem discussed. In other words, the latter type of fact is concerned with the values, however vague, held by others or it is a *fact about value. Decision-making* in a democracy becomes more complicated to the extent to which: (a) such facts or probabilities about other people's values remain basically incalculable, and (b) no final allocation of authority can ever be made to any one body to decide about other people's values. As traditional bodies, such as Parliament or even cabinets, prove less and less adequate to cope up with the fast-increasing number of occasions for such decisions, two complementary developments take over. On the one hand, civil servants are asked and expected to decide on other's values (of the sectional, or whole, public). On the other hand, several interest groups organize themselves to make public their values.

There are two further complications arising from the mutual influence of values on one another and the mutual influence of facts and values. Thus, democracy involves the freedom to persuade others to change their values to coincide with one's own. A decision-maker in authority, thus, operates over a long continuum – stretching from a struggle to find out the facts about other's values in combination with one's own value-neutrality to a concentrated attempt to persuade other's to accept one's own value without any corresponding effort to find out theirs. In this continuum, the fact-value relation becomes rather complex.

This may be better represented by a graph with the X-axis representing increasing effort to find out other's values and the Y-axis representing increasing commitment to persuade others to one's own value orientation. A public administrator or a politician may take any position – among the infinite possible relations between fact (about other's values) and (one's own) value – in this quadrant.

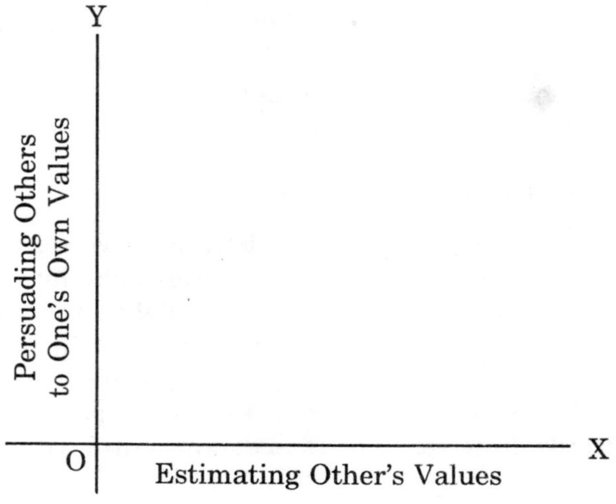

Secondly, some desirable values enter the realm of administration only when a patient assemblage of facts and probabilities proves their achievability. Thus, values connected with social welfare entered serious administrative discussion only after Beveridge's garland of facts and figures proved them possible even though they had been advocated for long as desirable by left-wing idealists. Similarly, progress in increasing the total feeling of security in western society was made possible more by actuarial calculations than by pleadings about the value of security itself.[7]

The Specialist and the Administrator

The fact-value distinction also helps to throw new light on the specialist-administrator controversy made stale by traditional argument.[8] It shows us how the responsibility for fact and value may be so flexibly divided as to tilt the balance in favour of one or the other under different social conditions. We can see that, in general, a major decision involves:

(a) more than one value,

(b) not each of which is clearly postulated,

(c) several facts, it not being always clear what facts need to be assembled, and

(d) nor easy to assemble those needed.

In regard to (a) and (b) the specialist has no advantage. The decision-maker must be sufficiently alert to the values involved in the decision through sympathy, experience and training. By popular definition, the professional has little time and training to do this and can do it only at the expense of practicing his own specialism. He also suffers the attendant difficulty (c) of not knowing what facts to assemble as this depends on the values taken into account, but in regard to (d) he may be particularly good at assembling facts in his field. The difficulties of the non-specialist administrator (or politician) are the reverse of these. His training and experience might have fitted him to recollect the values involved in the situation (his own and those of others) and he can, therefore, define the area of facts to be explored but he may not be fitted to explore that area as the professional is. He can produce a reasonably correct decision only if the specialist willingly supplies all the necessary material and scientific facts in a given organizational (and social) climate. Conversely, the specialist who would produce a correct decision must be aware of, and in tune with, the values involved either through his professional training (as in a medical question involving doctor-patient relations) or a general organizational training, and collect all his facts quickly though professional colleagues. It is a *priori* impossible to say whose difficulties are greater or predict who can produce the better decision. It would depend, in each case, on the number and complexity of the values involved, the degree of expertise necessary to assemble and understand the facts and the suggestive relation between the facts and values. But organizations, in general, cannot be bothered to make a decision in each case about the best procedure to make a decision and would rather vest the responsibility for all major decisions over a period in some definite persons. The identification of decision-makers is based partly on the anticipations about the character of the average run of decisions to be made, partly on the bargaining position of different participants in the organization and partly on extra-organizational factors. We will look briefly into the first of these as it is related to the fact-value distinction.

The image of the average decision differs from society to society and organization to organization in the same society. The government of a traditional society with a Burkean sense of continuity and responsibility for the past and future can see a multitude of complex values involved in each decision. In contrast to this, the government of a young society traces certain basic material values as obvious and settled. In the case of Britain, the traditional propensity to discover many complex values in each decision was heightened by her imperial commitments and ramifications with the distinct possibility that every decision in London could affect world events and the destinies of millions. All this put a premium on value-sensitivity, as against fact collection, and favoured the general administrator against the specialist. On the other hand, isolation and scarce resources were added to a lack of tradition in Australia and settled her basic value as development by government itself. This laid emphasis on the material facts of development and on the specialist, who could discover, process and use them. General administrators helping the statesman to balance complex values were seen as pointless parasites in Australia just as they were considered the steel frame of the empire in Britain where each decision was seen to involve a multitude of complex values.

Secondly, the degree of public expression of each value plays a great part in making the image of government decision. Broadly, when nearly all the values have and are known to have vocal advocates in organized interest groups, their balancing in each decision may be done in the open almost wholly by politicians, so that their close advisers in administration tend to take on a specialist character. Where there is a low degree of vocal organization of interests, much care is needed in taking into account all the values involved and the politician may be thankful for the help of a politically astute and anonymous administrator in spotting the multitude of values involved. Both types of body politic may retain this character for a considerable time as cause and effect reinforce each other; the guaranteed interest sensitivity of administrators keeps off many interests from organizing and a high degree of interest organization does not encourage demand for interest-conscious administrators. British central government, till recently, belonged to the former type though this is changing fast; British local government belongs to the latter type, while U.S.A. and Australia are probably foremost among societies where practically every interest is vocally organized.

There is a third way in which values lose their importance by their very eminence – through inclusion in a dominant ideology, such as communism. The assumption of its universal validity and the vesting of the right of interpretation in a small political group, leave no room for the value-sensitive administrator but give all power of executive administration to the specialist master of the facts concerned. A similar situation obtained in the absolute monarchies of Europe in the 18th century leading to the higher position of the specialist in Europe in comparison to Britain. In short, the generalist tends to dominate any administrative situation where values are not assumed as settled and open, while the specialist comes on top in the opposite situation.

Tools of Management

Lastly, let us see how the fact-value distinction clarifies the position of tools of management in relation to organization theory. In most university teaching and in general management training, tools – such as network analysis, operations research, linear programming and computer simulation – were, in the first instance, treated as mere techniques. It is rather recently that they have at all come to be regarded as aids to decision-making.[9] But even so, they are not fitted in the proper manner into decision theory. It is recognized that they perform different functions in terms of alternatives and choice: tools like computer simulation formulate alternatives while others, such as linear programming, help evaluate several alternatives in terms of given restrictions while still others, such as network analysis, help locate the quickest (and most efficient) way of carrying out a chosen alternative. The fact-value distinction goes further in providing a more analytical way of looking at the tools. The limit on rational decision making may be classified on the basis of this distinction as: (a) the cognitive limit deriving from lack of the necessary fact, and (b) the emotive limit deriving from the common predicament of never knowing for sure what one really wants. All management tools may be understood in terms of reducing the cognitive limit in some way or the other. Information retrieval and survey research do it directly by amassing the necessary facts as such. At the next level, some tools "process" the separate facts into meaningful groups, that is, alternative courses of action. Operations research and linear programming are examples of this. This "processing" is achieved by using the already existing mathematical tools on several sequential and repetitive movements by operations research and by the mathematical expression of various restrictions to demarcate feasible alternatives, by linear programming. This processing also helps to relate facts to value for the raw facts themselves cannot seem to be logically related to any value till this place. A third type of management tool, such as network analysis, helps in carrying out a decision effectively rather than making one, by working out the most efficient combination of successive and simultaneous activities into a network.

The present favourable attitude to management tools in university courses is not concerned with making an analysis of their proper place in theory. It is, however, necessary for the academic to identify the exact component of decision-making to which they belong and the exact stage at which they should come in. We can see that they serve mainly as fact-finders or fact-processors before decision-making and less frequently as fact-processors again in regard to execution after decision-making. They, thus, establish a close relation to decision theory through its fact component.

Notes

* From *Indian Journal of Public Administration*, Vol. XVII, No. 1, 1971, pp. 1-9.

1. To my knowledge, the only published paper which attempts an answer to these criticisms is mine, i.e., V. Subramanian, "Fact and Value in Decision-Making," *Public Administration Review*, Washington, Vol. XXIII, No.4 (Dec., 1963).

2. W.J.M. Mackenzie, "Models of Collective Decision-Making," *International Study of the Main Trends of Research in the Sciences of Man*, U.N.E.S.C.O./S.S./41/3.244.1/4/18, 1966 refers to agony that cannot be wished away.

3. For example, there are three horses, Today, Tomorrow and Dayafter, the odds offered being 2 to 1, 5 to 2 and 7 to 3 respectively. The probability of each winning, let us say, is ½ and ½ respectively. Then the net utility is given by the following table:

Horse	**Utility, i.e. odds**	**Probability**	**Net Utility**
Today	2	½	1
Tomorrow	5/2	½	5/6
Dayafter	7/3	½	7/12

Naturally, Today is chosen by the punter.

4. Simon's famous example in *Administrative Behaviour*, Free Press Paperback, 1965, p. 48, includes two fact statements namely: An attack is successful only when carried out under conditions of surprise; and the conditions of surprise are concealment of the time and place of attack. These two are clearly general statements with a high degree of probability. In fact, one can argue that absolute facts, which are simply a *priori* definitions, are normally useless in decision-making and only inductively-derived high-probability general 'facts' are useful therein.

5. This is only making explicit the assumption in the statistical calculation of probability from past events.

6. Regarding subjective probability, the work of Professor Cohen and others suggests this gets closer to objective probability after several attempts – in the case of gamblers. In the first attempt, this is more likely to depend on temperament.

7. Value, in the sense of the vaguely desirable, in a social context remains a 'myth' in the Sorellian sense, producing purely mass psychological effects. It comes into administrative discussion only when hard facts concerning its 'cost' show its possibility or impossibility.

   Apart from instances given in the text, one may refer to the free education policy of Ceylon based partly on a factual report on costs (1947) as an example of possibility-demonstration. Conversely, an exercise in the Netherlands showed that accepting all the suggested programmes in the National Plan would require four times the existing national income.

8. This Section is mostly taken from my paper "Specialists in British and Australian Government Services: A Study in Contrast," *Public Administration* (London), Autumn, 1963, pp. 370-72.

9. Most books on management tools refer to them now as decision-making tools, *e.g.*, Edward C. Bursk and John F. Chapman (eds.),

New Decision-Making Tools for Managers, Mentor, 1963. In the nineteen forties and fifties, however, these tools were taught as part of Industrial Engineering courses, and were known to the manager and the academic essentially as techniques.

3

Dror on Policy Making*

V. Subramaniam

This paper attempts to introduce to the Indian reader Yehezkel Dror's *Public Policy Making Re-examined* (Chandler Publishing Company, San Francisco, 1969, p. 370) probably the most important book on public policy making published in this century. It is a remarkable book by any standard and deserves a ruthless review as well.

It is original in two senses, it puts together with a tinge of passionate urgency a lot of widely scattered material on decision making and policy making at a high level of aggregative originality – and it puts forward original ideas in the pristine sense of that adjective. It is therefore appropriate to draw a detailed outline of the book before launching into appreciation and criticism.

Argument of the Book

Dror's point of departure is the patently low quality of public policy making in all countries and its continuous deterioration. Knowledge of all kinds, useful and necessary for policy making is being created faster and faster. As things have been till now, only a small part of the *existing* knowledge is *made available* to policy makers and only a small part of the *available* knowledge is used. This, at any time, creates a wide gap between actual policy and policy possible in terms of available knowledge, and a still wider gap *vis-à-vis* the best policy in terms of existing knowledge; and the latter widens alarmingly fast as knowledge accumulates faster. Indeed, according to the author, from this view point, the quality of policy making in the more and less advanced nations is *almost* equally bad.

How do we evaluate public policy making? We need to look into this first, before we can discuss improvements. The author finds existing decision-theory-literature alarmingly narrow, sectoral and specialized to help in the study of such a complex, non-deterministic and multi-contribution-made activity as policy-making.

The obviously acceptable method of evaluation is estimating the net output, that is the difference between the total input into policy making and the total output. In practice, it is extremely difficult to make even a complete list of the outputs, leave alone estimating them quantitatively. Thus a policy of expansion of secondary education – through more schools – has many products and by-products, such as more educated young men, more educated voters, more disappointment, more demand for tertiary education, more skill for production or more unwillingness for manual work. Some outputs are conveniently forgotten, some surface only after years, and some are combined by-products of several policies. Similar difficulties occur in listing and estimating the inputs too.

Dror's solution is to use some secondary criteria which influence the primary criterion of net output (and input) in an evidently proportionate way. Thus the employment of properly qualified civil servants and the use of well indexed reference libraries in regard to a problem increase the probability of a high input of knowledge and, therefore, of a high net output, even as their absence wipes out such a probability. Dror divides such secondary criteria into two groups: (a) those related directly to the output, e.g., the feasibility and acceptability of a policy; to the structure of policy making, e.g., units specially devoted to thinking, surveying or researching about policy; and (b) those criteria related to input, such as qualified manpower and organized knowledge used in policy making.

Such criteria help ascertain factually the existing quality of policy making. With what standard can it be compared to grade it? Dror discusses six existing standards used in different contexts and dismisses them all as unsatisfactory and some as even dangerous. Comparison with the past is the most widely used as people in general tend to look at today's achievement as an "improvement" on yesterday's. It is also the most dangerous. The past is most often completely irrelevant in a changed situation; as for example, in newly independent countries or in a 'nuclear' world. What was good enough in a less demanding past would be inadequate even for survival now even if it is "improved" twice over. The second standard of comparing with other systems (countries) is in a way the same as the first. The present of a "less developed" system is the past of a "more developed" system. The standard of "desired" quality, or quality considered satisfactory by the policy maker, is highly subjective and of doubtful value for objective evaluation. It is useful, however, in "understanding" the mind of policy makers. The fourth standard of "professional" quality can be applied only to limited areas, such as engineering where universal professional standards are developed. The fifth standard of survival quality can be useful – but the snag lies in the difference between objective and subjective needs for survival. If the former is more, it is disastrous, if otherwise, resources are wasted on bare survival. The sixth standard of planned quality is simply, the 'desired' quality made public; but in democracies, there is a tendency to 'plan' what is almost inevitable – to claim success, or plan far too vaguely to avoid pointed criticism. Having thus rejected the commonly used standards, one is left with the optimal standard – of how good a policy can possibly be.

Before going on to describe his optimal model in detail, Dror comes back to his point of departure – the low quality of contemporary public policy making. While this is an interesting section of the book, it is not so important in presenting cogently the argument of the author. We need only refer to the three alarmingly true criticisms made therein. The present "empirical" studies of public policy making, i.e., mainly case studies, are unstructured, unanalytical, unoriented and not related to any theoretical or conceptual framework. Theories of decision-making are highly developed in a narrow way, less developed in regard to collective organizational decisions and refuse to come to grips with the complex policy making process. Actual public policy making suffers from many defects; the author lists sixteen – a formidable list according to himself but still too forgiving.

Before detailing his own optimal model, the author indirectly argues the need for it through a critical survey of six existing (normative models) models. The pure rationality model comes in for most detailed criticism. Its first step, namely, establishing a complete set of operational goals is 'politically' more difficult than stating general goals and then letting operational goals evolve themselves. As a result, politicians abdicate this to administrators who are timid and conservative. The next two steps, namely, making a complete inventory of values and resources and preparing a complete set of alternative policies are even more difficult with the present manpower allocated to policy making. The next three steps, namely, preparing a valid set of predictions of cost and benefit for each alternative, calculating the net differential expectation for each and then choosing the best are indeed extremely difficult. The steps from four to six are at all attemptable only for certain quantifiable problems in transportation or business policy. The economical-rational model may be dubbed as the pure rationality model with a tack on it "as far economically possible". The sequential decision model involves trying out two alternatives till one proves obviously better than the other less than half way through the trial. The total cost of carrying out the one alternative finally chosen and a part of the other on trial is quite often less than the risk of choosing the second one only. The incremental model of step-by-step decision-making, using past experience – advocated by Lindblom, comes in again for very sharp criticism. It can possibly succeed only when the future is a reasonable continuation of the past with small desirable changes but it is ridiculous in the present world situation. It conforms, however, to actual behaviour insofar as the average policy maker depends on the past to study the future as well as to avoid discord arising from any radical change. The satisficing model is essentially Simon's satisfying model of the normal human being choosing the first satisfactory alternative without going further. The extra-rational model is no model as such but is brought in to emphasize the need to use extra-rational abilities. Dror states in the course of this critique that his own optimal model is a fusion of the economical-rational model and the extra-rational model.

The optimal model is best described briefly by using the author's own terms as far as possible. It consists of three major stages, namely, meta-policy making, policy making and post-policy making and each of these is sub-divided into several phases. Thus meta-policy making, that is, policy making about policy making includes: (1) processing values (specifying to a reasonable extent values relating to the policy); (2) processing reality (getting the facts as distinct from subjective images of reality and also evaluating some probabilities); (3) processing problems (distinguishing subjective problems, people may be observed with, from objective problems); (4) surveying, processing and developing resources (an important phase, including the survey of knowledge resources); (5) designing, evaluating and redesigning the policy-making system (this is Dror's most important contribution, that of analysing how to design a policy making structure, sub-divide it into parts and integrate it); (7) determining policy making strategy (i.e., asking questions such as: Should it be purely rational, incremental?, etc.). The (middle) stage of policy making itself involves seven phases, namely: (1) sub-allocating resources (to the various phases, e.g., fact collecting, experimenting or support-mobilizing); (2) establishing operational goals with some order of priority (considered most important by the people and civil servants); (3) establishing a set of other significant values (mainly those values likely to be affected within the execution-period of the policy); (4) preparing a set of major alternative policies including some 'good' ones (that is not stopping with the first plausible or satisficing alternative but searching on to include at least one less than common one real good alternative; (5) preparing reliable predictions of the significant benefits and costs of the various alternatives (using extrapolation from the past, theoretical analysis, focussed research, pilot testing, the Rand Corporation's Delphi method – in making these predictions and fixing definite time-limits or "cut-off horizons" for doing it); (6) comparing the predicted benefits and costs of the various alternatives and identifying the best ones (sometimes "synthesizing" the best alternative from a few 'good' alternatives); and (7) evaluating the benefits and costs of the 'best' alternatives and deciding whether they are good or not. The post-policy making state is essentially one of execution, evaluation and feedback and consists of four stages, namely, (8) motivating the implementation of the policy (winning support through coalitions, etc., even in the earlier phases); (9) executing the policy (including interpreting it in detail); (10) evaluating policy making after the policy has been executed (and identifying unexpected results openly and honestly); and (11) communication and feedback channels, connecting all phases (see diagram on page 77) The author supplements his detailed description of each phase with a chart summary and a diagram showing the interconnections of the phases through communication and feedback loops. Elaborating his main contribution, namely, the structuring of policy-making (or meta-policy-making), the author admits that the total work needs to be first sub-divided into several specialized units for "sub-optimization" (i.e., getting the best in regard to each special sub-goal) and then aggregated so as to avoid conflict and get the best out of the sub-optimal total. The known aggregative relations between units include: (a) the straight and simple hierarchy where each unit is under a larger unit, (b) the complex hierarchy where some units are subordinate and other interlace, through staff-advising and committeeing at equal levels; and (c) polycentric structures with few or many autonomous units. Without passing judgement on any of these or suggesting a new structure, the author specifies some conditions necessary for the best aggregation – including some *deliberate redundancy* or "multiplexing' deliberate isolation of some units for independent contributions and the general expectation and the relishing of the necessary complexity.

The rest of the book is devoted to examining the existing barriers against policy improvement (to the level of the optional model). The author attempts a long and exhaustive list but it is sufficient for our purpose to refer to a few interesting ones. In regard to changes needed in knowledge, apart from referring to the need to incorporate the extra-rational, nine barriers are listed particularly in the social sciences, as hindrances to the development of policy knowledge, namely, blaming the complexity of social phenomena as an excuse for non-research, initiating the physical sciences and thereby looking for certainty, the alienation of academics from policy makers; the favouring of incremental-change in social theory, the divorce of pure from applied knowledge with prestigious stress on the former, the normal isolated disciplinary organization of universities, the youth of the social sciences – and external restraints, such as lack of funds, and restriction by vested interests or social prejudice against research into several social phenomena as for example into the Jury system or the conditions for surrender in case of nuclear war. Two important suggestions are made to correct this situation – the encouragement of inter-disciplinary policy-oriented studies at a high level – creating respectable new fields thereby – and the establishment and pursuit of a definite "policy-science".

Among the changes needed in personnel are included the good old ones of "educating our masters", the politicians, into some policy-knowledge, selecting the best talent for the civil service and training the civil servants more rigorously in university institutions. In regard to changes in structure and process, the main stress on meta-policy-making in the model is reinforced by further suggestions for establishing independent policy analysis organizations, such as the Rand in U.S.A., establishing meta-policy-making and systems management units and explicit specialized staff unit for policy knowledge – apart from greater contact between universities and administration and the better "aggregation" of policy sub-optima at the political level – through functional representation and changes in legislative procedures. The book closes with a passionate plea in the last chapter to choose openly between "shaping the future and muddling through".

Positive Contributions

As an ambitious pioneering venture covering a wide and complex field, the book has remarkable merits and important defects. Let us, however, look at the positive contributions first.

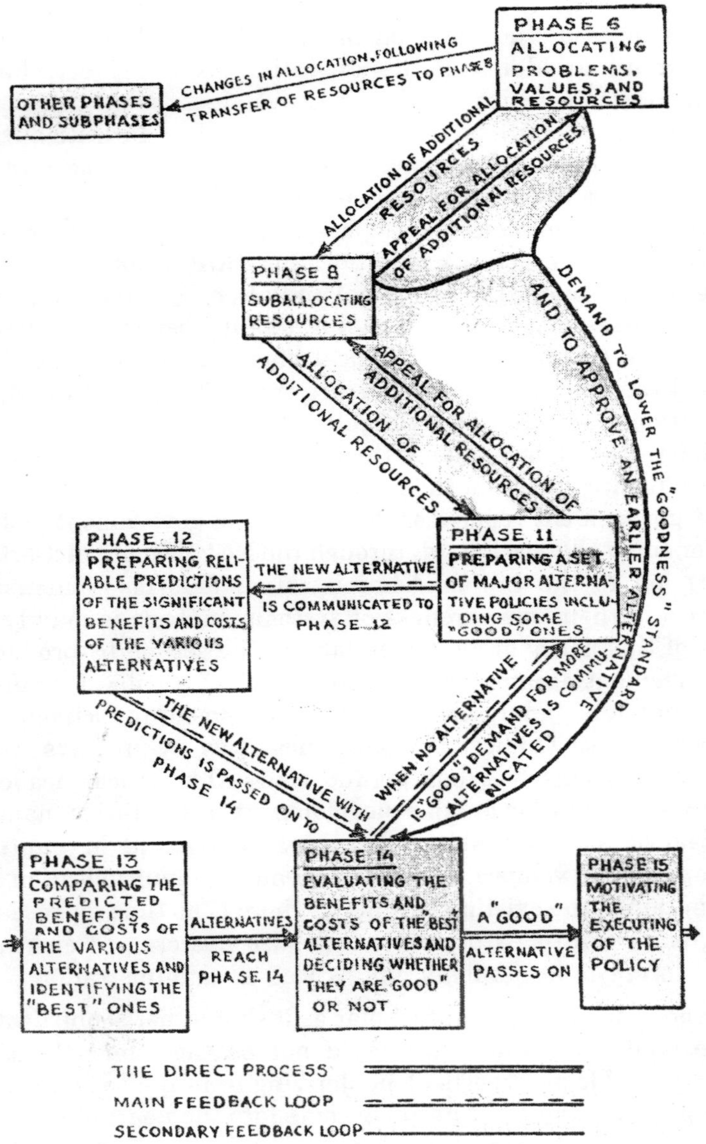

ALTERNATIVE SEARCH FEEDBACK LOOPS

From the point of view of University teaching and civil services training, the book makes a real break-through so obviously that it will be difficult to find excuses and alibis for continuing the older methods of case study and patchy moralizing. Through several unfortunate accidents in its evolution as a subject, Public Administration teaching both in the Universities and in civil service training institutions, has suffered a measure of vulgarization which no other subject has. It started its career as a subject in the U.S.A. around the turn of the century riding on the crest of a wave of reformism seeking to separate (good) administration from (bad) politics, in practice and in teaching. Swift came the reaction in the thirties under the New Deal and after, with the "discovery" that they were mixed up and cannot be fully separated. The two by-products (not necessarily logical ones) of this reaction have plagued the subject mercilessly since then. The first of these, the reassertion of an unbridgeable gulf between Public and Business Administration, has insulated the former firmly against any study of the advances made in the latter. The elementariness of all the recent government reports on "machinery of government" – from the Canadian Glassco Report, through the New Zealand McCarthy's Report, on to the Indian Administrative Reforms Commission Report and their unawareness of systems analysis is mainly the result of this policy of mental isolation. The second by-product is the convenient assumption that so "complex" a subject as public policy cannot be "analysed" but only "understood" inductively by a number of case studies. Perhaps, these two by-products would have worn themselves out in due course by critical academic commonsense but for another development in the fifties, namely, the gigantic boom in (public) administration training in countries, developing or developed. Any boom means the multiplication and distribution of the existing product as there is no time for research and quality control, a process which also has created enormous vested interests in academic life as well as administration.

Dror's book is important insofar as it shows that sophistication in the study of public policy need not be the monopoly of its economic and legal aspects alone deriving from the sophistication of the parent subject but needs to come into the heart of it. It will become more and more difficult to maintain the Peter-pantheist stance that it need not grow out of the case study stage at all.

The second major contribution is the "aggregation" (to use Dror's own phrase) of all the relevant material from varied fields, such as decision-making, political control, behavioural psychology or economics, into a coherent readable exegesis on the improvement of public policy making. In this process, the author has made his own original contributions, the most important of which we are discussing in the next paragraph. But the level of aggregation by itself shows enough originality to spark off good work by others both in aggregation as well as specialized fields. One thinks of the beginnings of scientific psychology in the study of small pieces of behaviour of Pavlov and Watson. While this was precise, dissatisfaction arose with its piece-meal character and led to the study of the whole personality – by personality psychologists and depth psychologists. While the two streams still remain identifiably separate, their regular interaction has been on the whole profitable to the subject. In administration, sound work on decision-making or human relations has been so far of a piecemeal character and aggregative work even when it was practically useful as in management manuals, has been conceptually hollow. A first rate aggregative achievement like Dror's may, let us hope, set in motion some profitable interactions as in Psychology. All this does not amount to saying that Dror's aggregative work is faultless. Indeed the faults are many and varied and we shall look into them a little later.

His discussion on meta-policy making is perhaps his conceptually most original and also most useful contribution. That the structure of any institution determines its policy output to some extent has been well known for a long time. Sociologically oriented history in general tries to explain decisions and events as flowing out of the social structure. Weber's efforts were also directed that way and he seemed to feel that bureaucracy was the final perfect structure of social evolution and, therefore, the most efficient in regard to output. Classical organization theory discussed the achievement of a perfect structure through unity of command and certain 'principles', such as span of control and departmentalization by purpose or process. But the rigidity of the Weberian or classical structure has been experimentally and conceptually shown to be self-defeating from the thirties onwards and criticism and even ridicule has poured fourth aplenty on it. Positive suggestions for change, however, have been few, such as Rensis Likert's, based on interlacing informal groups (*New Patterns of Management*) or Victor Thompson's advocating all round looseness against all round rigidity. To sum up, there has been plenty of discussion about the relation between structure and policy – but only minor isolated conceptual contributions about changing the former. Dror's discussion is fundamental in this regard, for meta-policy making is a continuous re-examination, for every policy question, of the policy making (bureaucratic) structure itself so as to change it, so as to make it produce not a "predetermined policy" but the optimal policy. It is more fundamental than the continuous re-examination of "the machinery of government" advocated by the Brookings report of 1937 to avoid large and showy investigations. It is turning the structure policy flow in the opposite direction so as to control it. We will discuss the shortcomings of the author's concept in a while, but let us first admit that it is fundamental, original and useful.

Another original contribution of a less fundamental and less conceptual character is the author's passionate plea for the establishment and recognition of a "policy science". Inter-disciplinary contact, rapport and collaboration are actually senior common-room 'old hats', useful in reviving conversation, after exhausting the available academic gossip. The author's plea for this inter-disciplinary action-oriented science takes on originality mainly because of its practical basis. One can also vouch for its sincerity – as the author did plead with strong arguments for a policy science institute in his own country, Israel. Even if the institution was not established during his time therein, one can see the success of that "orientation" in Israel's recent history.

I have concentrated on the major contributions and have ignored the several minor ones in my appreciation – but that is enough to demonstrate the importance of the book to policy makers and students of (Public) administration.

Some Criticisms

One can and needs to be ruthless about the shortcomings of such a remarkable book. These are many and again we will concentrate on the major ones relating to his 'aggregation' of relevant knowledge on policy-making and his concept of meta-policy making – and in particular his optimal model born out of his aggregative originality.

No aggregator is effusively thankful to the suppliers of machine parts. In Dror's case, however, this is more apparent than real. Quite apart from his scrupulous and copious footnote-references to earlier contributions, he forgets to claim originality for what is more or less his, for example, meta-policy making. His failure, essentially consists in making a somewhat inflated distinction between precise piecemeal decision theories and complex public policy making – and to this he adds an unawareness of the process of successful aggregation in the social sciences. Let me illustrate this.

It is easy enough to show that many, indeed most of the pieces going into his optimal model have been used discretely both in concept and practice, for some years. The feedback concept apart from its precise use by systems analysts, was employed in a lay fashion by market researchers and policy makers and was indeed specifically made a part of a decision execution cycle by Litchfield.* Benefit cost analysis has been used for about two decades by welfare economists, choice models by psychologists and decision-theorists and even such ideas as the examination of relevant neighbouring values and fixing a cut-off horizon, by Appleby and Keynes. The latter repeated his famous piece of cynicism, "In the long run, we are all dead", often enough to stress the need to fix a cut-off horizon for any economic policy. Similarly, Appleby's explanation of, how some important values discussed at the top one day are relegated to lower administrative levels another day and values from lower level are suddenly pushed up for examination, in his *Policy and Administration*, is essentially an insightful warning stressing the need to examine several neighbouring values.

All this legitimate borrowing does not in the least detract from Dror's aggregative contribution. What does, is his seeming unawareness of the process of successful aggregation in a social science. To refer back again to the example of Psychology, a total aggregative view of the human psyche as presented by philosophy or even by insightful men like William James led nowhere, till discrete explorations of discrete phenomena by Pavlov or Watson drew Psychology in a new direction. A total view of the psyche, thereafter could not be entirely speculative and even the Freudian view, while evoking strong criticism, still had to base itself on experiments. Other aggregative views of human personality too have drawn profitably from discrete experimenting. Similarly, a total, almost didactic view of management as presented by classical organization theory was a dead end, till discrete behavioural studies either of the manager's decision-making or the reactions of the managed to it, put administrative studies on a new basis. The time was ripe in the sixties for good aggregative work. While Geoffrey Vickers tried and did not exactly make it, Dror, I feel has. But his effectiveness in this regard can only be judged by the extent to which new areas of discrete research are discovered and explored. In other words, aggregation and specialized research need to be looking at each other all the time for mutual profit. A

*Edward H. Litchfield, "Notes on a General Theory of Administration", *Administrative Science Quarterly*, New York, Vol. I, No. I (June 1956)

worker in one field is not much good unless he keeps a foot in the other, much the same way as a "a chemist, who is not a physicist, is neither" – according to Ostwald.

Fortunately, Dror's work suggests many important special areas for exploration. Yet there are three crucial areas, very central to his own optimal model, which he forgets to mention.

In the first place, he claims his optimal model to be a fusion of the economically rational model with the extra-rational. The former modifies the pure rationality model in two directions: (i) with a definitely limited time for the search of alternatives (instead of an endless exhaustive search), and (ii) definitely limited supply of resources for the search (as determined in the meta-policy making stage). With these two modifications, there is every danger that only a satisfying (or satisficing) alternative will be found. Yet Dror stresses the need to keep searching till at least one "good" alternative is found and does little to explain how (p.179) – except suggesting *all too briefly* some devices, such as generally improving the climate of creativity, operational gaming, random computer synthesis of new alternatives, and (elsewhere) the use of men of extra-rational abilities. Surely, this crucial part of his model deserves more analytical treatment than providing an annotated list of devices.

The problem may be stated thus in a simplified way. In the normal search for alternatives, the human being may have a minimum satisfying standard say S. An alternative below this standard may be denoted by b_1, b_2, etc. (for bad), ones approaching it closely by s_1, s_2, etc., and good alternatives well above it by g_1, g_2, etc. In most cases, according to Simon's satisficing model, the alternatives occur in a series, such as b_1, b_2, b_3, b_4 – so long – that as soon as the series produces an s_1 it is grabbed. In some hardy cases, the series may go on – b_1, b_2, b_3...s_1, b_{10}, b_{11},..s_2...b_{100}, b_{101} – still producing satisficing alternatives of varying marginal qualities. The aim is to produce alternatives in a series where g_1, g_2 and g_3 will start appearing long before the point of psychological frustration or resource exhaustion. While I am sure that improving creativity, by extra-rational resources or computer synthesis of alternatives, will produce alternatives in this desirable way, one needs to do a lot of *specific* research on how the alternatives occur in a particular series, in a particular situation. The nature of the series is probably a function of the searcher(s) and the environment of existing knowledge. We need to know the precise nature of this function – apart from the fact that it improves under certain inducement – through special research. The economist will not help at the moment as they still keep going back to the maximizing model, while changing the object maximized, from profit to sales, to production or to power. The model which I personally use in teaching, the "maxificing" model, assumes that the series improves with every actual decision so that over a given time of similar decision situations, an attempt is made to push up the "satisficing" standard towards the maximizing one. This too is unsatisfactory and the problem needs to be stated as one of identifying the order in which alternatives occur under different conditions and should be subjected to specific intensive research.

Dror's call for the use of extra-rational abilities, while fully justified in theory is unfortunate in some regards in the present state of administrative studies. Life is too short, and every problem situation is so urgent that we cannot wait to get every piece of knowledge from the crucible of reason and so must use extra-rational ability to the safest maximum extent. That is the simple commonsense justification for the use of the extra-rational. There are, however, some snags. In the first place, extra-rational judgment has itself to be judged continuously and we need to do more than use the Delphi method. Secondly, the author's main suggestion for increasing its use is to discover men with such abilities and use them. The obvious snag is that there are desirable and undesirable types in the category; and the latter cannot often be exposed until it is too late. Thus a man like 'Paniwala Maharaj' who was able to divine water easily was used successfully by the Government of India to find new water resources for a while but one like Adolf Hitler, who also had extra-rational abilities, took control of a nation and brought it to disaster. The central problem of controlling the extra-rationally able person from controlling and destroying others has not been successfully solved. It is unfortunate that the author shelves this problem somewhat casually and gives a handle to the counter-reformationists, who are ready to enthrone the administrator "with a feel for things" and practices "the art" of administration.

In regard to his major contribution, of meta-policy making, again, the author has failed to pinpoint the problems for special research. Basically, all social theory, including the Marxist, has been structurally deterministic in one sense. The social structure is the prime mover dictating policies and events. Marxists simply shift the stress according to the context; a capitalist structure *inevitably* goes on to its own destruction in one sense – and in another sense, the great man gives it a push and the task of philosophers is not to explain but to change the world. Meta-policy making goes against this mainstream of sociological imagination and this reverse action, even in small or medium organizations, is never too easy. On this score alone, it needs closer analysis. Dror reaches something of an anticlimax when he goes over from meta-policy making to simply describing the "existing" structures, such as simple and complex hierarchies, and polycentric structures, very much like a textbook on organization theory. He takes off from there, but not far enough upwards, when he lays down certain conditions, such as deliberate duplication of some units, isolation of other units for independence and ensuring that every *sub-optimised* task has at least one unit to look after it. One must here stress the need for more research into deliberate structural changes and their results on policy. The existing literature almost entirely concentrates on resistance to change and not the aftermath.

I hope, I have said enough about the contents, merits and shortcomings of the book to provoke interest. One can easily notice also its urgent relevance to the Indian situation – but I should now leave it to the reader to pursue this interesting question.

Notes

* From Indian Journal of Public Administration, Vol. XVI, 1970, pp. 84-96.

4

The Paradox of Policy Science*

STEPHEN BROOKS

The present state of policy science is paradoxical. Coincident with the ubiquity of the policy orientation, one finds widespread doubt expressed as to the contribution which social science analysis can make to the policy process. The decade of the 1970s, which began with the confident prescriptions of Lasswell[1] and Dror[2] closed with the sober reassessments of Scott and Shore[3] and Lindblom and Cohen[4]. This is, of course, an oversimplification and is not intended to suggest a neat progression from unbridled enthusiasm to sober scepticism. Trenchant critiques of policy science from Horowitz[5] and Tribe[6] and the recent publication of Nagel[7] believe any suggestion of unambiguous movement over the course of the decade. Contemporary evaluations of policy science range from the tempered optimism of Quade's *Analysis for Public Decisions*[8] to the outright pessimism expressed in Lindblom and Cohen's *Usable Knowledge*.[9]

In a recent editorial article in *Policy Sciences*, Peter deLeon describes the explosive growth in policy analysis and remarks that "the pervasiveness of the genre leads one to question the heritage, present condition, and future of the discipline and profession".[10] Indeed, deLeon's stock-taking causes one to inquire into whether the amorphous body of research and vast army of practitioners he describes constitute in any meaningful sense a coherent 'discipline', or whether policy science is not more accurately characterized as an approach to the understanding and solution of social problems. This point will be developed subsequently.

David Garson's criticism of policy science as "a discipline notoriously neglectful of its heritage,"[11] provides a springboard for the subsequent discussion. In his essay,[12] "From Policy Science to Policy Analysis: A Quarter Century of Progress?", Garson explains the theoretical divisions in contemporary policy studies by arguing that developments in this field cannot be understood apart form the traditional issues of contention in political science. This article endeavours to broaden Garson's inquiry into the intellectual underpinnings of the policy orientation, while remaining focused upon policy science as against the broader scope of Scott and Shore's recent book.[13]

More specifically, the analysis will proceed through the following stages:

(i) a discussion of policy science as a method for grappling with social problems;

(ii) a review of Lindblom and Cohen's argument that social science analysis is of very limited value as an approach to social problem solving;

(iii) the argument that the policy science movement represents an attempt to escape from 'messy' politics; and

(iv) an examination of the beginnings of an alternative approach to policy-making which: (a) allots primary importance to culture, and (b) transcends what van Gunsteren describes as the quest for control.[14]

Policy Science as an Approach to Policy Formation

Policy science involves an approach to the making of decisions, an approach which is rational and centres around the systematic application of scientifically-collected knowledge to social problems. V. Subramaniam's characterisation of policy science as "The practical application of all relevant knowledge in the social physical sciences, to specific policy problems identified well ahead of time"[15] expresses succinctly this understanding of policy science as a decision-making approach. From Lasswell through Dror to the present, the idea that policy science entails a theory of choice remains central. Nagel's recent book entitled, *The Policy-Studies Handbook*, is solidly in this tradition: "As social science does more analysis of hypotheses, predictions, causation, and optimising, there develops a body of potential premises that can be used in deducing conclusions, just as chemistry was able to deduce the existence of new elements before they were empirically discovered."[16]

The decisions theory implications of policy science are widely recognised. In his article "Policy Science: Analysis or Ideology?", Tribe provides a selective review of the intellectual and methodological roots of policy science, focusing upon: (1) the emergence of operations research, (2) the influence of von Neumann and Morgenstern's *Theory of Games and Economic Behaviour*[17] and (3) development of welfare economics. Similarly, White suggests that the origins of policy science lie in management science and the classical management literature.[18] Its association with management science suggests an instrumental relationship between social research and choice. This problem-solving approach informs the policy science model of the relationship between knowledge and action. Carol Weiss describes this instrumentalist understanding as a decision-driven model of research use. This sequential model has the following stages: (1) definition of the social problem, (2) identification of missing knowledge, (3) acquisition of relevant data using social research techniques, (4) interpretation for problem solution, and (5) policy choice.[19]

Policy science is, at bottom, a systematic and rational approach to public policy-making. Scott and Shore's observation that applied policy-relevant work in sociology entails a prescription as to how policy should be done is equally valid as an assessment of policy science. The rationalist model involves a "commitment to scientific planning".[20] As innumerable commentators have remarked, this implies a dramatic overhaul of traditional patterns of public policy-making. However, the specter of Vonnegut's Ilium[21] is warded off by the suggestion that a policy science culture be encouraged in order to ensure democratic participation in the policy-making process. Duncan MacRae's book, *The Social Function of Social Science*,[22] contains a typical statement of this position. MacRae advocates greater rationality in policy-making, achieved through the deliberate creation of a policy analysis culture. This policy analysis culture has three principal features: (1) technical experts who are sensitive to the ethical implications of decisions; (2) close cooperation between researchers in academic and research institutes, and policy practitioners in government; and (3) an informed citizenry to fend off the anti-democratic spectre of an expert ruling class. This is squarely in the tradition established by Dror's pioneering writings on the contours of a policy science culture.

The idea of policy science as a guide to public policy-making has, however, not gone unchallenged and a number of alternative roles have been suggested.

Legitimation

Horowitz demonstrates that, at least until 1970, social research in the United States was used as legitimation rather than impetus to policy action. Describing what he considers to be the usual sequence of policy-making, he argues that a policy decision is first arrived at through traditional political processes, after which occurs: (a) "a frantic search for precedent in the past, justification in the present, and rationalisation in the future," and (b) the application of social science research in order to lend the weight of 'dispassionate' analysis to a policy choice already decided upon.[23] This is substantially identical to Lindblom and Cohen's suggestion that professional social inquiry is, in large part, ritualistic, i.e., "practiced for the same reason as, say, dancing in tribal societies.... It also brings assurance because it appears to apply the prestigious effective methods of natural science to the study of the social world."[24]

Ideology

This characterisation is related to that of legitimation, and suggests that policy science is laden with utilitarian assumptions. Tribe argues this case and describes its implications as follows:

> (The) policy sciences' intellectual and social heritage in the classical economics of unfettered contract, consumer sovereignty, and perfect markets both brings them within a paradigm of conscious choice guided by values and inclines them, within the paradigm, toward the exaltation of utilitarian and self-interested individualism, efficiency and maximized production.[25]

Conceptualisation

Policy science may contribute to the way in which policy-making is structured and, indeed, what choices and even issues are considered. Policy science as conceptualisation has two thrusts: (a) social research may sensitise policy practitioners to relationships and consequences of which they were unaware; and (b) the findings of policy-relevant research may percolate into society, influencing "the way that a society thinks about issues, the facets of the issues that are viewed as susceptible to alteration, and the alternative measures that it considers".[26] In brief, policy science can have an influence upon the political agenda through sensitising both decision-makers and the general population.

Notwithstanding these alternative characterisations, the idea of policy science as an approach to the determination of policy choice remains vigorous. The impressive number of chapters and articles devoted to the teaching of policy studies and the training of policy analysis/scientists reflects the fact that policy science involves primarily the development of professional analysts who are expert in rational decision-making.[27] The orientation of these professionals is apparent from Nagel's discussion of methods of policy analysis, which consists mainly of a review of the principles of optimisation in decision theory. The theory question of how to accommodate values within a rational model of choice is faced in a cursory way by: (1) acknowledging the significance of the matter, and (2) suggesting that policy analysts be required to submit "sensitivity analyses" along with their recommendations, in order to demonstrate how the optimal policy choice varies with changes in the relative weight assigned to the values being maximised. In response to the often made criticism that the methods of policy analysis are open to abuse, lending themselves as readily to the maximisation of undesirable ends as to desirable ones, Nagel advocates the development of a code of ethics, professionalisation, and institutionalised checks.[28]

A considerably more profound criticism of policy science contends that the analytical approach is only one, and not always the most appropriate, of the means of solving social problems. In other words, the shortcomings of policy science lie in the approach itself, rather than in its misapplication in the service of undesirable ends. This is the essence of Lindblom and Cohen's critique of professional social inquiry (PSI) – a critique which is undiminished in its application to policy science ("Imperial PSI").

Some Shortcomings of the Policy Science Approach

Notwithstanding Nagel's judgement, "The policy studies field is only in its infancy,"[29] large claims have been made for the analytical approach to solving social problems. A recent textbook on policy analysis declares, "no sensible policy choice can be made without careful analysis of the advantages and disadvantages of each course of action,"[30] This position is concurred in by Nagel, who argues that policy analysis provides "new insights" and enables policy-makers to make better-informed choices and, by implication, better policy.[31] These confident assessments echo Dror's belief that institutionalised policy science would result in improved policy choices. In part, this belief is based upon the assumption that the knowledge generated by social science research is considerably superior to that which commonsense understanding affords the decision-maker.

The argument against policy science as an approach to the determination of policy is presented most forcefully by Lindblom and Cohen in their recent book.[32] Their critique is three-fold: (1) analysis is but one approach to dealing with social problems, and only infrequently is it the appropriate approach; (2) the policy process is too amorphous to allow for the rational model of policy-making proposed by policy science; and (3) the knowledge generated by policy-relevant social research is dependent upon "ordinary knowledge" to an extent unacknowledged by policy science.

Lindblom and Cohen contrast the analytical and interactive approaches to social problem solving, and suggest that the latter is frequently more appropriate. This interactive model describes a market situation, encompassing the countless forms and forums of bargaining. This is the traditional approach to problem resolution, characterised by outcomes arrived at through the interaction of two or more actors. In explanation of its neglect, Lindblom and Cohen write:

> The problem-solving capacity of interaction is ... obscured because the interactions often do not result in a decision by an official or collective authority explicitly resolving a recognized problem. Resource allocation by buying and selling requires no decision *about resource allocation* by anyone, nor need anyone articulate the problem of resource allocation or articulate the answer.[33]

Though the process is more reactive than analytical analysis may well contribute to the decision-making process at the level of the interacting actors, so that "analysis need only attend to limited questions."[34] Consequently, interactive problem solving is commonly mixed with some degree of analytical problem solving. The significance of the interactive model is elaborated upon by Lindblom in *Politics and Markets*.[35]

Similar to interactive problem solving is social learning. It too involves resource allocation in the absence of centralized analyses and choice. Briefly, social learning refers to an incremental process, grounded upon action, in which the tension deriving form a mis-match between values and action is reduced through an adjustment of either one or the other (or both). Lindblom and Cohen explain, "the learning we have in mind in such cases comes from actual experience that upsets old attitudes and dispositions."[36] This is not significantly different from what Sir Geoffrey Vickers describes as appreciative behaviour in situations of multi-valued choice.[37] At bottom, social learning entails policy adjustment by accretion, not unlike the development of case law out of the dialectic between the concrete circumstances of present litigation and the values distilled from past decisions.

Lindblom and Cohen's second criticism of the analytical approach to policy-making is directed at the assumption of identifiable decision-makers. This point is related to the preceding argument. Analytical problem solving implies the existence of a manageable number of decision-makers whose choices are decisive and who, themselves, are isolatable. Dror attempted to make allowance for the reality of an amorphous policy-making system through his advocacy of both a decentralized network of policy science centres and the deliberate promotion of a policy science culture.[38] However, Lindblom and Cohen suggest that the policy analysis approach is invariably misleading in that it identifies problem understanding as both necessary and prior to problem solving, and thereby neglects the interactive and social learning approaches to social problem solving. These latter approaches, they suggest, are more appropriate to the reality of an amorphous policy process in which outcomes are seldom attributable to the choices made by one or a small number of identifiable actors.

The third criticism denies that policy analysis involves a distinct and superior way of comprehending social problems, but is simply more systematic in approach. This is premised upon the argument that the knowledge generated by policy-relevant social research is dependent upon ordinary knowledge, i.e., knowledge that is based upon "commonsense, casual empiricism, or thoughtful speculation and analysis."[39] The same point is made by John Hughes in *The Philosophy of Social Research*.[40]

A different argument is introduced by Cohen and Weiss. They remark that intensive research of a policy problem generally produces a picture of greater complexity rather than clarity. This, they suggest, is unavoidable, and the expectation that a convergence in understanding ought to emerge is based upon an implied parallelism between the development of physical science and that of social science: "(If) the result of scientific improvement in some aspects of physical science is convergence – at least for a time, within important conceptual limits – the result of improvement in the social science is a richer, more diverse picture of things."[41] By this reasoning, the expectation that policy-relevant research will provide unambiguous guidance for policy is misplaced. Cohen and Weiss propose a more modest role for social research, suggesting that it can contribute to 'social wisdom'. Important as this is, it is certainly a smaller role than that envisaged by policy science.

Flight From 'Messy' Politics

It is only a mild overstatement to suggest that policy science proposes analysis as a substitute for politics. Horowitz goes so far as to speak of "the rise of genteel fascism in America, or for the faint hearted, a modernised Platonism, in which every man knows his 'place', and in which information is held to be equivalent to wisdom."[42] This is immoderate in that it fails to acknowledge the unmistakable Deweyism which pervades policy science. While not anti-democratic, the analytical approach to public policy-making aspires to the de-politicisation of the policy process. An understanding of how support for democratic participation is reconciled with de-politicised policy-making requires a review of the intellectual history of policy science.

The policy orientation was evident in the beginnings of American social science. In their discussion of the origins of scientific planning, Scott and Shore quote Albion Small, founder of the *American Journal of Sociology*, who in the first issue of that journal wrote, "The work of the discipline was to increase our present intelligence about social utilities.... (to achieve) more effective combination for the general welfare than has thus far been organised."[43] Nor was Small's a lone voice. Scott and Shore remark upon the optimism which characterised fledgling sociology and social philosophy in America: "Ward Ross, Small, Dewey, James and Cooley all exude a sense of confidence in the possibility of creating a sociology relevant to the great social challenges of the day. They felt certain that this new science would be equal to the task of ameliorating social evils."[44]

Influenced by the methodological rigour of German social science, American sociology was confident of its role in shaping a better society in the Age of Progress. Traditional methods of historical research and philosophical inquiry increasingly became unfashionable as empirical methodology waxed prominent. The 'Wisconsin Idea', involving the participation of social scientists in the policy process through consultation and, generally, as a source of expert advice, embodied what Hugh Hawkins has described as the "Ideal of Objectively."[45] The sense of mission which informs the policy science writings of Lasswell and Dror is no less evident in the work of America's first social scientists. Universal public education and sociological training for legislators were measures advocated by Lester Ward in order to embed rational decision-making into the very culture and political institutions of American society. The tradition of rationalism in the service of democracy runs undiluted from Ward to Dror. These visions of a new politics share a conviction that the institutionalization of scientific analysis into the policy-making process is a necessary condition for the attainment of democratic government in a modern society.

The influence which Deweyism has had upon policy science is profound. Lasswell acknowledged the intellectual debt when he wrote, "policy sciences are a contemporary adaptation of the general approach to public policy that was recommended by John Dewey and his colleagues in the development of American pragmatism."[46] In an article entitled "The Relevance of John Dewey's Thought", Sidney Hook discusses the relationship between freedom and science in Deweyism. Of particular significance is Dewey's commitment to the scientific attitude and the knowledge generated by this approach, alongside an unwavering belief in the necessity and possibility of an intelligent citizenry as the bulwark of democratic government. Faith in human intelligence is central to Dewey's thought. As Hook explains, "for Dewey the survival and expansion of democracy depends upon its use of scientific method or creative intelligence to solve its problems."[47] This is not merely a rationalism of means, but a rationalism of ends as well. Dewey maintained, "if ever we are to be governed by intelligence, not by things and by words, science must have something to say about *what* we do, and not merely about *how* we may do it most easily and economically".[48]

A more detailed picture of the intellectual history of policy science emerges from the accounts provided by Scott and Shore, Horowitz, and Tribe, respectively. However, the foregoing review is sufficient to demonstrate that policy science is but the most recent manifestation of a long-standing tradition in American social science, *viz.*, the flight from 'messy' confrontational politics. This phenomenon reaches its apogee in the technology of value trade-offs, being a utilitarian approach to policy choice. Ward Edwards explains:

The essential idea of multiattribute utility measurement is that every significant value can in effect be partitioned into a set of sub-values on each of a number of dimensions. Technological devices exist for ascertaining what these dimensions are, for locating each one of the actions, objects, or whatever is being evaluated on each of these dimensions, for judging how important each dimension is to the aggregate value of the thing being evaluated, and then for performing the aggregation.[49]

Ward acknowledges that this approach has limited applications. An example of the sort of policy-making situation in which, presumably, an analytical methodology would be appropriate is provided by Hammond and Adelman.[50] In the context of a dispute over the choice of bullet to be used by a police force, they identify three discrete operations in the policy-making process: (1) the externalisation of social value judgements, (2) the externalisation of scientific judgements (i.e., factual assessments), and (3) the integration of fact and value.

Method occupies the central position in this analytical approach to policy making. Value resolution is the outcome of an analytical process rather than, for example, resulting from market interactions. As Scott and Shore remark, policy analysis implies that "such procedures will lead to more frictionless situations than we now have, situations that maximize the good and minimise harm done to those affected by them."[51] However, the analytical model presumes a coherence which does not characterise the policy-making process. As Lindblom and Cohen observe, "policy is actually made not by a policy maker but by interaction among a plurality of partisans."[52] A rather different argument is made by Tribe in his critique of quantitative techniques of decision making. Arguing that the analytical approach structures in certain concerns while structuring out others, Tribe accuses policy analysis of "*reducing entire problems to terms that misstate their underlying structure, typically* collapsing into the task of maximising some simple quantity an enterprise whose ordering principle is not one of maximization at all."[53]

Prominent in the policy science tradition is the theme of unity of knowledge. Thirty years ago Lasswell lamented, "The unity of the intellectual life and the harmonizing of science and practice have been undermined by... 'centrifugal' forces,'[54] *viz.*, rampant specialisation in both the social and natural sciences. Policy science was proposed as a centripetal solution to this tendency toward increasingly segmented knowledge. Dror is the most forceful advocate of this role, arguing that the maturation of policy science would have three consequences for the state of knowledge: (1) the separation between basic and applied research would be bridged through a "synergetic relationship" between normal science and policy science,[55] (20) the specialist/generalist dichotomy would be rendered irrelevant with the emergence of the policy scientist, a "specialist in general approach and method,"[56] and (3) interdisciplinarity in policy research would eventually give way to supradisciplinarity, as a result of: (a) continuous exchange between social, natural, and administrative scientists working on common policy problems, and (b) deliberate development of professionals trained in the policy orientation.

Charles Frankel's comments on the idea of an independent and objective social science are also appropriate for an understanding of this aspiration of unified knowledge. Frankel suggests that the idea of an autonomous science of man represents an attempt to establish an Archimedean point; a rational perspective not dependent upon particular circumstances of time and place. He ascribes this quest a mythical significance: "The notion of an autonomous science of man is a liberal, secular civilisation's effort to achieve something like this perspective of immortality on itself."[57] Policy science is the most recent, and certainly the most explicit, manifestation of this quest for an independent vantage point, above the political fray, affording objective criteria upon which policy decisions can be made.

Beyond Analysis

The missionary admonitions of Dror today seem quaintly passe. Nonetheless, the analytical approach to policy making, which he advocated, is firmly entrenched, though it is often described as either policy analysis or policy studies rather than policy science. Alongside the analytical approach has developed a substantial body of criticism, the main currents of which are represented by Hughes,[58] Scott and Shore,[59] Lindblom and Choen,[60] Tribe,[61] and Horowitz.[62] In addition to such widely recognised difficulties as the possibility of value resolution through analysis, and the tendency for analysis to structure problems (and solutions) along certain paths owing to the fact that some phenomena are more readily accommodated in a mathematical model than others, there is increasing recognition that the analytical approach to policy-making is bounded by limitations of method and language.

The alternative is not altogether clear. Certain directions are suggested by Vickers[63] and Eric Jantsch though[64] little has been done to follow the leads they provide. While Vickers' conceptualisation of decision-making as 'appreciation' is acknowledged to be an important corrective to the rationalist model of purpose-driven man, the fact that his work has not attracted a greater following can be ascribed, mainly, to the ineffable character of appreciative behaviour. Moreover, the 'elitist disposition'[65] evident in Vickers' treatment of policy-making is alien to the Deweyist assumptions which underpin policy science. As to Jantsch, the less-than-enthusiastic reception accorded to his approach to the policy process is due to its excessive reliance upon parapsychology.[66] Jantsch argues the importance of such problematic concepts as

Teilhard de Chardin's 'noosphere'[67] thereby situating himself far outside the mainstream of policy study.

Central to the work of both Vickers and Jantsch is the idea that meaning and action are inextricably bound, therefore, the rationalist assumption of control at some remove from the process being directed is untenable. Instead, policy is understood to evolve out of the continuous interaction of meaning and action, with emphasis upon process and relations rather than ends. This is evident in Vickers' following observation; "policy making may be regarded as the by-product of a *situational* process; a process, that is, by which the conjunction of a particular situation in the world of events and the world of ideas produces a new situation in both worlds, which in turn gives rise to new acts of judgement and decision."[68] Policy choice and implementation are inseparable aspects of a regulative cycle. They are bound together in the appreciative system of the policy maker through the continuous dialectic between judgements of fact (instrumental judgement) and judgements of value (appreciative judgement), tending toward a balance in the relations being regulated.

Vickers suggests that methods of analysis suited to the study and regulation of organisations may be inappropriate at the level of society and public policy. The difference is due primarily to the far greater complexity of the communications system at the societal level. Indeed, Vickers considers that problems of communication represent the major obstacle to more effective policy making. Commenting upon the rapid obsolescence of plans, he explains:

> But the condition which produces this unhappy result is not primarily due to exploding technology but to the limitations of human communications. The long lead times which intervene between the emergent need for action and its achievement are partly due to the delays inherent in the processes of generating a sufficiently agreed view of the situation, a sufficient consensus on the course to pursue and sufficient common action to achieve it; and all these are collective processes, mediated by communications.[69]

This stress upon society's communication network leads Vickers to identify social learning as the key to improved policy making.[70] His suggestion that institutions be designed so as to facilitate learning at all levels, from that of individuals and discrete organisations to entire systems of organisations, anticipates Lindblom and Cohen's advocacy of interactive problem-solving as an alternative to analysis.

Jantsch follows Vickers in attributing the ungovernability of society to the breakdown of the system's appreciative system. His own approach to the policy process is characterised by two additional features: existentialism and an insistence on self-regulation as a universal principle of systems. Jantsch is critical of analytical approaches to policy, arguing that they are informed by an unrealistic separation between regulators and the system being regulated. Policy science, and the rational analytical approach generally, are of course located squarely within the mainstream of western rationalist thought. According to Jantsch, this implies that human systems can be understood merely as networks for processing information and marking decisions. This approach to human systems introduces two related distortions: (1) it stresses technological solutions to social problems, to the exclusion of cultural design (i.e., social change through value adaptation:; and (2) it is reductionist in that it denies that human systems are "more than the sum of individual expressions of their members". Jantsch maintains that society and its sub-systems possess a "life far richer and deeper – a life which heightens, magnifies, focuses, and restrains the life of all the human members which express themselves through these systems".[71] These systems are characterised by evolution toward increasingly complex forms within a harmonic whole. Whether this is more than an exotic reification in the spirit of Teilhard de Chardin is a moot point. Nonetheless, it does suggest an alternative approach to policy formation, involving social regulation through deliberate adaptation of the appreciative system.

Summing Up

Despite persistent expressions of doubt as to the appropriateness of the rational/ analytical approach to social problem solving, the growth of the amorphous policy science field has continued unabated. The paradox of policy science is precisely this wide acceptance by governments, especially in North America, of analysis and all that is attendant upon it (*viz.*, modeling, computer simulation and suchlike) as a guide to the identification and choice (optimisation) of policy alternatives, coincident with unremitting criticism of both the premises and actual contribution of the analytical approach. This criticism comes not only from academic, but from the politicians and administrators whom policy science is presumed to liberate from the vagaries of traditional policy making.[72] Relevant here is Lindblom and Cohen's suggestion that increasing awareness of the "competing attractions of science and art in problem solving" has tempered enthusiasm for policy science.[73] Social regulation through cultural design, as proposed by both Vickers and Jantsch, and interactive problem solving, as advocated by Lindblom and Cohen, give much-needed recognition to the 'art' of policy-making. Far from being a backward-looking condemnation of the rational/analytical approach, this is an attempt to establish an appropriate balance between the art and science of public policy making.

Notes

* From *Indian Journal of Public Administration*, Vol. XXIX, No. 2. 1983. pp. 215-228.

1. H. Lasswell, *A Pre-View of Policy Sciences*, New York, American Elsevier, 1971.
2. Y. Dror, *Design for Policy Sciences, and Ventures in Policy Sciences*, New York, American Elsevier, 1971.
3. R. Scott, and A. Shore, *Why Sociology Does Not Apply: A Study of the Use of Sociology in Public Policy*, New York, Elsevier, 1979.
4. C. Lindblom and D. Cohen, *Usable Knowledge*, New Haven, Yale University Press, 1979.
5. I. Horowitz, "Social Science Mandarins: Policy Making as a Political Formula", *Policy Sciences* 1 (3), 1970, pp. 339-360.
6. L. Tribe, "Policy Science: Analysis or Ideology?", *Philosophy and Public Affairs* (Fall), 1972, pp. 66-110.
7. S. Nagel, *The Policy-Studies Handbook*, Toronto, D.C. Heath & Co., 1980.
8. E. Quade, *Analysis for Public Decisions*, New York, American Elsevier, 1975.
9. Lindblom and Cohen, *op. cit.*
10. P. deLeon, "Policy Sciences: The Discipline and Profession", *Policy Sciences*, 13 (1), 1981, pp. 1-7.
11. D. Garson, "From Policy Science to Policy Analysis: A Quarter Century of Progress?", *Policy Studies Journal*, 9 (4), 1981, (Special Issue, No. 2), pp. 535-544.
12. *ibid.*
13. Scott and Shore, *op. cit.*
14. H. van Gunsteren, *The Quest for Control*, Chapter entitled "Anxiety and the Quest for Control", New York, John Wiley & Sons, 1976. See also Hannah Arendt, *The Human Condition*, Ch. VI, Sections 36-40, 1958.

15. V. Subramaniam, "The Science of Public Making: Towards a New Discipline" (transcript from a six-part series of radio lectures), Division of Postgraduate Extension Studies, The University of New South Wales, 1980.

16. Nagel. *op. cit.*, p. 204.

17. J. von Neumann, and O. Morgenstern, *The Theory of Games and Economic Behavior*, N.J., Princeton, 1944.

18. D.J. White, Decision Methodology: *A Formalization on the O R Process*, London, John Wiley, 1975.

19. Carol Weiss, *Using Social Research in Public Policy-making* Lexington, Mass. D.C., Health, 1977.

20. Scott and Shore, *op. cit.*

21. K. Vonnegut, Player Piano, New York, 1952.

22. D. MacRae, *The Social Function of Social Science*, New Haven, Yale University Press, 1976.

23. Horowitz, *op. cit.*, p. 340.

24. Lindblom and Choen, *op. cit.*, p. 84.

25. Tribe, *op. cit.*, p. 105.

26. Weiss, *op. cit.*, p. 16

27. Refer to the "Bibliography on Teaching Policy Studies", pp. 72-74 in Nagel, *op. cit.*

28. Nagel, *op. cit.*, ch.9.

29. Nagel, *op. cit.*, p. xi.

30. E. Stokey and R. Zeckhauser, *A Primer for Policy Analysis*, New York, W.W. Norton & Co., 1978, p. ix.

31. Nagel, *op. cit.*

32. Lindblom and Cohen, *op. cit.*

33. *ibid*, p. 26.

34. Lindblom and Cohen, *op. cit.*, p. 22.

35. C. Lindblom, *Politics and Markets*, New York, Basic Books, 1977, see especially Ch. 19, pp. 253-8 and Ch. 23, pp. 314-6.

36. Lindblom and Cohen, *op. cit.*, p. 18.

37. G. Vickers, *The Art of Judgement*, New York, Basic Books, 1965.

38. Dror, *op. cit.*

39. Lindblom and Cohen, *op. cit.*, p. 12.

40. J. Hughes, *The Philosophy of Social Research*, London, Longman, 1980.

41 D. Cohen and C. Weiss, "Social Science and Social Policy: Schools and Race", in Weiss (ed), *Using Social Research in Public Policy Making*, Toronto, D.C. Heath & Co., 1977, p. 68.

42. Horowitz, *op. cit.*, p. 341.

43. Scott and Shore, *op. cit.*, p. 7.

44. *ibid*, p. 13.

45. H. Hawkings, "The Ideal of Objectivity Among American Social Scientists in the Era of Professionalization, 1876-1916", in Frankel (ed.), *Controversies and Decisions*, New York, Russell Sage Foundation, 1976.

46. Lasswell, *op. cit.*

47. S. Hook, *Philosophy and Public Policy*, Carbondale, Southern Illinois University Press, 1980.

48. J. Dewey, "Science as Subject-Matter and as Method", *Science* 31 (1910), p. 217.

49. W. Edwards, "Technology for Director Dubious: Evaluation and Decision in Public Contexts", in Hammoned (ed.), *Judgement and Decision in Public Policy Formation*, Boulder, Colorado, Westview Press, 1978, p. 86.

50. K. Hammond and L. Adelman, "Science, Values and Human Judgement" in Hammond, (ed.), *Judgement and Decision in Public Policy Formation*, Boulder, Colorado, Westview Press, 1978.

51. Scott and Shore, *op. cit.*, p. 71.

52. Lindblom and Cohen, *op. cit.*

53. Tribe, *op. cit.*, p. 97.

54. H. Lasswell and D. Lerner (eds.), *The Policy Sciences*, Stanford, Stanford University Press, 1951, p. 3.

55. Dror, *Design for Policy Sciences, op. cit.*, Ch. 5.

56. Dror, *Ventures in Policy Sciences, op. cit.*, Ch. 22.

57. C. Frankel (ed.), *Controversies and Decisions*, New York, Russell Sage Foundation, 1976, p. 30.

58. Hughes, *op. cit.*

59. Scott and Shore, *op. cit.*

60. Lindblom and Cohen, *op. cit.*

61. Tribe, *op. cit.*

62. Horowitz, *op. cit.*

63. G. Vickers, *Freedom in a Rocking Boat*, New York, Basic Books, 1970; *Making Institutions Work*, London, Associated Business Programmes,

1973; *Value Systems and Social Process*, New York, Basic Books, 1968.

64. E. Jantsch, *Design for Evolution*, New York, George Braziller, 1975.
65. V. Subramaniam, "A Disposition Towards Decision Theory," *Indian Journal of Public Administration* 18 (10), Jan.-Ma., 1972, pp. 1-6.
66. V. Subramaniam, "Reflections on trends in Organization Theory," *Australian Journal of Public Administration*, December 1980.
67. P. Teilhard de Chardin, *The Phenomenon of Man*, New York, Harper and Row, 1959.
68. Vickers, *The Art of Judgement, op. cit.* p. 169.
69. Vickers, *Value Systems and Social Process, op. cit.*, p. 81.
70. This emphasis is evident in Vickers' brief article entitled, "The Future of Culture," in *Futures Research: New Directions* (1977).
71. Jantsch, *op. cit.*, p. 73.
72. An especially articulate expression of this criticism was delivered by Richard D. Lamm, Governor of Colorado, to a public policy symposium held in 1978. See his article, "The Environment and Public Policy" in *Judgement and Decision in Public Policy Formation* (1978).
73. Lindblom and Cohen, *op. cit.*, p. 91.

5

Politics of Implementation: The Achilles' Heel of Public Administration*

S.R. MAHESHWARI

Implementation of what has been planned and intended is a problem dogging almost all administrative systems today and has acquired a high degree of urgency in the developing countries. At the same time this area of administration continues to be under-researched one, demanding a closer and comprehensive look at this knotty issue. The first and foremost requirement for effective implementation is the need for sustained political and administrative commitment and support for the decided course of action. To improve policy making and its implementation, administrative reforms in the broad sense of the term must be carried out urgently.

Historically, Policy making did not accord much importance to implementation. It was assumed that implementation, its other terms being delivery of services and programme effectiveness, was a simple, pedestrian task raising no issues worthy of the attention of serious scholars. Implementation of a public policy was viewed as a mundane affair. In the early years of the recently decolonised nations the emphasis was naturally laid on plan making, and implementation was hardly viewed as a problem worth attention. But the evaluation of plans and programmes disclosed recurring weakness in implementation. So much so that it was universally, admitted that implementation is truly the Achilles heel of Indian

Administration. Its study easily constitutes a critical policy need across all levels of business of government. Since the early 1970s there has been a burgeoning literature focused on implementation. Mention may particularly be made of the following publications focusing attention of public policy makers:

1. Kaufman, H. and Couzens, M: *Administrative Feedback: Monitoring Subordinates' Behaviour*. Washington, the Brookings Institute, 1973.
2. Pressman, J.L. and Wildavsky, A.B: *Implementation: How Great Expectations in Washington Are Dashed in Oakland*. Berkeley, University of California Press 1973.
3. Hood C: *The Limits of Administration*, London, John Wiley, 1976.
4. Dunshire, A: *'Implementation Theory' in Implementation, Evaluation and Change*, Milton Keynes, The Open University, 1980.
5. Levitt, R: *Implementing Public Policy*, London, Groom Helm, 1980.
6. Hood, C: *The Tools of Government*. London, Macmillan, 1983.
7. Lewis, D and Wallace, H: *Policies in Practice: National and International Case Studies in Implementation*, Heinemann Educational Books, 1984.

Implementation of what has been planned and intended is thus a problem dogging almost all administrative systems today and has rightly acquired a high degree of urgency in the developing countries. Indeed, the national planners today find implementation a knotty area, defying easy and simple solution. At the same time, this area of administration still constitutes an under-researched one, demanding a more detailed dispassionate examination.

It was Woodrow Wilson (1856-1924), regarded as the father of the study of administration, who first, emphasised the need for sound implementation of policies and programmes while propounding his case for separateness of administration from policy. The Wilsonian dichotomy has today been firmly rejected. Yet the soundness of his observation that 'it is getting to be harder to run a constitution than to frame one'[1] made in 1887 is universally acknowledged. And in no other country is perhaps this realisation sharper than in India, a country which is glorious so far as policies are concerned but is verily a dwarf in the matter of implementation. India has been ceaselessly producing a plethora of social and economic plans ever since the start of economic planning in the year 1950 but their implementation has been poor and tardy. One should note that each Five Year Plan routinely devotes a chapter on implementation, where it does suggest ways and means of toning up of the country's public administration to improve execution even if the remedial measures are too superficial in kind.

A policy or programme is necessarily implemented in the field though it is made in the secretariat. The implementation process thus necessarily gets tied up with the dynamics of relationship between the headquarters and the field as well as between different agencies in the field. The discrepancy between a policy and its implementation may become wider when the policy depends on longer-run allocations. The original intent of the legislation may get obscured or diluted when it is funded year after year.

Traditional Approach to Implementation

The field holds the key to successful implementation. Brian Hogwood and Guy Peters rightly observe: The field staff must actually put the new policy into effect on the ground and it is therefore crucial to coopt the field staff into acceptance – if not support – of a new policy. It is perhaps more important to influence the field staff than the top leadership. They continue: It is at that level that real decisions about clients will be reached, and perhaps as importantly as it is at that level of the organisation that the new programmes will have to be 'sold' to clients who may be skeptical or outright hostile to the changes in their programme'.[2]

It has already been said that unpreparedness of the field is a reason for poor implementation. The field is seldom taken into confidence in determining policies and programmes; nor does it possess an appreciation of the overall plan or objective. It is not even sure of the methods and techniques it is using for executing these programmes. The only channels of communication open to it are 'noting on files' and manuals. Communication is usually one way, i.e., from top to bottom in the form of orders, directives, notification, circulars and memoranda. Above all, there are the 'sacred' manuals laying down in categorical terms the role of officials at various levels. Feedback from below upwards is not encouraged, if not even frowned upon. As regards manuals, the complaint of the field personnel is that the procedures and rules prescribed therein do not always fit the situation and often do not take into account operating ground level realities. Dimock and Dimock call this phenomenon "Manualities" which is defined as "an occupational disease, generally found in Government... that causes people to assume that everything in administration can be reduced to rule and embalmed in a procedure manual for the guidance of all employees in the organisation".[3]

Another aspect of this relationship is the mode and mechanism of control by the headquarters over field agencies. A number of commonly accepted techniques and devices exist by which administration at one particular level of an organisation may control the performance of subordinate field agencies. Such techniques may be in the nature of control before action is taken, for example, prior approval of individual projects before initiation by an operating unit; the promulgation of service standards; budgetary limitation upon the magnitude of operations; and approval of key subordinate personnel.[4]

It is not uncommon for field agencies to find themselves particularly handicapped by the imposition of detailed financial control by the Finance Department as also by an insistence on prior approval of the departmental headquarters office before any programme can be executed.

Control after action presently takes the form of reporting, audit, inspection and investigation. Indeed, one of the traditional methods of exercising control is for the headquarters to insist on receiving information from the field agencies in the form of returns, reports and statistics relating to the progress of field operations. The trouble with this method is that the returns and reports tend to multiply, thus entailing untold burden on the offices concerned without gaining commensurate advantages. Audit may be defined as an independent examination of every financial transaction, its main purpose being to prevent embezzlement, fraud, carelessness, errors, unauthorised expenditure, expenditure of excess allotment, and non-compliance with rules and laws. Two things to be noted about audit are: first, audit is a post facto function and is basically in the nature of a post-mortem scrutiny; and second, it has the limited function of examining compliance with rules and regulations in financial transactions.

Inspection, literally speaking, means looking carefully at or over, viewing closely and critically. Inspection is designed primarily to ensure that the existing rules, regulations, procedures and practices are observed. In order words, it ensures compliance with instructions. In this respect, it resembles the audit function. What audit is to financial transactions, inspection is to administrative activities. Such a limited view of inspection, however, is out of date in the present context of administration. Inspection, to be useful and effective, must develop a positive and affirmative character, and its scope should be widened to include some sort of audit of performance. These devices impair action-mindedness, which is India's requirement. Lastly, inspection is not a mere fault-finding process, and one of its essential elements should be instructing and guiding the person working in the inspected field agency, and actually demonstrating on-the –spot as to how defects have to be rectified and discrepancies reconciled. In an ideal system of inspection, the inspectors have to regard themselves as a part of the administrative process and assume responsibility for the successful working of the office or project in the same sense as other officials engaged in the work. Investigation is an inquiry into some alleged or suspected malpractice or abuse of authority. Its main purpose to discover the guilty person and prosecute him. Investigation is often personal and particular in character and, is usually on an ad hoc basis. All these devices have turned out to be too formalistic and mechanical that they only add to the confusion of the field level personnel without helping them in the implementation process. A comprehensively designed well-integrated plan of reform of headquarters-field relation is thus a pre-requisite of more efficient implementation.

Among the essential prerequisites to successful administration of field offices, the following may be enumerated: Effort should be made to create, at the headquarters as well as in the field, a full appreciation of the particular field situation so that they get induced to arrive at a decision appropriate to the situation. Orders should be, in the words of Mary Parker Follett, 'the composite decision of those who give and those who receive them' and this will maximise the chance of their acceptance. Follett calls this process as the 'law of the situation'. Field offices must be staffed by trained and competent personnel in adequate number, who can take sound decisions on matters falling within the sphere of their responsibility. The responsibility of the field officers must be clearly defined, and their limitations, too should be made clear to them. There should be free, frank and frequent communication between field officers of different departments in the same area on related problems. The powers given to field officers must relieve the headquarters of unnecessary work because powers have been handed down, it does not follow that they will be used. Special facilities including financial incentives should be provided in 'hardship' areas to attract competent staff. Periodic transfers from field to headquarters and *vice versa* and between fields are useful in inculcating a balanced outlook on local requirements and national policies. The existing 'tenure system' needs to be strengthened. Formal inspections, submissions of periodic returns and reports should be supplemented by informal visits by headquarters officers. These help build up rapport between the headquarters and field. Training courses and conferences between field officers and headquarters officers make them more competent, and keep them aware of each other's problems. This also results in the building up of community of interests. Field and headquarters officers must possess adequate knowledge of local needs and opinions, and, within the framework of the governmental policy and procedures, strive to meet these.

Finally, before a person is posted in the field, he should be given briefing by the headquarters on his own assignment and the problems and issues involved in it. This helps him in understanding his new job quickly and more completely. Likewise, there should be debriefing when he completes his field assignment. Debriefing may take the form of a few terminal interviews with the headquarters personnel wherein he communicates the operational problems and difficulties he encountered in his work. This would provide the much needed feedback to the headquarters.

The word 'implementation' is derived from the verb 'to implement', which means to 'put (a decision, plan, etc.) into effect'. Implementation is thus a central theme in public administration, which must not surprise a reader. "To administer' is nearly a synonym of 'to implement'.

New Insight into Implementation

A policy is not worth the paper on which it is written if it cannot be – and is not – implemented. The utmost care must therefore be taken to ensure successful implementation of whatever is finally decided. Implementation is not easy, not even in presidential form of government with its strong and effective executive. Henry Kissinger, former United States Secretary of State, has rightly warned. "The outsiders believe a presidential order is consistently followed. Nonsense. I have to spend considerable time seeing that it is carried out and in the spirit the President intended". This statement confirms two points: First, simply because an order has been issued it is not to be assumed that it will be carried out. Implementation requires concerted efforts. *Secondly*, the senior administrators will have to watch and see that what has been decided gets properly implemented. The implementation process inevitably throws up problems and challenges and administrators are called upon to act as trouble-shooters.

In the eighties, the Economic Administration Reform Commission headed by L.K. Jha, a former member of the legendary Indian Civil Service, was confronted with the widely held belief that India's 'major failure has been on the administrative front and that the machinery for the implementation of plan has not been equal to the tasks' emphasised the need for 'steps which can be taken to improve the implementation of plans'.[5] Implementation depends on the nature of the programme to a large extent and is thus not simple or easy. To improve implementation of plans included in India's five year plans, attention has to be given not only to the frame-work of policies and procedures, which public administration pursues, but also to the question whether the formulation of plans themselves need a measure of re-orientation to narrow down the gap between promise and performance.[6] Implementation inevitably highlights the multi- organisational nature of public administration. Implementation is an extremely complex process and involved in the process are a large number of agencies and personnel formally reporting to different authorities and thus subject to duality or even multiplicity of command. It is plainly wrong to believe that a programme is implemented by a single organisation alone and that it is solely responsible for its success. One may give an example. The implementation of a health programme is inevitably affected by other agencies involved in delivering integrally related facilities like housing, nutrition, educational services, etc. In a federation, different levels of government controlled by different parties may be involved thus pursuing differing goals in the same policy area. Implementation highlights the crucial role, which the lower echelons of administration necessarily play. As B. Guy Peter observes: "It is the cop on the beat as opposed to the commissioners, chief of police or other upper level personnel, who determines what the operational policy is going to be. ... As a general rule, it is necessary to discuss and to understand the operations of the lowest levels of administration in order to fully understand administration. Unfortunately, most of the literature on administration deals only with the upper echelon".[7]

Implementation in short demands the existence of a wide range of factors either in simultaneous or sequential operations. As a public policy necessarily seeks to accommodate a variety of interests operating in the society, it is a more or less balancing exercise. What may – in fact does – happen in many cases is that a law is deliberately made stiffer and stricter to satisfy one lobby but no adequate administrative arrangement is provided to enforce the law, apparently under pressure from the opposing lobby, resulting in implementation failure. A large number of laws in India have been enacted to satisfy the shouting 'brigades' but the policy makers ensure their defeat by not providing enforcement personnel that might upset the *status quo*. It is not an uncommon practice either to see a policy formally proclaimed by the government with great fanfare but the implementing agency is not provided with adequate funds to complete the job, the hidden motive being to please both sides of the demand. The policy on prohibition is an apt example. Implementation is much more intricate, complex and difficult in public administration.

First and foremost requirement for effective implementation is the need for sustained political and administrative commitment and support for the decided course of action. Indian experience is that such support is either hypocritical or at any rate begins to decline steeply in the course of implementation process. Such support must be evidenced by action – that is by the specification of the well-endowed agency or organisation made responsible for implementation. It would preferably be necessary to specify the legal and financial resources including the implementation personnel. This is mentioned here in view of the existing lacunas as at present hardly a sufficiently clear and detailed indication is given as to how its effective implementation is to be achieved. Functions and structures are not clearly and comprehensively defined. Add to this rather poor definition of responsibilities and authority at various levels of administration. All this aggravates confusion, which cannot but adversely affect implementation.

Executive agencies are continually buffeted by various interest groups and lobbies to score sectional gains. The political environment inevitably affects implementation processes in varying ways. Even organisational hierarchies have to contend with problems of rationality, sub-unit loyalty, distorted communication flow, weak supervision over subordinate behaviour, etc., - factors which impair implementation. Implementation cannot be ensured by mere reliance of promulgation of formal rules and instructions. These have to be heavily and continually supplemented. One such supplement is knowledge of alternative organisational structures to enable the planners to predict how alternative structures will behave over a period of time. Organisations, one must note, can be both barriers to implementation as well as facilitators.

Implementation shortfalls and gaps in many areas may be explained by insights thrown up by other researches. Implementation in many areas threatens the locally entrenched interest groups and such lobbies become aggressive and thwart execution. Implementers thus confront substantive problems and the locally entrenched vested interests impale their performance. It is common for the implementing or regulatory agencies to become dominated by their clientele. Studies by Selznick, Kaufman, etc., have shown that execution of programmes gets moulded by local pressure groups. Researches in rural development in India eloquently prove that many rural development programmes have become 'captives' of the local dominant social groups.

One should not overlook the organic relationship between formulation and implementation of policies. Public policy is framed by the political executive (even when the policy-administration dichotomy is firmly repudiated), but its implementation is the sphere of career bureaucracy, which is rule-bound and inflexible. Its sole concern is with its own procedures and evinces an inborn habit of moving in circles. Let this be said emphatically, formulation and implementation of policies constitute a continuum so to say and the various players throughout the process engage in mutual adjustment of goals and strategies. Implementation problems, equally, must be explicitly considered when policies are made. This precautionary measure will take care of the pitfalls, which often derail a plan and impede its execution. A plan when it is chalked out must be backed by an administrative plan also. This is not attempted in the country thus resulting in shoddy and poor implementation. A far saner course of action on the part of the national planners would indeed lie in the preparation of a concurrent administrative plan underpinning a general plan. This is done in China.

Some policies entail a long implementation process. This is particularly true in the case of the Central Government policies and programmes whose implementation generally rests in the hands of the lower state government. The Central Government agencies can in such cases exercise only indirect control over the remotely located executive bodies. The procedures and sanctions which can be invoked by the Centre are as a result weak and of uncertain efficacy in bringing out the desired change in the behaviour and motivations of implementing bureaucracy, especially the frontline functionaries. Planners generally adopt top-down hierarchical approach thus not fully recognising the crucial role of the implementing agency. This must change. Nor is there a free flow of information between the headquarters and the field. Rather, a nearly complete blockage of communication between organisations characterises the headquarters – field relationship. What is called for is an imaginative development of policy and procedures manuals as well as holding of regular meetings. There must be capacity building particularly at the point of service delivery. Implementation is apt to become weak as one goes down the administrative hierarchy. Real execution takes place at what is called 'the cutting edge of the administration'. Personnel at these levels lack clarity of policy. Sometimes they even see a contradiction between a part of the policy they are implementing and some other policy being executed by the same department. Besides, the present administrative practice in India of consigning the field posts to rather junior personnel with insufficient experience must be abandoned. It must be asserted that implementation highlights the crucial role which the lower echelons of the administration necessarily play: actual implementers are really the ground level functionaries. The cutting-edge bureaucrat -- the street-level bureaucracy as many Americans call him – wields considerable discretion in influencing the delivery system of welfare programmes. A student of rural development in India knows the central truth of this observation. By the same token, the policy making personnel sitting at the headquarters of the government show inadequate understanding of the cutting edge of administration. Studies of the British Civil Service amply show the weaknesses in the delivery system; the policy making senior management levels are found to possess little experience of managing or working where services are actually being delivered, that is the field. Indian experience is not otherwise.

Implementation is inevitably intertwined with the nature of the policies. Policies and programmes broadly fall into two areas. Erecting a factory is a policy – area where what is primarily required is technological skills and competence. But family planning falls into what is called discrete area where its success depend on larger social processes and changes, some being seemingly intractable. Implementation of family planning programmes – most programmes of development fall in this category is thus vastly more intricate calling for, among others, large – scale acts of social engineering and capacity building at the point of service delivery. Other problems could be: paucity of staff; financial and infra-structural constraints; unrealistic targets; and shortage of time.

The World Conference on Agrarian Reform and Rural

Development (WCARRD) organised by the FAO of the United Nations in July 1979 emphasised that the effectiveness of agricultural and rural development administration, especially at the field level, was the key to successful implementation of strategies for small farmer development. Its observations impart valuable lessons to national policy makers. Implementation of policies and programmes is replete with problems but the critical factor in it is the nature of the programme itself. If the policy, to be implemented, entails adverse effects on interests deeply entrenched then it can be neutralised only by firm sustained political determination. If the public policy focus is on change, opposition becomes all the more resolute and determined. The quality of public personnel is generally high at the headquarters and low in the field where implementation takes place. It is thus poorly trained and inadequately motivated functionaries who constitute the delivery system, resulting in implementation gap. This has already been referred to. Nor are policy makers in the area of development fully conversant with the field level realities.

As a result, field level beneficiaries of rural development programmes do not see any difference between the career bureaucracy and the local elite who have been traditionally exploiting the rural population. The field level bureaucracy too adopts a passive attitude and lacks zeal to improve receptivity of beneficiaries to developmental programmes. Also, one major cause of weak implementation is that organisational structure of government is incompatible with the functional requirements of national development. This anomaly leads to low morale in professional functionaries particularly in the field. Implementing agencies in many cases are not able to attract and retain high caliber personnel largely because of defective personnel policies but partly also because of poor working and service conditions. In developing countries, institutions engaged in policy planning and implementation are generally weak and low performing. This is more or less true all along the line and even non-governmental bodies and voluntary agencies have a weak base and wrong motivations. Finally, difficulties in implementation arise also from the very nature of rural development. Inputs and services in rural development are provided by several agencies which must function in well coordinated harmonious manner. Then alone, inputs and service are likely to reach small farmers scattered all over the area.

Poor implementation in many cases owes itself to poor designing of many development projects. As a result, time and cost overruns have been widespread, their target beneficiaries have remained deprived because of weakness in administrative planning and delivery mechanism. A more effective implementation demands a tighter project planning. Implementational shortfalls reveal imperfect knowledge about the micro-situation, inadequate data base and time and resource constraints. A designing of an irrigation project, for instance, requires correct and detailed information about water availability, land acquisition, irrigation intensity, cropping pattern, land productivity, cooperation of the water users to name a few. Very often assumptions made on them turn out to be woefully unrealistic as shown by subsequent studies. It is therefore absolutely desirable to go into all the necessary details to undertake extensive groundwork. The World Bank has rightly commented: 'Administration is not geared to identifying the people to be served, increasing their access to services, adapting services until they are appropriate, delivering them efficiently and observing (and reacting to) the public response'.[8]

To improve policy making and its implementation, therefore, administrative reform in the broad sense of the term must be carried out urgently. What is crucial is administrative reform all along the line. It must particularly be emphasized that improvement of administration at the periphery – in the field – is vastly more complex and difficult than at the centre. While improving implementation of programmes one must be absolutely clear that there is no single implementation model which might work in all situations. Generally speaking, conditions contributing to success in implementation are situation-specific and thus custom-made and peculiar to the soil. Improvement in administrative performance is imperative and to this purpose training of appropriate personnel is very necessary. To optimise its effectiveness, the training faculty must possess knowledge of even the practical issues involved in the development process. At present, training in many cases is not well led and well fed which produces no durable impact on the administrative situation. Training must also be integrated with the larger personnel management.

Coordination is a very weak feature of policy implementation in the country. Many district level developmental functionaries do not even show evidence of remembering, much less understanding of all development programmes under way in their jurisdiction even though there is a district coordination committee. The situation is really confusing, even chaotic as is explained by Paul H. Appleby, the well-known American expert who reported on India's public administration in the fifties: the district collector is made the jack of all trades. But 'no ministry knows how much of his time it is entitled to, and none has any capacity for ensuring that it receives that portion of his time and energy. The result has been a halting and rather unclear removal of certain functions and personnel from his direct jurisdiction, but this arrangement involves in turn an interaction of the responsibilities and personnel of the ministries of health, education and agriculture, along with the home ministry and the ministry of finance, in association with the development and/or community projects officers, and some lingering associations with the collector. In a technical, administrative sense, no one is really responsible for anything of much importance and all share in responsibility for almost everything'.[9]

To recall, reasons impeding implementation of public policies are thus multiple. The foremost in the list, of course, would be political considerations including political interference and apathy. As the implementation of a public policy, especially when it is designed to promote social equality threatens the status quo, those directly affected-and these are locally influential groups, the elite deeply entrenched in the local society-mobilise themselves, enlist political support to sabotage and neutralise the policy. It is well known that in India the pressure groups bend policy making to their advantage, more particularly at the implementation stage. Other barriers may be (i) financial difficulties, (ii) bureaucratic corruption, (iii) bureaucratic indifference, (iv) lack of people's participation, and (v) shortage of experts, especially in the field, etc. Other weaknesses could be in poor implementation strategy.

Efficient implementation, according to C. Hood[10], requires the fulfillment of the following conditions:

1. The subject matter of implementation must gain complete political acceptability and import. This is a pre requisite.
2. The resource availability of required scale and quality must be ensured.
3. The administrative system for the programme must be organised on the army lines with a single line of command. The administrative system must in other words, be unitary.
4. Rules to be enforced must be uniform and objectives must be clearly ascertainable.
5. Existence of well enforced obedience and administrative control.
6. High level communication and coordination should prevail between administrative units.

According to C. Ham and M. Hill,[11] successful implementation must require satisfactory solution of the following problems:

1. Nature of the policy – the policy should be unambiguous.
2. The links in the chain of the implementation structure must be kept to be minimum.
3. Prevention of outside interference.
4. Control over implanting actors.

Concluding Observation

One should conclude this paper with the advice which Machiavelli gave to his prince: "It must be considered that there is nothing more difficult to carry out, nor more doubtful of success, nor more dangerous to handle, than to initiate a new order of things. For the reformer has enemies in all those who would profit by the new order, this lukewarmness arising partly from fear of their adversaries, who have the laws in their favour, and partly from the incredulity of mankind, who do not truly believe in anything new until they have had actual experience of it. Thus it arises that on every opportunity for attacking the reformer, his opponents do so with the zeal of partisans, the others only defend him half-heartedly, so that between them he runs great danger.[12]

Implementation is not a problem exclusive to public administration. It depends in varying degrees on environmental inputs, legislative outputs (decisions), etc. In other words, implementation must be linked with and studied from, a more comprehensive systems angle calling for a wide-ranging strategy of action. Implementation acquires added significance in India in view of the alleged speculative bent of the Indian mind resulting in a certain 'lack of action-mindedness' in its people. This fear was diplomatically aired by Paul H Appleby in what has since become a classic report on Indian administration (1953). Referring to Indians 'lack of action-mindedness', Appleby elaborates:

This does not imply sloth, lack of social consciousness or irresponsibility. It refers to a way of thinking about and addressing action problems. It may be elaborated to the obverse side of the shield, which is one of India's distinct virtues – a bent towards and capacity for speculative thought. It is certainly related to a history that provided little opportunity for large scale action responsibility, it is a lack of highly developed capacity to conduct action institutions, which is to say an administrative lack. There is here, on the other hand, a new and extra-ordinary determination to overcome this lack.[13]

Notes

* From *Indian Journal of Public Administration*, Vol. XLIX, No. 4, 2003. pp. 679-692.

1. Woodrow Wilson, "The Study of Public Administration", *Political Science Quarterly*, June 1887, p. 4.
2. Brain Hogwood and Guy Peters, *Policy Dynamics*, Brighton, Wheather Books, 1983. p. 125.
3. Dimock and Dimock, *Public Administration*, New York, Rinehart, 1959, pp. 320-21.
4. See J.D. Millett, Management in the Pubic Service, New York, McGraw Hill, 1959, pp. 99-107.
5. Report of the Economic Administration Reform Commission on "Towards the Successful Implementation of the Seventh Plan: An over-view of Economic Administration", New Delhi, Planning Commission, 1984, p. 3.
6. Mohan Kaul, *An Inside View: Management Reforms in Government IIAS and CAPAM*, Commonwealth Association for Public Administration, 2000.
7. B. Guy Peters, *There Polities of Bureaucracy*, USA, Longman, 4th Edition, 1995, p. 10.
8. World Bank, *World Development Report*, The World Bank, Washington, D.C, 1982, p. 76.
9. Paul H. Appleby, *Public Administration in India: Report of a Survey*. New Delhi, Cabinet Secretariat, 1953, p. 20.
10. C. Hood, *The Limits of Administration*, London, John Wiley, 1976, pp. 6-7.
11. C. Ham and M. Hill, *The Policy Process in the Modern Capitalist State*, Sussex, Wheatsheaf, 1984, p. 99.
12. Niccolo Machiavelli, *The Prince and the Discourse*, New York, The Modern Library, 1940, pp. 21-22.
13. Paul H. Appleby, *Public Administration in India: Report of a Survey*, Delhi, Cabinet Secretariat (Organisation and Methods Division), 1953, p. 4.

6

The Use of Policy Evaluation in Policy Making*

ARIE HALACHMI

Rossi and Williams note that, "government and the academic community have recently focused much attention on evaluative research."[1] The government's interest is shown by its provision of special funds for evaluation research that are estimated to run as high as $ 130 million this year;[2] that of the academia, by the growing number of symposia and publications containing both evaluation results and methodological discussions.[3] The interdisciplinary interest in evaluation[4] is similar to the interdisciplinary interest in policy making. Consequently, it is of interest to find out if evaluation can generate policy-related knowledge. A positive answer to this question depends on the extent to which evaluation provides that understanding both of : (a) the policy, and (b) the environment in which it takes place. If these two are the initial goals of policy analysis,[5] we may assume that policy analysis that follows the methodology and convictions of evaluation research may constitute a preferred approach.

This paper attempts to illuminate some theoretical aspects of policy evaluation. It points out a number of dimensions evaluation research can add to policy analysis and some of its advantages *vis-à-vis* other approaches to policy analysis.[6] The paper does not elaborate every methodological aspect of policy evaluation, nor does it touch upon every aspect of the problematic inter-relationship between the policy maker and the analyst or the role of the latter as a "change agent."[7] Rather, the paper presents those points that should be considered if policy-evaluation is to be used in order to improve policy making.

Policy Evaluation: What is it All About?

Policy evaluation is an inquiry motivated by an "intellectual passion."[8] It "represents the application of social science research methods to discover information of importance to programmes practice and public policy."[9] Policy evaluation tries to link in an empirically demonstrable manner organizational settings, procedures and the impact of programmes. Thus policy evaluation generates the benefits of learning from past experience to create a basis for action the policy makers may want to consider.

Policy evaluation is an intellectual activity because it calls for judgment on the use of formal and tacit knowledge. Before the policy analyst applies knowledge, he has to judge the quality of the knowledge (or information) – e.g., its validity and adequacy for evaluating the policy in question. By passing judgment, the analyst creates an essential basis for his own conviction in the merit of his work. As the analyst builds up this conviction, by checking and rechecking whether the evaluation satisfies his own criteria of scientific demonstrability and moral values, he is building the case by which to persuade the policy maker to use the findings in subsequent decision making. Therefore, policy evaluation has to determine whether the fact that these were not found to be wrong and rejected to start with, makes them worthy of pursuing in the long run as well. Policy evaluation verifies whether the alleged issue with which a policy is concerned is the real issue that has to be dealt with and, that the policy can be carried out in the prescribed way, to reach the desired results. Policy evaluation attempts to establish the validity of all these before the actual course of events reveals a huge cost resulting from a fallacy in the policy. Therefore, the cost of policy evaluation can be looked upon as a premium paid to insure against possible future damages.

What Distinguishes Policy Evaluation From Other Modes of Policy Analysis?

One difference between policy evaluation and some other modes of policy analysis (such as benefit-cost analysis) is that policy evaluation is carried out before a decision is made, while it is being implemented, and after it is terminated – while others are used mostly before the decision is made, to help in the initial choice.

Another difference is that it does not assume a narrow definition of decision- making. Policy evaluation assumes that the choice is not completed when a particular option is singled out for implementation. Rather, it attempts to verify the soundness of the initial choice, and to make room for alteration if the choice is doubted as additional insight is gained through implementation.[10]

For that purpose, policy evaluation involves an early specification of the indicators that will be used to determine what has been attained, the trend of the policy's impact, and the economic and political efficiency of the implementation process. Above all, it involves a conscious definition of what constitutes a satisfactory level of achievement. Agreement on these definitions and measures before implementation of the policy starts may facilitate brave decisions later on. An open debate about evaluation standards may reveal the policy's value loading and contribute to its evaluation in the proper context. No less important is the possibility that a discrepancy between practice and standards would force a policy maker "to modify the real world or to change his standards."[11]

The conduct of policy evaluation as an integral part of all the phases of the policy making process may help the policy maker to review his decisions, prevent inertia, and cause the making of new decisions to become a joint product of the emergence of new needs and the consideration of previous decisions. Even when the policy maker is not faced with the need to reallocate resources, policy evaluation may bring him to reconsider the way in which he is trying to meet the demands of the past. Thus, it enables him to have initiative and be innovative not only in regard to present or future events, but past developments as well. It follows that policy evaluation is necessary even if an incremental strategy of policy making is used, if incrementalism is not to become identical to inertia.

The incremental approach to policy making as suggested by Lindblom[12] was criticised for being reluctant to make badly needed innovations.[13] Lindblom initially defended it by the need to limit risk taking. A related approach is expressed by Allen Schick, who calls for a move from analysis to evaluation. Schick suggests that analysis is appropriate for a situation "when underutilized slack resources are available, when there is a great deal of confidence in the efficiency of public action."[14] However, questioning the value of both suggested and established practices and goals does not make policy evaluation a conservative approach to policy making. Rather, policy evaluation creates the forces for innovation whenever the progress of past behaviour slows down or when new needs have to be answered. Policy evaluation demands a demonstration of an *a priori* capability, and the use of predetermined indicators to monitor progress encourages innovation but guards against uncalculated adventures.

Another difference is that policy evaluation does not attempt to base a decision on a simple consideration. Hill criticized benefit-cost analysis for using a narrow consideration of economic efficiency,[15] and suggested the use of the goals-achievement matrix instead. Matrix evaluation techniques[16] look at each policy or programme as a package of sub-goals. Evaluating each of these sub-goals on its own, and assigning proper weights to results, (according to their relative desirability for a policy maker, for a particular constituency, etc.) permits a more comprehensive evaluation that (unlike other modes of analysis) is sensitive to the complexities of social intervention[17] This satisfies the demand for contextuality, and assures that the evaluation is capable of giving the policy maker useful decision-making information.

Policy evaluation provides the policy maker with a direct reference to the substantive impact of a policy. so that he can make a normative judgment based on his attitudes towards risk taking, ideology, etc. In other modes of policy analysis, there is an indirect reference to the policy's impact – because such considerations as benefit-cost ratio create a halo effect and distort the policy maker's value judgment. For instance, if the policy maker compares the 3:2 benefit-cost ratio of a preventive programme to its previous rate of 4:2, and disregards the need to keep its momentum, he may decide to cancel the programme. But if it is a programme to control the plague, it can be successful only if no affected persons are left without treatment. The scattered and remote location of the last few untreated people – who carry the seeds of a new epidemic – involves a greater cost per person than do the first cases, which were easy to locate. A policy maker who judges the ratio rather than the substantive impact, and cancels the programme – leaving some affected people without treatment – reduces the effectiveness of the total programme, and thus the overall benefit-cost ratio. The consideration of short, medium and long range goals[18] in policy evaluation, helps the policy maker keep the real problem(s) in focus.

Experimentation and the Use of Controls in Policy Evaluation Policy evaluation is an attempt to prove the merit of a hypothesis expressed as a policy i.e., that an alleged problem can be dealt with in a certain manner so as to cause the desired changes in the environment.

A rigorous examination of merit is a common demand in any mode of policy analysis. In the context of policy evaluation, it has a special connotation. This special attribute is well expressed in Campbell's call to use experimentation in the policy making process and to build an experimenting society "which will make hard headed and multi-dimensional evaluations of the outcomes a key element in policy making."[19] In evaluation research, experimentation (or quasi experimentation when experimentation is not possible) has to do with the use of adequate controls. Their use makes it possible to define the elements that constitute the action and compare its impact on reality with a similar setting where the action did not take place.[20] This notion of looking at evaluation as a research paradigm was presented in the 1930's by Ralf Tyles as a way of developing curricula. Tyles' notion was based on the specification of hypothesis (what is expected to be found in class-room experimentation) providing the condition that would enable to generate information and the analysis of results. Indeed, this approach still dominates educational evaluation.[21] Experimentation as a part of policy analysis makes it possible to verify a causal relation – and, thus, to test the validity of the sponsor's assumptions about a policy's ability to lead to specific outcomes. Reflecting on the role of experimentation in social science, Stephan concludes: "Adequate social planning demands a knowledge of the field of operation of the planning programmes (it) calls for a rigid observation and 'control' over the possible factors which may affect a given situation. 'Control' is an attempt to observe and measure the forces put into operation and the results produced by these forces."[22]

The use of 'control' in policy making can logically be derived from the desire to assure its rationality. Policy making is an expression of intentions which are not necessarily coherent. They result from assumptions concerning the desirability of certain goals and of the ways they can be achieved. The implementation of a policy is, therefore, a test of the internal consistency of the policy maker's intentions and the validity of his assumptions. Through adequate controls, a policy's failure or success (determined by its observable impact, within a given empirical setting, on reality) provides a basis for conclusions about the compatibility of intentions, the feasibility of the goals, or the way they are reached. Without the ability to trace the results of a policy to their cause, the policy maker cannot generate the necessary information to guide him when he has to consider the continuation, modification or termination of the existing policies or the initiation of new ones.

The lack of adequate built-in controls may prevent the policy maker from anticipating the need to change the policy. However, by introducing 'controls' as a part of a policy evaluation scheme, he can avoid becoming subject to the course of events. The control that is used for purposes of evaluation constitutes, therefore, a mechanism that guarantees that the content of the feedback the policy maker gets would not be full of random noise. It follows that the analysis of a policy, *i.e.*, its evaluation, must be designed during the initial stages of the policy making process – the metastages, as Dror calls them.[23] When the use of simple experimentation or control is not possible, policy evaluation concentrates on the verification of the indicators, change levels, etc. that are claimed to suggest the merit of the policy. Dealing with these, policy evaluation must consider very carefully the inter-relation and the relative value of short, medium and long range effects and side-effects[24]. Since a full elaboration of this point is beyond the scope of this paper we would like to emphasise that such considerations constitute always a natural part of policy analysis because they have to do with the way the policy aims are understood and defined.

Policy Evaluation and Contextuality

The general quality of a policy evaluation cannot be better than the scientific value of its initial methodology and theoretical basis. In addition, the conduct of policy evaluation must satisfy the demand for contextuality. Moynihan states that "programmes relate to a single part of the system; policy seeks to respond to the system in its entirety"[25]. Therefore, the demand for contextuality that Lasswell suggests as essential in any form of policy analysis has a special importance in policy evaluation.[26] The evaluation of a policy may be a liability – both economic and political. Consequently, it is always important to clarify in advance 'what decisions about the programme or its objective will be affected by the results of the evaluation?' As Suchman sees it, "further development of this question could force consideration of why the evaluation was being done. What alternative courses of action were being considered, who was in favour or opposed to the evaluation, how much would the results of the evaluation carry and what resources existed or could be marshaled to support the recommendations of the evaluation."[27] Suchman refers mainly to evaluation that takes place after a policy or a programme is implemented. Nevertheless, these considerations are no less important when the evaluation is done before a policy is adopted. The question concerning the impact of the evaluation on decision-making is always true, because every decision involves either approval or departure from an old decision. Contextuality is, therefore, an attempt to influence the evolutionary nature of decision-making.

When we refer to policy evaluation, contextuality is understood to include at least the following components:

(1) Substantive Contextuality – those aspects of the issue in which a change is or was desired. These aspects can be identified by the influence of the policy on 'social indicators' – e.g., how does a particular zoning policy influence the ratio of family members per room?

(2) System Contextuality – the functional importance of the issue not only on its own merit, but also its value for the political environment of the policy maker. For example, how does state regulation of public utilities relate to the values of free enterprise, on one hand, and the public interest, on the other? A case in point is Title I of ESEA. Six years after its passage, Murphy questions whether this spirit of reform was translated into educational practice. "Has state and local administration reflected these new priorities?" These questions are important, he claims, because their answers "provide useful information about the limits of federally-initiated reform....(and) a better understanding of the problems of implementation."[28]

(3) Policy Making Contextuality – the decision the policy maker must take, not only among alternative policies concerning the same goal, but about the priorities among competing goals. For example, he must decide on financial aid to big cities and deal with it, while he tries to curb inflation; or, he has to respond to demands and, at the same time, solve environmental problems when the only way to do it is to reduce the consumption and availability of energy.

Policy making contextuality always has to do with the basic facts that "everything relates to everything", and that "there are no social interests about which the national government does not have some policy or other, simply by virtue of the indirect influences of programmes nominally directed to other areas."[29] Therefore, policy making contextuality suggests the need to reach a minimal level of comprehensiveness. This level is dependent on: (1) the general complexity of the environment within which the policy maker is acting – i.e., its political, socio-organizational and economic characteristics, and

(2) the organizational characteristics and the distribution of

programmes and projects by which a policy is expected to be implemented.

The organizational settings, programmes and projects involved in the implementation of one policy also concern other policies, including the so-called "hidden policies". The latter may include policies that prohibit the abolition of existing institutions or programmes. The critical level of comprehensiveness a policy evaluation needs in order to answer the demand for contextuality is, therefore, largely determined by the constraints it should consider. To ignore these constraints may sharply limit the value of any assessment for the policy maker. For example, the evaluation of an urban renewal policy cannot be limited to measures of the land that is 'recovered', the number of families that are relocated, the economic cost and benefits. Such evaluation must consider the initial attitudes of the population in the 'target area' towards the local authorities, and their attitude after they have been relocated, the attitudes of other groups towards the proposed projects, general and local economic conditions, constraints imposed by state and federal authority on the practices and scope of the urban renewal, etc. Even these numerous examples do not add up to an exhaustive list. An evaluation that fails to consider such factors – to the extent that they have to do with policy impact – is distorted and thus has limited value for the policy maker. As Carol Weiss has suggested, "Decision makers respond to a host of factors besides evidence of programme effectiveness. They are concerned with the political and organisational feasibility of the programme; its acceptability to funders, staff and constituents; the availability of money. They may have an ideological commitment to the programme or an interest in maintaining the agency's position in the field. They may fear the unknown consequences of change and feel more comfortable in the *status quo*."[30]

The importance of all the three dimensions of a policy's context is illustrated by the Westinghouse-Ohio evaluation of Head Start,[31] where they were partially ignored. In 1967, two years before the Westinghouse-Ohio evaluation was published, Clara Riley and Frances Epps told the story of one of the Head Start programmes. As they saw it, "Head Start has captured the hearts and the imaginations of those persons concerned with the welfare of children and their development. It truly provides the proving ground for the oft-voiced concept, which has tended too often to be mere lip service, of dealing with the 'whole child'. Through Head Start, teachers, doctors, psychologists, social workers and families are planning and concentrating their efforts in a 'package' for the true concern and development of the 'whole child'."[32]

A year later, but still almost a year before the release of the Westinghouse-Ohio report, McDavid summarized the general problems in evaluating Head Start programmes as follows:

(1) Head Start is a comprehensive, multi-dimensional programme, not a stable, uniform, easily described form of intervention.

(2) Goals are pursued simultaneously for immediate and ultimate impact.

(3) There is a paucity of information about the disadvantaged population.

(4) It is extremely difficult to describe pre-school programme elements for clarity of comparison and contrast.

(5) There is a conceptual problem of formulating researchable questions.

(6) Methodological problems are many – especially the difficulty of sampling, in view of the non-random variations in the population and the difficulty of locating control groups.

(7) Logistic problems have to be considered. The nature of the Head Start programmes requires evaluation to be unobtrusive and subordinate to programme demands.

(8) There are problems of middle-class researchers dealing with lower-level adults in data collection.[33]

The Westinghouse-Ohio evaluation was intentionally limited[34] to one aspect of the educational merits of the programme – the improvement of cognitive ability – leaving out all other aspects, including the value attached to it by the administrators of the programme, the children who participated in it, and their parents. A possible discrepancy, therefore, results among the goals assumed for Head Start by the Westinghouse-Ohio team in the actual study (cognitive and effective development), the question posed in the Executive Summary ("To what extent are the children... who attend Head Start programmes different in their intellectual and social personal development from comparable children who did not attend?"),[35] and the goals assumed by administrators, parents and children. This discrepancy may be responsible for the different assessments of Head Start by different parties.[36]

The improvement of cognitive ability with which the Westinghouse-Ohio evaluation was concerned has to do with substantive contextuality. However, it does not necessarily constitute the only substantive aspect, or the most important aspect, by which the whole educational concept that underlay Head Start can be appreciated. John W. Evans, who contracted for the Head Start evaluation, is aware that "since its release, the Westinghouse study has occasioned considerable, even bitter debate." Evans' explanation of this is illuminating: "If we are to understand the heat that spiced this controversy, we must look less to the purely methodological issues in the exchange and more to the fact that the findings of the study have been difficult to accept."[37] Evans accepts the possible existence of some methodological problems, but does not give up the validity of its findings. To be sure, he overlooks the fact that Westinghouse-Ohio evaluation passed a verdict on the idea of Head Start by referring to questionable measures of teaching effectiveness. The Westinghouse-Ohio report concludes that children did not get a head start as a result of the programme they attended. It implies that the idea of Head Start is wrong without a demonstration that the teaching methods, the quality of the teachers, the material studied and the exams (by which effectiveness of the programmes is concluded) are adequate and capable of creating the desired effect. For purposes of policy making, this implication is misleading. It comes as an answer to a policy question – should the idea of Head Start be further pursued or should it be abandoned – while it refers to a narrow research problem that the evaluating team defined for itself.

The Westinghouse-Ohio evaluation of "head start" should be looked upon in connection with the observation offered by Lewis Anthony Dexter some years before it was carried out. According to this observation, good researchers that are qualified to undertake technical research on attitudes, for instance, are not equipped to answer the policy questions underlying their particular assignment. The right way to utilise such experts is to bring them in after the problem has been analysed "at the highest relevant policy levels with informed social scientists able to think in policy terms *from the standpoint of the enterprise*."[38]

The Westinghouse-Ohio report testifies that parents of Head Start children participated more actively in school affairs. This indicates a willingness to cooperate, and acceptance of the idea by the target population. It means that the policy may be effective in reducing the need to spend resources just to overcome resistance or the alienation feeling of that population toward the government. Such conditions would have crippled the project even if it was capable – technically – to produce the desired change. The negligence of system contextuality in the Westinghouse-Ohio evaluation is reflected in the low emphasis it gives to this cooperation. This paper does not speculate on the possibility that 'cognitive improvement' cannot be achieved under hostile conditions. Rather, it suggests that cooperation is a precondition for efficient intervention; its existence, therefore, indicates a potential change, even if such a change does not materialize or is not directly measurable. Since the report does not establish beyond doubt that 'cognitive improvement' is not conditioned by attitudes, the substantive contextuality of the evaluation is also deficient.

Harry Passow notes that "the Westinghouse-Ohio University evaluation was not the first study of Head Start, but the timing and the nature of the release of the findings resulted in wide spread impression that such programmes were of very limited value and such efforts were generally futile.[39] This observation testifies to the evaluation's relevance for purposes of policy making. President Nixon referred to the Westinghouse-Ohio evaluation for purposes of policy making.[40] Thus, it is of secondary importance whether this particular evaluation influenced the making of one or another decision. The important thing is that it influenced the attitudes of administrators and the subjects of such programmes, making them suspicious of the government's real intentions and even more reluctant to cooperate with policy evaluators. In sum, lacking rigor and contextuality, this evaluation did not contribute much to the betterment of policy making. As Campbell notes, "Head Start was a disastrous example of good intentions and bad methodology producing worthless evaluation."[41]

What Concerns Policy Evaluation

Policy evaluation attempts to verify whether a certain action caused (or is capable of causing) a particular impact. It deals with the adequacy[42] of the impact and the way by which it was brought about. Thus, it is concerned with effectiveness.

To prove effectiveness, the evaluation attempts to establish:

(1) That the policy is capable of bringing about the desired substantive results. Friedland *et al.*, for example, found that determinants of compliance with rules depend upon whether both the law maker and the individuals are going to benefit from the individual's compliance or only the law maker will. If only the law maker benefits Friedland et. al., call this relation 'correspondent'. If on the other hand, if both the individual and the law maker benefit from the law they call it 'non-correspondent'. In the first case, rule enforcement

methods are likely to become irrelevant factors. In the other, however, variations in enforcement methods have differential effects upon the individual's compliance with the rules.[43] Thus, the question concerning the ability to cause a particular change of behaviour – e.g., to make drivers use seat-belts by law, depends on the ability to create 'correspondent' relations between the individual and the law maker or, on the selection of an appropriate enforcement method – e.g., in their absence.

(2) That the alleged results are products of the specific characteristic of the policy, and could not be achieved through any other policy – e.g., that safe streets are the result of taking young men off the streets to participate in sports, and cannot be achieved to the same extent by putting more police cars on the streets.

(3) That the policy is feasible for a given policy maker and his political environment – e.g., that a Senator who proposes a clean water bill can survive a confrontation with big business. This, for example, was not the case of Senator Muskie in 1963 when he tried to pass his clean water bill. Even though the bill was finally accepted in 1965, it might have contributed to his failure as a presidential candidate in 1972.[44]

(4) That the policy, or the organisations' programmes and projects by which it is implemented, indicate the future feasibility of the existing level of results and the durability of the achieved results.[45]

(5) That the policy or some of its principles can be expanded to include other segments of the population or other related issues.[46]

Once the expected or actual impact of the policy is defined, policy evaluation goes on to evaluate the process and organization by which this impact is brought about – i.e., the efficiency of the policy. For that purpose, the evaluation attempts to establish several things.

(a) That the chosen process is indeed the preferred course of action for reaching the prescribed goal. [47]

(b) That the relation between the resources used and the output is such that it is not possible: (i) to increase the output substantially by marginal change (e.g., increase) in the input, or (ii) to decrease the output marginally by a major change (e.g., substitution) in the needed resources.[48]

(c) That it is not possible to generate the desired results as a by-product of the attempt to reach another goal.

By application of the experimental and quasi-experimental approaches, the policy analyst may relate the elements of the input and the implementation process to the change attributed to the policy. The policy maker is then in a position to appreciate the efficiency rating of the procedures he uses to make this impact. A policy maker may even want to look for evaluative indicators and build them into the programme before they are launched.[49] The use of such indicators can facilitate evaluation once the analyst verifies that changes in the indicator are the result of the programme and not of a host of other factors.[50]

In programmes like Head Start or crime control, where the realisation of results may take time and prevent the use of direct indicators, such factors as cooperation and interest may be used as indirect indication that the policy may have a desired impact. The policy maker is then able to decide whether he wants to use another procedure (which he assumes has other political and economic characteristics) in order to carry out the policy. In view of such indications, the policy maker may try to differentiate the political value of the policy and the political value of the way in which it is carried out.

Policy Evaluation and Policy Revision

Writers tend to see decision-making as an evolutionary process in which new decisions evolve from previous ones.[51] These observations imply that the unmaking of old decisions is the result of making subsequent decisions, not of a deliberate intention to alter or to abandon the old ones. The termination of a decision is not explicit, but rather implicit and indirect. It follows that policies are abandoned because their relative saliency decreases, and not because of their inadequacy.

When policy making is coupled with an ongoing evaluation, the abandonment of a decision is made explicit. The policy maker and his constituency can judge not only the value of the policy that is ended, but also the value of the trade-off – i.e., the relative value of the new policy whose adoption became possible by the reallocation of resources. Policy evaluation, therefore, calls for an updating of standards according to changes in expectations, values, environment, etc. This facilitates the estimation of the trade-off between the political and economic benefits and costs of the policy, and assures that the policy is considered in the proper context. Such an estimation is important when either the economic or the political results are not enough in themselves to end a project. A policy maker may face such a situation when he decides whether to trade with a boycotted country – paying a high political cost for economic benefits – or to refrain from trade, paying an economic cost for political benefits. A policy maker may choose to continue old policies until a more promising policy can be identified. In that sense, policy evaluation is not concerned with the assessment of past performances as a retrospective yardstick of accountability (marking a policy maker's score card);[52] it has to provide indicators of future performance as a sound basis for decision.

Terminating a policy on the basis of an explicit consideration should be considered from still another angle. In a society of scarce resources, worthless policies (including "hidden policies")[53] should be abandoned so that resources can be saved for future needs. Evaluation can make a policy maker aware that a particular policy is worthless or even disfunctional for the conservation of resources. A case in point is the U.S. policy concerning the import of oil. For many years, the American government imposed a quota on the import of American oil. This policy did not serve the genuine interests of the U.S., but it was reconsidered only after the 1973 oil embargo.

Policy Evaluation and Values

Policy evaluation is not a value-free analysis. First of all, there are the values of the policy maker; these influence the definition of the goals and the constraints (both on the achievement of goals and the evaluative process itself).[54] Then there are the values of the analyst; these influence the way the evaluation is carried out and the way its findings are presented.[55]

Other modes of policy analysis are not free from this deficiency, either. However, the influence of this bias on the normative judgment of the policy maker can be controlled in policy evaluation more than in other modes of policy analysis. Nash, Pearce and Stanley suggest that, "whatever technique is used should allow the decision maker and interested persons to identify its underlying value judgments and examine how evaluation results change with changes in the value judgment."[56] If this prescription is followed, the claim that administrators and policy makers are excluded from influencing the mode of evaluation does not hold.[57]

The design and tools of evaluation and the goals it assumes, can be established after they are seen to be consistent with the value judgment and preferences of policy makers and administrators. If no single evaluation design is acceptable to the policy makers, administrators and subjects of a policy or a programme, there is a problem. However, this problem has nothing to do with policy evaluation; it is a political problem that concerns whose values and preferences will prevail.

Even after there is an agreement about the proper value judgment, a prediction of 25 per cent, 35 per cent, 50 per cent or 75 per cent effectiveness for a programme does not imply that a particular decision must be made. The normative judgment whether X per cent of success is sufficient to continue, halt or change a programme is always at the discretion of the decision-maker; equipped with evaluation results, he responds on the basis of his own convictions. He can halt a programme even if it is found to be 75 per cent effective, or he may choose to go on with it even if it is found to be only 10 per cent effective. In both cases, the decision is subjective and political; it has nothing to do with the judgment made in the evaluation.

This prerogative of the policy maker does not always hold in other modes of policy analysis. For instance, when the benefit-cost ratio constitutes the core of policy analysis, a normative judgment is expressed by the analyst in his decision to include some quantitative benefits and costs but not others, and to overlook the qualitative ones, or some of them, because they are hard to handle. This may be the case, for example, when the gains from new jobs (even with the monetary value of the feeling of economic security) are measured against the cost of investment in industry, but no consideration is given to the cost or benefit from the environmental impact of new industries. This deficiency may have a special significance in the case of broad-aim programmes, where the possible difference between the ability to reach a specific sub-goal and the ability to change – even marginally – the overall situation may render a policy unworthy and cause its rejection. Weiss and Rein observe that "the administrators of a broad-aim programme are apt not to know in advance exactly how the system change they hope to achieve will itself change."[58] Even when the policy maker presumes to know what he is expecting, "what at first seems clear often evaporates when the test of measurability is applied. The language use turns out to be ambiguous precisely where it should have to be specific in order for evaluation to be useful.[59] Walter Williams notes that "in the Community Action Programme it is not at all clear whether such things as resident participation or community organization are to be viewed as goals or means."[60] Some of these difficulties occur because of the better insight that results from the implementation itself. Therefore, the policy maker who gains this extra insight can help the analyst make the evaluation accurate and useful.

In policy evaluation, the experimental approach (that is lacking in other modes of policy analysis) encourages the policy maker to participate actively in the exploration of new opportunities, definitions of goals, results and processes without unintentionally turning such exploration into costly adventures. These approaches allow value judgments to be postponed until insight is gained; in this respect, policy evaluation is not much different from Klein's sequential model approach to decision making.[61] The discretion of the policy maker to make his own value judgments is even more evident when policy evaluation takes the form of goal-free evaluation – when reference is made not to nominal plans and goals, but rather to the actual achievements of a programme.[62] In this case, the policy maker has to decide not only how the results correspond to his initial aim, but also whether to go on with a policy when the results are judged on their own merit.

It was suggested at the beginning of this paper that policy evaluation should be viewed as the premium paid for insurance against possible future costs. The relationship between an analyst and a policy maker has some similarity to the relationship between an insurance agent and his client – particularly in regard to trust and reliability. Therefore, policy evaluation does not suggest that a value bias be eliminated by excluding the policy maker from the evaluation process.[63] Both policy maker and the analyst are in a position to influence the values of the other; both have the freedom to decide whether they are willing to accept this influence. The possibility that a policy maker will be unable to resist the influence of an analyst is a problem that concerns the policy maker's readiness and ability to carry out his job; it has nothing to do with policy evaluation's capability to improve policy making.

Notes

* From *Indian Journal of Public Administration*, Vol. XXIII, No. 4. 1977. pp. 1035-1054.

1. Peter H. Rossi and Walter Williams (eds.), *Evaluating Social Programmes*, New York, Seminar Press, 1972, p. XIII.
2. This estimation is suggested by Thomas D. Lynch in his editorial introduction to the *Bureaucrat's* special issue on Program Evaluation, Vol. 5, no. 1, April 76, p. 3.
3. The *PAR* devoted its Summer 1974 issue to a symposium on program evaluation and the Bureaucrat did the same thing frequently in the first issue of its 5th volume April 76. Other examples include the *Bibliography in Program Evaluation* complied by Sangmon State University, Program Evaluation

Center; the *Project Formulation and Evaluation series* published by the U.N. Industrial Development Organization, Vienna, New York, 1972; the magazine *Evaluation,* published by the Program Evaluation Project of the University of Minneapolis, Minnesota; and the collection *Public Policy Evaluation* edited by Kenneth M. Dolbeare and sponsored by the Policy Studies Organisation and published by Sage (1975).

4. Charles N. Brownstein, "The Experimental Evaluation of Public Policy: An Overview," (paper delivered at the 1974 meeting of the American Political Science Association, Chicago), p. 2.
5. Yehezkel Dror, *Ventures in Policy Science*, N.Y. Elsevier 1971, pp. 230-231.
6. For elaboration on some disadvantages of other approaches to policy analysis cf. Christopher Nash, David Pearce and John Stanley, "Criteria for Evaluating Project Evaluation Techniques", *American Institute of Planners Journal*, Vol. 41, no. 2 March 1975, pp. 83-86.
7. For elaborations on the role of the change agent in the context of policy evaluation see Aaron Wildavsky "The Self-Evaluating Organization", *Public Administration Review* 32, 5, Sept.-Oct. 1972, pp. 509-519. The concept of the "Change Agent" was developed initially in connection with the introduction of planned change. In that context the change agent performs several roles including those of an organization analyst, a broker of knowledge. See Ronald Lippitt et. al., *The Dynamics of Planning of Change*, N.Y. Harcourt, Bruce & Co. 1958, chap. 5, Warren G. Bennis *et. al., The Planning of Change*, 2nd Ed., N.Y. Holt, Rinehart and Winston Inc. 1969, chap. 11.
8. Michael Polaney, *The Study of Man*, London, Routledge, 1959, p. 13.
9. Carol H. Weiss, *Evaluating Action Programs*, Boston, Allyn & Bucon 1972, p. 4. For other attempts to define the objectives of evaluation v. John Wholey, *Federal Evaluation Policy,* Washington, D.C. The Urban Institute 1970, p. 23; Francis G. Caro, "Approaches to Evaluative Research: A Review" *Human Organizations*, Vol. 28, no. 2 (summer 1969), pp. 87-89.
10. It is important not to confuse policy evaluation with Klein's sequential model of decision-making in which the choice is postponed until a better insight into the problem becomes

available. cf. Burton H. Klein, "The Decision Making Problem" in National Bureau of Economic Research. *The Rate and Direction of Inventive Activity*, Princeton University Press, 1962.

11. Malcolm M. Provus, "Evaluation for Decision-Making, Choice and Value", *Journal of Research and Development in Education* 3, no. 4, Summer 1970, p. 1.

12. Lindblom, "The Science of Muddling Through", *Public Administration Review*, Vol. 19, no. 2, 1959, pp. 79-88.

13. Y. Dror. "Muddling Through – Science or Inertia", *Public Administration Review*, Vol. 24, no. 3, 1964, pp. 153-157.

14. Allen Schick," From Analysis to Evaluation", *The Annals of the "American Academy of Political and Social Sciences,* 394, March, 1971, p. 57.

15. Maurice Hill, "A Goal Achievement Matrix for Evaluating Alternative Plans", *American Institute of Planners*, 34, no. 1, 1968, pp. 19-29.

16. W.D. Jessiman, *et al*., "A Rational Decision-Making Technique for Transportation Planning", Washington, D.C., Highway Research Record No. 180, 1967.

17. Daniel P. Moynihan, "Policy vs. Program in the '70s", *The Public Interest*, 20, Summer 1970, pp, 97f.

18 Edward A. Suchman, *Evaluation Research*, N.Y. Russel Sage Foundation 1967, pp. 51f.

19. Donald T. Campbell, *Methods for the Experimenting Society*, mimeograph 1971, p. 1.

20. Robert S. Weiss and Martin Rein, "The Evaluation of Broad Aim Programme: Experimental Design, its Difficulties, and an Alternative", *Administrative Science Quarterly*, 15, 1 (1970), pp. 97-109; and a reply by Donald T. Campbell, "Considering the Case Against Experimental Evaluations of Social Innovations", *Administrative Science Quarterly*, 15, 1 (1970), pp. 110-113.

21. Malcolm M. Provus, "Evaluation for Decision Making, Choice and Value", *Journal of Research and Development in Education*, Vol. 3, no. 3 (Summer 1970), p. 9.

22. A. Stephen Stephan, "Prospects and Possibilities: The New Deal and the New Social Research" in Francis G. Caro (ed.), *Readings in Evaluation Research*, New York, Russel Sage, 1971, p. 38.

23. Yehezkel Dror. *Public Policy Reexamined*, San Francisco, Chandlere, 1968, p. 8.
24. The side effects constitute this part of the impact that is considered secondary in importance whether intended and planned for or not.
25. Moynihan, *op. cit.*, p. 91.
26. Harold D. Lasswell, *A Pre-View of Policy Sciences*, New York, Elsevier, 1971, p. 4.
27. Edward A. Suchman, "Action for What: A Critique of Evaluative Research" in Carol H. Weiss (ed.) *op. cit.*, p. 55.
28. Jerome T. Murphy: "Title I of ESEA: The Politics of Implementing Federal Education Reform", *Harvard Educational Review* 41, 1, Feb. 1971, p. 36f.
29. Moynihan, *op. cit.*, p. 93.
30. Carol H. Weiss, *op. cit.*, p. 11.
31. V.G. Cicirelli *et al.*, *The Impact of Head Start: An Evaluation of the Effects of Head Start on Children's Cognitive and Effective Development*, Washington, D.C.: O.E.O. June 1969.
32. Clara M.D. Riley and Frances M.J. Epps, *Head Start in Action*, West Nyack, Parker Publishing Co., 1967, p. XIII.
33. J.W. McDavid, "What Kinds of Changes Occur in What Kind of Children Under What Kind of Programs: The National Evaluation of Head Start", Wash., D.C. HEW 1968.
34. John W. Evans, "Head Start: Comments on the Criticisms" in Francis G. Caro (ed.): *Readings in Evaluation Research*, N.Y., Russel Sage Foundation 1971, p. 400.
35. V.G., Cicirelli, *op. cit.*, p. 1.
36. For other claims that have to do with the methodological aspects of the study, cf. Walter Williams and John W. Evans, "The Politics of Evaluation: The case of Head Start" in Peter H. Rossi and Walter Williams (eds.), *Evaluating of Social Programs*, N.Y., Seminar Press 1972, pp. 247-264.
37. John W. Evans, "Head Start, Comments and Criticism", in Francis G. Caro (ed.), *Reading in Evaluation Research*, New York, Russel Sage Foundation, 1971, p. 40.
38. Lewis Anthony Dexter, "Impressions About Utility and Wastefulness in Applied Social Science Studies", *American Behavioural Scientist* 9, 3, (Nov. 1965), p. 9.

39. A. Harry Passow (ed.), *Opening Opportunities for Disadvantaged Learners*, New York:, Teachers College Press, 1972, p. 15.

40. Williams and Evans in Rossi, op. cit., p. 261, See also *Public Papers of the Presidents*: Richard Nixon 1970, Wash. D.C. Government Printing Office, Document No. 66, pp. 231-232.

41. Carol Tavris, "The Experimenting Society: A Conversation with Donald T. Cambell", *Psychology Today* 9, no. 4. (Sept. 75), p. 52.

42. O. Lynn Deniston *et al.*, "Evaluation of Program Effectiveness and Program Efficiency" in Fremont J. Lyden and Ernest G. Miller (eds.) *Planning Programming Budgeting*, 2nd Ed., Chicago, Markhan 1972, p. 142.

43. Nehemia Friedland, John Thibaut and Laurens Walker, Some Determinants of the Violation of Rules", *Journal of Applied Social Psychology* 3, 2, 1973, pp. 103-118; and, John Thibaut, Nehemia Friedlandand Laurens Walker, "Compliance with Rules: Some Social Determinants", *Journal of Personality and Social Psychology*, 30, no. 6, 1974, pp. 792-801.

44. James L. Sundquist, *Politics and Policy*, Washington D.C. The Brookings Institution 1968, p. 363. *Newsweek*, Aug. 23, 1971.

45. Walter Williams, *Social Policy Research and Analysis*, N.Y., Elsevier, 1971, pp. 85-86.

46. *ibid.*

47. Dror defined a preferred alternative as one "which is clearly superior to all known alternatives, but which is not necessarily optimal." Yehezkel Dror, 1971, *op. cit.*, p. 4.

48. The third possibility – increasing the input as long as the output is multiplied by factor x – is senseless in the context of policy making, since rationality is defined not as the most efficient use of *resources* but rather as a function of the utility of the goals they serve.

49. Walter F. Mondale, "Social Accounting, Evaluation and the Future of Human Services', *Evaluation*, no. 1, (Fall, 1972), pp. 30-31.

50. Carol H. Weiss, *op. cit.*, pp. 24-25.

51. This tendency is articulated especially well by Charles E. Lindblom in *The Policy Making Process*, Englewoods Cliffs N.J., Prentice-Hall, 1967.

52. Williams, *op. cit.*, p. 85.
53. Moynihan, *op. cit.*, pp. 94-95.
54. cf. Marcia Guttentag, "Evaluation of Social Intervention Programmes", a paper presented at the N.Y. Academy of Science Conference on Critical Human Behavioural Research issues, Oct. 1972, p. 2.
55. This problem of value projection was raised in connection with the role of the analyst's bias in determining the attainment of the organizational goal. cf. A. Etzioni, 'Two Approaches to Organizational Analysis: A Critique and a Suggestion", *Administrative Science Quarterly,* Vol. 5, no. 2, September 1960, pp. 257-278.
56. Christopher Nash, David Pearce & John Stanley, *op. cit.*, p. 83.
57. Marcia Guttentag, *op. cit.*, pp. 2-3.
58. Robert S. Weiss and Martin Rein, "The Evaluation of Broad-Aim Programmes: Difficulties in Experimental Design and an Alternative" in Carol H. Weiss (ed.) *op cit.*, p. 237.
59. Pamela Horst, *et al.*, "Programme Management and the Federal Evaluator," *Public Administration Review*, 34, 4, July-August 1974, p. 302.
60. Williams, *op. cit.*, p. 86f.
61. Yehezkel Dror, (1968), *op. cit.*, p. 142.
62. Michael Scriven, "Pros and Cons about Goal Free Evaluation", *The Journal of Educational Evaluation*, 3, 4 (Dec. 72), Evaluation comment, pp. 1-5.
63. Marcia Guttentag, *op. cit.*, p. 2.

7

Analysis of Policy Failure : A Three Dimensional Framework*

THOMAS B. SMITH

In almost every policy arena, one can observe some persons declaring that a policy is a 'failure' while at the same time the policy is being defended as a 'success' by others. In India, major policy areas are battlegrounds for divergence of opinions and analysis. Is the atomic energy programme a success or a failure? Has land reform succeeded? Is poverty being eliminated by the IRDP? Is the government's policy on Punjab a success? Has compensatory discrimination failed?

Differences of opinion about public policies and policy performance are bound to prevail in open, democratic political systems, and India is no exception. Groups and organisations demonstrate their views on public policies on the streets and in the villages. Government and opposition political leaders are engaged in verbal duels over public policy. The print media's newspapers reflect varying shades of political opinion and perceptive periodicals, such as the *Economic and Political Weekly, India Today* and *Seminar* provide a forum for divergent views. Policy research organisations also contribute to the evaluation of success and failure analytical studies on particular issues and programmes. By contrast, in authoritarian political systems, public policies are, by nature, deemed a 'success' and a critique, whether by a citizen, by academic, the media or political leader, is unwelcome and discouraged by authorities.[1]

Making judgements about the success and failure of public policies is not confined to policy analysts. The concepts are used in everyday conversations of citizens, programme managers, politicians and by scholars who devote their teaching and research to the study of public policy and administration. Considerable effort in the past two decades has been made in trying to find out *why* policies fail, and in attempting to devise policies that will be successful. Rarely much thought is given specifically to analyse what is meant by failure or success. The concepts are used very loosely even by writers on policy analysis. More often than not, the concepts remain undefined, with the implication that the readers will know what the authors mean.[2]

For teachers and researchers in public policy and administration, it is important to understand the meanings of policy success and policy failure and to refine the usage of these concepts when applying them. This especially is the case in developing countries where solutions to serious problems may rely upon government action based upon judgements about success or failure. The purpose of this article is to examine these concepts and to develop a three-dimensional framework for assessing failure and success judgements which takes into account the policy analysts' perspectives as well as the participants in the policy arenas.

Ingram and Mann provide a useful insight to understanding the multi-faceted meaning of policy failure and success. They note, "Success and failure are slippery concepts, often highly subjective and reflective of an individual's goals, perception of need and perhaps even psychological disposition toward life."[3] I think Ingram and Mann correctly define how success and failure are used in the policy arena. The issues at hand are partly matters of implied, often unconscious, definitions and of the choice among the range of alternatives and techniques for evaluation. However, a more fundamental issue is at stake than techniques. The act of making a judgement about a policy's success or failure is itself a political act in that there can be a myriad of individuals, groups, organisations and other stakeholders involved in making evaluations in the policy process. What is success in the eyes of one beholder can be regarded as failure in the view of another. Different entities apply different dimensions and standards when assessing a policy or programme's worth or 'goodness'. They also have differing views about what is a public policy and about what aspect, facet or stage of a policy is being subjected to judgement.

Many policies are initiated and implemented over the protests and vehement opposition of some individuals or groups. Just because a policy is legitimised by the government of the day is no indication that those opposing it will change their views towards the policy. Some policies are designed, consciously or unconsciously, so that the costs and benefits of the programme do not fall evenly upon all stakeholders – there may be some victims as well as some beneficiaries. Success and failure become subjective evaluations if this is the case. Another consideration in judging success and failure is that public policies and the policy process are not static and stable, but policy is a 'moving target' to use to the phrase of Wittrock and deLeon.[4] Views change as policy unfolds, there can be "changing conceptions of policy failure."[5] Judgements also may be made by 'neutral' professional policy analysts who utilise theoretical constructs and methods which in themselves reflect values and beliefs neither understood nor acceptable to everyone in society.

Defining Policy Success and Failure

What can the literature of policy analysis and evaluation contribute to defining success and failure? The question of what constitutes success or failure has not attracted a great deal of direct attention or analysis in the public policy literature. Ingram and Mann edited a book with an appealing title *Why Policies Succeed or Fail*, but did little to define success or failure or even to keep the contributors to the book on the theme of the title.[6] Larson in *Why Government Programs Fail* has attempted to clarify the concepts, but provided a most unhelpful definition of policy failure as "...not as a total failure, but as any significant shortcoming in a government program. Thus all programs are viewed as a failing in part even if they are successful in toto."[7] With this definition, all policies are bound to 'fail'. Majone and Wildavsky and Wolman examined programme design and programme implementation factors which might lead to why policies fail without defining in acceptable detail what was meant by failure.[8] In general, it appears as if failure to achieve policy objectives is implied. Mayntz quite specifically indicates effectiveness as the evaluative criterion and notes, "An effective program is ... defined by its ability to induce, under given conditions, such behaviour as will bring about the desired change."[9]

Few analysts have considered alternative ways in which policies can fail beyond the criterion of effectiveness. Kerr describes *implemental failure* as, "... a policy cannot be implemented...," and *instrumental failure* as, "... it does not fulfil the purpose or purposes of the policy," and failure in *normative justification* as whether,

"...the purpose or goals for the policy is normatively justifiable to the relevant public."[10] Poister argues that criteria "... to evaluate policies and programs all relate to goals and objectives, either focusing on the objectives themselves or on the means/ends relationships between strategies and objectives."[11] He then outlines performance variables as effectiveness, adequacy and appropriateness. More recently, Linder and Peters deal with three types of failure: *implementation* failure occurs, "...when a program or policy is sabotaged during implementation," *policy design* as "The failure of those making the policy to formulate a program which had any possibility of being successful," and *policy failure* as "...a program may or my not achieve its goals, but creates so many negative side effects that the cure may be worse than the disease."[12]

More elaborate frameworks are provided by Suchman and Dunn. Suchman proposes a five dimensional scheme for evaluating success or failure. *Effort* refers to, '...the quantity and quality of activity that takes place.' *Performance* '...measures the results of effort rather than the effort itself.' *Adequacy of performance* measures the, '...degree to which effective performance is adequate to the total amount of need.' *Efficiency* concerns the question, *'Is there a better way to attain the same results?' Process* deals with the complex problem of, "how and why a program works or does not work."[13]

Dunn's six dimensional criteria for evaluation provides the following: Effectiveness concerns, "Has the valued outcome been achieved?" *Efficiency* measures, "How much effort was required to achieve a valued result?" *Adequacy* is, "To what extent does the achievement of a valued outcome resolve the problem?" *Equity* involves the question, "Are costs and benefits distributed equitably among different groups?" *Responsiveness* concerns the question, "Do policy outcomes satisfy the needs, preferences or values of particular groups?" *Appropriateness* seeks an answer to "Are desired outcomes (objectives) actually worthy and valuable?"[14]

The perspectives presented so far provide a useful starting point to examining the facets of policy success and failure. However, these perspectives are the analysts' perspectives, rather than views which take into account the various interested individuals and groups who also make judgements about public policies.

A variety of perceptions about criteria for judging policy success or failure exist. In clarifying the diversity, I think three major categories for policy judgements are evident. First, there is the criterion of the *policy design* which views the policy from the perspective of its appropriateness and agreement with its objectives and means. A second criterion deals with *policy process* in terms of how the policy is dealt with in the context of the policy arena. The third criteria relates to *policy achievement* and concerns the effectiveness and adequacy of the policy in achieving its goals. Within each category, there are several sub-criterion.

Policy Design

Appropriate Perspective: Is the policy based upon an appropriate ideology and acceptable values? Are there moral, political or theoretical grounds upon which the policy is accepted or rejected?

Consensus and Agreement: To what extent are those involved in making and implementing the policy and those affected by it in agreement that it is a 'good' policy? Will the policy lead to disruption, conflict and violence, or greeted with agreement and acceptance by stakeholders?

Policy Process

Ratio of Costs to Benefits: Is the policy an efficient one? Is there value for money and effort in the policy?

Implementability: Has the policy been implemented? How well? Is it a feasible policy in terms of implementation, or is it the case that it cannot be implemented or is {or will be} sabotaged in implementation?

Sustainability: Has {or will} the policy be terminated or substantially altered? How well has the policy become institutionalised into the social, political and economic systems of the community?

Policy Achievement

Achievement of Goals and Objectives: How effective is the policy? Is it attaining the goals it was set out to achieve?

Adequacy and Sufficiency: is there a possibility that the policy will lead to solution of the problem to which the policy is addressed. Is the theoretical base of the policy sound?

Policy Design

Public policies can be judged in terms of their design and how they were formulated. Success and failure using this dimension often is in the realm of clashes of values and interests with little awareness or concern about other evaluative criteria, such as efficiency and effectiveness.

Appropriate Policies: Values, Ideology and Partisanship

One form of success-failure judgement does not rest upon what could be called an objective analysis and may be completely unrelated to achievement or efficiency. This dimension is concerned with judgements about a policy's appropriateness—its suitability, pertinence and its fitness to be a public policy. Kerr refers to this as the "normative justification" dimension.[15] Dunn comments, "While all (of Dunn's) criteria take objectives for granted— ... the criterion of appropriateness asks whether these objectives are proper ones for society."[16] Judging policy failure and success by appropriateness is where disagreements are likely to be most intense. Several facets are evident in this form of evaluating a policy's success or failure. Some policies can be 'wrong' in themselves, others impact unevenly upon citizens, and some are deemed to be failures for partisan political purposes.

Wrong public policies inherently are seen to be failures by some individuals and groups. The policies are seen to be based upon or are promoting unacceptable values and are seen to be failures in ideological, ethical or moral terms. This represents making evaluating judgements about public policies from the perspective of an approach well divorced from the ends—means assessment of some other forms of evaluation. Evaluation is symbolic and emotive and can cover a wide range of issues in the public arena—health, welfare, the environment etc. Public policies which are re-distributive in purpose (such as land reform or compensatory discrimination), generate intense conflict by those who feel they are losing from the policy. It makes no difference if a current policy is achieving its stated objectives and is clearly 'efficient'—the objectives and goals themselves are in question. Gusking and Chester have noted that values and ethics often are overlooked in evaluation and that there is a place for 'partisan' evaluation strategies in the policy process.[17] An evaluation of various policies in India from an environmentalist perspective has been provided by the Centre for Science and Environment.[18]

Some policies are designed to serve the 'public good' in a general sense and resolve issues and problems which the society, as a whole, faces. However, not all policies register impact evenly upon the populace, and some in society are expected to bear the high costs of the resolution of a problem which they do not regard as their problem in particular. The view of public policy is one which sees a particular facet or project that becomes the focus of the evaluative judgement. For instance, the disposal of radioactive and other hazardous wastes is necessary for the public good, yet nobody wants it done in their backyard. Any policy to do that will be seen as a failure by those being disadvantaged.

Public policies can also be judged to be failures as part of the process of normal political activities. In many parliamentary democracies, it is the role and duty of the opposition to oppose. Whatever policy being promoted and implemented by the party or parties in power is fair game for criticism and a declaration that it is a failure. This type of partisanship also is prevalent in authoritarian regimes where the opposition is suppressed along with criticism of governmental activities. Any form of government activity is seen by the opposition to be wrong and a failure.

Consensus, Agreement and Consultation

Public policies also are judged in relationship with how they were formulated and what sort of reception they receive within the political arena during implementation. This can be called the agreement dimension. Some policies touch off bitter and open conflict, while others are 'agreeable' to those who are making and implementing it as well as those affected by the policy.

Lindblom argued that the governmental decision process often is one of 'muddling through' or 'partisan adjustment'.[19] Decisions are not necessarily made only on the grounds of 'rationality,' or on attempting to achieve effectiveness or efficiency. Instead policymakers place premium upon agreement and consensus among participants in the policymaking process. Compromise and accommodation become the central concerns, as the determination of ends and objectives become tangled with the search for suitable means and alternatives to achieve those objectives. Following consultation, compromise and accommodation, emerges a policy or decision with which stakeholders involved (such as planners, political leaders, implementers and target groups) are willing to live. With such a decision process, those involved have a stake in seeing the policy as a success regardless of outcome in terms of criteria, such as efficiency and effectiveness.

Many sound reasons exist for smooth implementation of policies for a consensus/compromise/accommodation style of decision-making to be promoted. Diverse interests get accommodation or at least feel some identification with the policy. The decision-making process requires consultation and discussion and is likely to result in policies and programmes which deviate little from what has been done in the past. Thus, implementation becomes less conflict prone because there is less likelihood of the policy being ambushed by aggrieved stakeholders (both implementers, target group citizens and policymakers) as it is being implemented. Nakamura and Smallwood argue that constituency satisfaction and clientele responsiveness are important factors in policy evaluation and Hays has provided a useful model of the feedback process.[20]

In this dimension for evaluation, the success of a policy is measured by the extent to which there is consensus and agreement that the policy is acceptable to the policy actors: those who have formulated it, the implementers and the affected target groups. Failure, on the other hand, occurs when a policy generates excessive conflict, dissension, opposition and perhaps violence. However, decision processes in many instances are based upon ideological assumptions or upon efficiency criterion where negotiation and bargaining are set aside in favour of a decision-making process which is seen to be ideologically pure or more rational. It must also be noted that not all policy issues are resolvable by a process in which there can be consultation, agreement and consensus among those persons and organisations involved. Single issue organisations expect to achieve what they are promoting or opposing and nothing less which means that agreement and consensus are hardly possible.

Some public policies are inherently without friends. Hansen has provided a useful analysis of what she terms 'unpopular decisions'[21] Some polices regulating people's behaviour (traffic and parking laws) and extracting resources (taxes) seldom are popular with the general public, but there is reluctant acceptance of their enforcement.

Policy Process

While policy design deals with the form and the making of the policy, process is concerned with the policy execution — in particular, its implementation, efficiency and sustainability. Examining policy process can provide answers about the effort put into the policy and serve to explain policy achievement. Efficiency is included in this dimension because it is a measure of benefits and costs as, or after, the policy is implemented.

Costs and Benefits: Efficiency

Policies can be also be judged in terms of the calculated relationship between costs and benefits which provides a measure of efficiency.[22] The general public and casual observer may make rough success or failure judgements based upon a simple assessment of value for effort or money. Efficiency can be unrelated to other criteria, as Scioli explains.

> — the efficiency model does not need to question the impact of the program on the community of its citizens. It questions merely intended output in relation to program input— An efficiency study would tell— how much time and cost is involved in providing these services and, hopefully, outline ways to cut time and cost by maintaining the same level of output. It would not question the effectiveness of the output or the effects of the output on the community.[23]

Sophisticated, contemporary economic analysis has permeated into policy formation and evaluation—especially in regard to physical projects (dams, roads, bridges, power plants, factories, etc.) and to development programmes in the Third World. Increasing numbers of planners and analysts promote the judgement of policies, programmes and projects on the basis of economic criterion. Through methods of determining the short and long-term costs and assessing benefits, the costs-to-benefits ratio can be calculated. Where alternatives are considered, economic analysis stresses that the programme or project with the highest benefit to cost ratio (rate of return) is inherently the 'best' and should be selected over others.

Economic analysis with efficiency as the key criterion can also be used regarding on-going or completed projects—those not returning 'profits' or services in relation to the amount of resources invested may be judged to be failures on the basis of efficiency. Masking judgements about efficiency requires a perspective of public policy in terms of identifiable sub-units, such as projects or particular work practices. This limitation restricts the use of this criterion. Not all policies or government agencies can be broken into small sub-units for analysis or can fit into a business oriented economic framework; although, some public enterprises can be assessed this way.

Some observers of the political realm see all government operations as inherently inefficient or money wasting exercises and see few successes in public policies—unless the policies are to cut spending. Advocates of small government and privatisation have been on the ascendancy in western democracies in recent years and their views have helped form the evaluative strategy based on efficiency.

Failure and Success in Implementation

The implementation process takes policies, which only are idea and plans, and advances them into reality. Recent overviews of implementation in theory and practice can be found in Sabatier and O'Toole.[24] Once a policy is formulated, there is no guarantee that the implementation process will be well executed and often it is the case that policies may not be implemented at all. This leads to what can be called implementation failure. Implementation failure can be the causes of other types of policy failure – in particular failure to achieve objectives and failure in terms of policy efficiency. Sabatier and Mazmanian have provided a "Guide to Achieving Policy Objectives" which is designed to satisfy an effectiveness criterion.[25]

Policy implementation is closely related to the feasibility of policies – some policies might have noble objectives, be based upon adequate theory, have wide support in the community, but be totally infeasible to implement. Chase attempted to detail "how hard will it be?" to implement human services programmes is a good example of the complexity of actors and processes in implementation.[26] Rural development policies in India in particular are prone to implementation failure.[27] Part of the problem of implementation failure can be due to the lack of capacity on the part of implementing organisations to implement. Some organisations have difficulty when attempting to put policy into practice due to lack of direction, leadership or shortages of skilled or dedicated personnel. Some policies are subject to the discretionary behaviour of lower ranked 'street level' implementers and the scope for policy distortion is high if those implementing the policy deliberately seek to obstruct, distort or ignore the goals and aims of the policy and if monitoring and control is ineffective.

While it is always fashionable to blame the implementing agency (and bureaucracies in general) for implementation shortcomings, target groups of recipients or beneficiaries also must respond to policy initiatives and their response influences the quality of implementation. Not all policies have a positive, beneficial effect upon a target group or interested groups and there can be resistance to accepting the change necessitated by the public policy. If they are recalcitrant and create opposition, the implementation can be slowed or stopped and the impact of the policies can be significantly lessened.

Other policies may be good ideas at the time of formulation, but resources and commitment are not forthcoming on the part of the government and they remain policies more in the symbolic sense than in terms of viable policies which are implemented. In Third World development planning, for instance, the results after implementation seldom match what is predicted, needed or expected.

Policies often take a long time to formulate and environmental conditions can change significantly during implementation to the extent that the policy, even if vigorously implemented, fails to address the problem at hand. In India, the recent drought severely undermined policy implementation in some areas.

Sustainability and Survival

'The policy has failed—it is being terminated.' This comment is heard in the corridors of power less often then one would think. Analysis and research into the elimination or termination of policies has shown that it is a difficult and not always a successful process. Hogwood and Peters provide a detailed account of policy succession and termination.[28]

Termination should be the ultimate failure if one assumes that a policy having severe shortcomings will not be continued. But, is this so? Not all policies have long-term, sustainable goals and objectives. Many are destined for a short life in that they deal with a problem or issue that can be resolved and no further need is apparent for a continued policy effort. Other policies may have 'sunset' clauses and expire due to statutory specification. Still others are caught up in times of financial constraints and are eliminated solely to avoid budgetary expenditure. Some policies are implemented during rapid social or economic change which renders a policy inappropriate. Policies which require the construction and operation of power plants, roads, communication systems, factories and similar physical entities may endure because of the life of these hard technologies.

Even polices designed to be terminated by sunset clauses survive. There is something life-like about a public policy. It generates and nurtures supporters—organizations, people and groups—who depend upon the policy for some form of reward or gratification (money, position, power etc.). With support from the public and the bureaucracy, it is difficult for democratic governments to eliminate entirely a particular function. Instead of elimination, it is more likely that the policy will be altered significantly or there will be cutbacks in activities or reduction in personnel. A more severe form of disapproval may be drastic changes to goals and objectives or shifting responsibility to another organisation. In times of a change of government, policy change may be less likely than a change of organisational arrangements. Major structural reorganisations or public bureaucracies seldom have the result of terminating public polices. The same people (though perhaps few in number) in a differently named organisation continue implementing the same policies. Policies, then, can become institutions to the extent that they survive even in adverse conditions. They adapt to their changing environment; they have a life of their own and have support in the political realm enough to make them endure long after their original goals and objectives have been achieved. Policies, of course, are what organisations are supposed to implement; and it is well documented that public organisations are very good at perpetuating themselves and promoting the policies they are implementing. As Kaufman has shown for the USA, only 27 out of his sample of 421 agencies had been terminated since 1923.[29]

Viewing policies as life-like entities which can be killed, be transformed or allowed to live is an important dimension when considering policy success and policy failure. Regardless of the rating of a policy on other dimensions of success, if a policy can survive and be institutionalised it is a clear success within the policy arena.

Policy Achievement

Assessing policy achievement, especially by the effectiveness criteria, is the most common method of formal evaluation. However, the adequacy of a policy to deal with the problem must also be considered.

Effectiveness: Achieving Goals and Objectives

The comment, "The policy is a failure, it is not achieving its objectives," must be the most widely used of evaluative judgements about public policies. Policies are supposed to have goals to be achieved and if they are not being achieved then the policy can be judged a failure. Indeed, this criterion is implicit in policy studies by academics and evaluators to the extent that this assumption is not explained as the meaning of success or failure.

There are good reasons for this, in part because it is a very important dimension and one about which policymakers and programme managers seek and receive information. Evaluation methodologies promoted in books and journals and utilized by practicing evaluators of the past 20 years have been concerned with the measurement of effectiveness. Quasi-experimental designs using time-series analysis, "Goal Attainment Scaling" and various other methods of measuring recipient or target group behaviour are part of this package of methodologies, and rarely a book on evaluation will not have effectiveness as the central criterion to determine policy success or failure. Although more recent attempts deal with 'process' rather than 'impact' methods of evaluation, effectiveness of the policy is still the key concern.[30]

Many of those who study public policy are wary of attempting to define policy goals and objectives and to measure whether or not they have been achieved. Governments and organisations seldom take goal definition for specific policies very seriously and the result has been obscure, hazy and ill- defined generalisations.[31] Rarely is there a clear statement about exactly what a particular policy is supposed to achieve over a specified time period and what will constitute success or failure. Evaluators may be faced with the task of defining and setting appropriate goals and objectives for the policies and programmes they are to evaluate.[32] This being the case, it may be difficult to judge the extent of success or failure of a particular policy to raise standards of living, improve housing, provide health services, reduce dependence on imported oil, prevent crime, and so forth. The exact specification for evaluation can take place after the policy has been implemented and not before, with success and failure standard generated by those with an interest in terminating or continuing the policy or by those who have to evaluate it.

Even if goals and objectives are clearly stated in policy formation, there is no guarantee that the same goals will be operational at a later time. Goals and objectives change as policy is being implemented and initial over-optimism about the power of a policy to achieve results is not uncommon.[33] This is tempered by time as the policy is being implemented and the realisation sets in that less is going to be achieved than thought possible.

Governments have many policies and many goals and not all of the policies and goals are coordinated. Goals and policies overlap (how many policies deal with road transport or rural development?); they may contradict each other (subsidise the tobacco industry, collect a lot of taxes on tobacco and attempt to stop people smoking tobacco); and, some may be in direct conflict with a government's ultimate goal of staying in power.

An added problem when assessing policy effectiveness is regarding the amount of change which should be attributed to a particular policy and what can be the result of the impact of market conditions, other public policies or changes in environmental conditions. Allison reminded us some time ago that organisations are 'blunt instruments'[34] Public policies also are blunt instruments — especially those which attempt to achieve goals by relying upon incentives or other indirect means of stimulating target or recipient groups.

A final point regarding effectiveness as the criterion for policy judgement is that some policies may not achieve very much of what they were supposed to achieve, but can have very beneficial (or very negative) secondary or spin-off impacts which can be of great value (or create real disasters). With only a specific primary goal oriented evaluation criterion, this can be overlooked.

In summary, there can be considerable debate over what a policy's goals really are, as well as conflicting views over whether their achievement (even if the goals are agreed upon) has been a success or a failure. Equally contentious and complex is the question of what causes policies to achieve or not to achieve objectives. This issue will not be addressed in this article, but it must be noted that establishing casual links is not easy.

Policy Adequacy

While the policy effectiveness dimension is relationship between policy goals and what is achieved, the adequacy of a policy refers to the relationship between the policy and the problem to which it is addressed (see Poister, 1978). A clear distinction exists between the two dimensions in the sense that a policy may be judged to be a success in achieving its stated objectives, but it has little impact upon the problem being addressed by the policy. There are many policy failures of this type in all public policy arenas. There are policies dealing with the homeless in Calcutta, policies to end poverty in Bangladesh, policies to end the power shortage, as well as policies to abolish terrorism.

Often insufficient resources are available to be directed toward serious and adequate problem resolution in many policy areas. Government financial and staff resources are not unlimited and the action taken may be token and piecemeal, but it is all that can be done given other policy priorities of the government. The uncertainty over which is the proper policy to pursue also may lead to a lack of resources being devoted to problem resolution. Enough may be done to satisfy election promises, but the problems remain.

This is a criterion for policy judgement in which there is bound to be a range of perspectives about the same policy. Beneficiaries and other target groups often view government action as never enough, while policymakers are prone to argue that what is being done is all that can be done in an imperfect world.

Policies are also failures when they are based upon the wrong 'theory' or a faulty problem definition. How one defines a problem significantly influences the solutions (policies) put forward for resolution; if the assumptions are wrong, the policy also can be wrong and a failure. In many policy arenas, there is incomplete or developing theory available for policy guidance; there may be even competing theories. Proponents of one path may be intolerant of other approaches and explanations. Approaches to problems often are dependent upon available theoretical perspectives and major policy areas may undergo significant policy change over time as new theories are put into action. In the case of rural development in India, Dantwala and Barmeda have outlined six approaches used since independence—each at the time of initiation seemed to have the proper theoretical grounding.[35] Much of the evaluation literature deals with policies as theories and evaluation as testing the validity of those theories.

Some problems are 'wicked' in that there may not be viable solutions which are implementable even without resource constraints. Some problems may be relatively immune from any government action having a major impact on their resolution. In cases such as this, policy never matches the seriousness of the problem and while a policy may be a success in achieving limited objectives, it is a failure in resolving the problem to which it is addressed.

Conclusions

The description and assessment of the three dimensions and seven subcategories to policy success and failure might make the concepts less slippery. However, it also makes them far more complex. From the discussion a number of conclusions, suggestions and new directions emerge.

Not much can be done about the varied use of the concepts of policy success and failure by policymakers, the media, interest group leaders and the common citizen. The terms are part of the political culture of democratic countries and various observers of the same policy will continue to argue about a specific policy's success or failure as viewed from particular interests and competing perceptions of what failure means. However, it is possible for those who teach, research and evaluate public policies to adopt a more precise as well as more complex use of the concepts. It should not be sufficient to use them either loosely or implicitly.

Policy and programme evaluators have focused attention primarily upon the dimensions of effectiveness and efficiency or in combination. The assessment of a policy's 'worth' on these dimensions is important and the judgements provide valuable information for planners, policy-makers and programme managers. However, the emphasis upon policy effectiveness and efficiency as the central criteria should not be accepted to the point where they dominate the analysis of success or failure. There is a tendency for some types of criteria to dominate particular substantive public policy fields. In terms of development progammes and projects, dominance of the efficiency criterion over others leads to the promotion of particular types of projects and the neglect of others. In health and welfare, effectiveness appears to dominate. If this is the case, why is it so? What could judgements based upon the other criteria provide?

With a number of dimensions for success/failure judgement outlined, it is important to investigate the question of why policies fail in each. The amount of research already conducted upon effectiveness, efficiency and implementation failure can serve as a starting point for an examination of the remaining four criteria. Effectiveness and efficiency have been closely linked in the past. Implementation failure can be closely linked with failure of goal attainment and efficiency. Implementation failure itself partly may be the result of lack of consensus or a clash of values.

If a policy is failing by one of the criteria, what can be done to correct this perceived failure? A less prescriptive approach to this issue is to examine the politics surrounding perceptions of failure and how remedies for each of the criteria are advocated and utilised. The possibility should be explored that adjusting for policy failure in one dimension may lead to increased failure in another dimension. Can increasing effectiveness lead to a decline in efficiency? Does promoting consensus reduce effectiveness?

Policy failure must also be considered within its overall political and societal context. In many developing nations, one finds what Hirschman has called the 'failure comples'.[36] Policies are expected to fail; governments are seen to be ineffective and a 'soft state' persists.[37] Policy evaluation in authoritarian regimes by analysts as well as the media and citizens is discouraged, and if conducted, tends to avoid focusing upon effectiveness or implementation.[38]

Policies are successes by official government decree. The feeling of futility over government action among stakeholders (implementers and target groups) and citizens in general leads to the perception of all public policies as potential failures and to the view that government is impotent. Policy arenas exist in the wealthy nations about which the same feeling prevails—drug abuse, housing for the poor and homeless and organised crimes are examples.

Policy evaluation as practiced by planners, policy analysts and programme managers often takes a very narrow perspective and can focus entirely upon the policy or programme as the key variable and unit of analysis. This can be a myopic view and can conceal from analysis the broader concerns of problem definition, the causes of the maladies the policy is to resolve, as well as the overall societal, economic and political context in which the problem and the policy occurs.[39] Perceptive analysis can be thwarted by narrowness.

A final issue concerns the dynamics of public policymaking, implementation and evaluation. Policies and the policy process are not static entities in an unchanging environment. Any consideration of success and failure must take this into account. Support as well as opposition to a policy may subside or increase over time. So too can indicators related to effectiveness of efficiency, or any of the five other criteria, However, those making judgements about a policy's success or failure and advocating policy changes seldom wait until the implementation and the impacts are settled. The point here is that policies may not be given the time to prove themselves before declarations of success or failure are forthcoming.

While this article has concentrated upon the meanings of success and failure, one can still examine and evaluate public policies without resorting to making judgements of success and failure. One can assess the process of implementation and the outcomes and impacts of policies without making a judgement about failure. While this approach satisfies many academic needs, those who make and implement policies, as well as citizens, have a desire and a need to hear judgements about success and failure. The planners and policymakers receiving and using success/failure judgements have a duty to beaware of the multiple criteria and how judgements about the same policy may differ. Those providing this perspective have an obligation to indicate clearly what they mean by success and failure, and to defend the choice or choices made.

Notes

* From *Indian Journal of Public Administration*, Vol. XXXV, No. 1, 1989, pp. 1-15.

1. Thomas B. Smith, "Evaluating Development Policies and Programmes in the Third World," *Public Administration and Development*, Vol. 4, April-June 1986, pp. 129-44.
2. *See*, for instance, Allen R. Hays, "Perceptions of Success or Failure in Program Implementation: The Feedback Loop in Public Policy Decisions." *Policy Studies Review*, Vol. 5, No.1, 1985, pp. 51-67; David Brian Robertson, "Program Implementation versus Program Design: Which Accounts for Policy 'Failure'? *Policy Studies Review*, Vol. 3, Nos. 3-4, 1984, pp. 391-403; F.W. Scharpf, "Policy Failure and Institutional Reform: Why Should From Follow Function?" *International Social Science Journal*, No. 108, 1986, pp. 179-89; and Michael G. Schatzberg, "Le Mal Zairois: Why Policy Fails in Zaire," *African Affairs*, Vol. 81, No. 324, 1982, pp. 337-48.
3. Helen Ingram and Dean Mann (eds.), *Why Policies Succeed or Fail*, Beverly Hills, Sage, 1990, p. 12.
4. Bjom Wittrock and Peter deLeon, "Policy as a Moving Target: A Case For Conceptual Realism," *Policy Studies Review*, Vol. 6, No. 1, 1986, pp. 44-60.
5. Susan B. Hansen, "Public Policy Analysis: Some Current Development," *Policy Studies Journal,* Vol. 12, September 1983. p. 21.
6. Helen Ingram and Dean Mann, op.cit.
7. James S. Larson, *Why government Programs Fail: Improving Policy Implementation*, New York, Praeger, 1980, p.1.
8. Giandominico Majone and Aaron Wildavsky, "Implementation as Evolution," *Policy Studies Review Annual*, Vol. 2, Beverly Hills, Sage, 1978, pp. 103-117; and Harold Wolman, "The Determinants of Program Success and Failure." *Journal of Public Policy*, Vol. 1, No. 4, 1981, pp. 433-64.
9. Renate Mayntz, "The Conditions for Effective Public Policy: A New Challenge for Policy Analysis," Policy and Politics, Vol. 11, No. 2, 1983, p. 127.
10. Donna H. Kerr, "The Logic of 'Policy' and Successful Policies," *Policy Sciences*, Vol. 7, No. 2, 1976, pp. 359-61.
11. Theodore H. Poister, Applied Research Methods. Baltimore, University Park Press, 1978, p. 9.
12. Stephen H. Linder and B. Guy Peters, "A Design Perspective on Policy Implementation: The Fallacies of Misplaced Prescription, "*Policy Studies Review*, Vol. 6, February 1987, p. 461.

13. Edward A. Suchman, *Evaluation Research*, New York, Russell Sage Foundation, 1967, pp. 61-66.
14. Willian N. Dunn, *Public Policy Analysis: An Introduction*, Englewood Cliffs, Prentice-Hall, 1981, p. 343.
15. Donna H. Kerr, *op. cit.*
16. William N. Dunn, *op. cit.*, p. 238.
17. Alan E. Guskin and Mark A. Chester, "The Partisan Diagnosis of Social Programs", in General Zaluman (ed.), *Process and Phenomena of Social Change*, New York, Wiley, 1973, pp. 353-76.
18. Anil Aggarwal and Sumita Narain, (eds.), *The State of India's Environment*, 1984-85, New Delhi, Centre for Science and Environment, 1985.
19. Charles E. Lindblom, "The Science of Muddling Through", *Public Administration Review*, Vol. 19, No. 2, 1959, pp. 79-88.
20. Robert T. Nakamura and Frank Smallwood. *The Politics of Policy Implementation*, New York, St. Martin's Press, 1980; and Allen R. Hays, *op. cit.*
21. Susan B. Hansen, "On the Making of Unpopular Decisions: A Typology and Some Evidence", *Policy Studies Journal*, Vol. 13, September 1984, pp. 23-44.
22. George W. Downs and Patrick D. Larkey, *The Search for Government Efficiency: From Hubris to Helplessness*, Philadelphia, Temple University Press, 1986; Theodore H. Poister, *op. cit.*; Jerome Rothenberg, "Cost-Benefit Analysis: A Methodological Exposition," in M. Guttenberg and E.L. Strening (eds.), *Handbook of Evaluation Research*, Vol. 2, Beverly Hills, Sage, 1975; Mark S. Thompson, *Benefit-Cost Analysis for Program Evaluation*, London, Sage, 1980.
23. Frank P. Scioli, Jr., "Problems of Improving the Efficiency of Public Administration," in H. Hanusch (ed.), *Anatomy of Government Deficiencies*, Berlin, Springer-Vertag, 1983, p. 166.
24. Laurence J. O'Toole, "Policy Recommendations for Multi-Actor Implementation: An Assessment of the Field", *Journal of Public Policy*, Vol. 6, No. 2, 1986, pp. 181-210; Paul Sabatier, "Top-Down and Bottom-up Approaches to Implementation Research: A Critical Analysis and Suggested Synthesis," *Journal of Public Policy*, Vol. 6, No. 1, 1986, pp. 21-48 and Paul Sabatier, "What Can We Leam From Implementation Research?", in F-X. Kaufmann, G. Majone and V. Ostrom (eds.), *Guidance, Control and Evaluation in the Public Sector*, Berlin, Walter de Grayter, pp. 313-25.
25. Paul Sabatier and Daniel Maznanian, "The Conditions of Effective Implementation: A Guide to Accomplishing Policy Objectives," *Policy Analysis*, Vol. 5, No. 4, 1979, pp. 481-504.

26. Gordon Chase, "Implementing a Human Services Program: How Hard Will it Be?", *Public Policy,* Vol. 27, No. 4, 1979, pp. 385-435.

27. Sandeep Bagchee, "Poverty Alleviation Programmes in Seventh Plan: An Appraisal", *Economic and Political Weekly*, Vol. 22, No. 4, 1987, pp. 139-48.

28. Brain W. Hogwood and G. Guy Peters, *Policy Dynamics*, London, Wheatsheaf, 1982.

29. Herbert Kaufmann, *Are Government Organisations Immortal?*, Washington, DC Brookings Institution, 1976.

30. Michael Q. Patton, *Utilization–Focused Evaluation*, Beverly Hills, Sage, 1980.

31. Carol H. Weiss, "*Where Political and Evaluation Research Meet,*" *Evaluation*. Vol. 1, No. 3, 1973, pp. 37-43.

32. Gerd-Michael Hellstem, "*Assessing Evaluation Research,*" in F.X. Kaufmann, G. Majone and V. Ostrom (eds.), *op. cit.*, pp. 279-311.

33. Bjom Wittrock and Peter del.con, *op. cit.*,

34. Graham T. Allison, "Conceptual Models and Cuban Missile Crisis", *American Political Science Review*, Vol. 63, September 1969, pp. 689-718.

35. M.I. Barmalla and J.N. Bimenda, "Rural Development", in R.S. Ganpathy, et.al. (eds). *Public Policy and Policy Analysis in India*, New Delhi, Sage, 1985, pp. 51-69.

36. Alben O. Hirschanan, "Policy Making and Policy Analysis in Latin America: A Return Joumey", *Policy Sciences*, Vol. 6. No. 12, 1975, pp. 385-402.

37. Gunnar Myrdal, *The Challenge of World Poverty*, New York, Pantheon, 1970.

38 Thomas B. Smith, *op. cit.*

39. R.S. Ganpathy, "On Methodologies for Policy Analysis", in R.S. Ganpathy, *et. al.*, (eds.), *op. cit.*, pp. 30-48.

8

Organization for Public Policy in Government*

Ishwar Dayal

This paper^ examines the organizational demands of effective policy formulation in public administration. Such an examination would have to be preceded by clarification and review of the decision process and an analysis of the characteristics of the task.

Since interpretations of terms differ in the literature in the field, I shall define the terms that are used here.

Decision is the commitment of the decision-maker to act, thereby committing the personnel, material and financial resources of the organization toward the action-objectives.

Policy prescribes the aims, the objectives, the targets that are to be achieved, and the methods, that would be used to achieve the objectives. Operationally, the policy statement in this sense must specify the expected results, the measures for achieving them, and the mechanism, or method, with which the results are expected to be achieved. In so far as this definition provides both a statement of *intent* by the decision-maker and the *method* of achieving it, it is specific and covers both the perspective and the choice of administrative action.

There is another issue that needs clarification here. Sometimes a distinction is made between policy formulation and decision-making. It is often suggested that policy formulation relates to tasks at the top levels of the hierarchy and decision-making refers to normal day-to-day functions of the administrator. In this paper, policy formulation refers to that aspect of administration which is concerned with defining the objective and determining the choice of action. Decision-making refers to the process by which this policy is determined. In this sense, policy and decision-making are inherent parts of administration at all levels of the hierarchy.

Neither policy formulation nor decision-making is a prerogative of any one level of hierarchy in administration. Indeed policy is formulated at all levels and decision processes are inherent in all administrative roles.[1]

The Decision Process

Simon[2] suggests that the process of decision-making includes three identifiable and essential phases.

"The first phase of decision-making process – searching the environment for conditions calling for decision – I shall call *intelligence* activity (borrowing the military meaning of intelligence). The second phase – inventing, developing, and analysing possible courses of action – I shall call *design* activity. The third phase – selecting a particular course of action from those available – I shall call *choice* activity."

The *intelligence* activity in formulating public policy requires search for the special, political, economic and technical aspects in the environment that impinge upon a particular decision-making situation. The *design* activity requires a search for relevance, inventing, developing and analysing the various decision choices and the consequences of these alternatives. *Choice* requires the selecting of a particular course of action with as complete a knowledge as possible of the consequences of the decision.

Before we examine the kinds of support systems required in an organization for improving decision-making, it may be relevant here to examine some special circumstances in the intelligence, design and choice activities in public administration.

There are several unique characteristics of the Government system that impinge upon decision processes, the most important of these being:

Environment of the Decision Situation

(1) *Diffused boundaries*: By the very nature and scope of the work in administration, the impact of the decision is felt by masses of people in addition to the employees within the office. I shall call this a *response system* suggesting that in public administration the characteristics of the response system are complex because it consists of multiple values within itself. The kind of data required to judge the impact of public policy on an on-going basis is difficult

and requires a wide data base and very careful interpretation of societal phenomena. Yet predicting the response to a decision is necessary, however sophisticated the methods required for doing so, may be.

In India, the responses on key issues are obtained more often through the channels of the political party than through the administrative machinery. The *mulki* rules dispute in Andhra was discussed and feelers of proposed solutions obtained through the party machinery of the ruling party and not through the administrative system; nor from direct sources, i.e. the public. The party machinery by its very nature is selective.

The political party machinery is indeed useful and has the capacity to provide data for policy formulation when one party rule is predominant as now. But when there are severe and matching pressures exerted by opposing parties, or when the party system represents a coalition, as it did after the 1967 elections in India, the feedback machinery of the party is likely to have inherent limitations that tend to make it less effective. Under pressure of competing positions among political parties, ranks tend to become defensive about their positions and often fail to receive, and interpret, valid public response. The lack of an administrative machinery to evaluate public response could become a handicap to formulating effective public policy in Government.

The response system working through administrative channels at present mainly consists of frequent exchanges between officers in the Centre and the States. This process is casual and inadequate; basically neither the Centre nor the State levels have adequate machinery for obtaining, collating and interpreting public response to their policies. Certain Ministries have set up policy research cells, notably the Home Ministry, but such units have had a habit of dying out in a short time, because of various inherent weaknesses.

(2) *The Political System*: Because the boundary conditions of public office are diffused and the elected representatives have a legitimised role in representing their electorates and because ideological differences and perspective of realities among parties are so vastly different, the assessment of the public response is difficult. The evaluation is often conditioned by the assumptions people make about social situations and how they are affected by their reference groups.[3] Often the data on effectiveness of public policy is slow in coming and sources of such data are uncertain. Both the party view and the administrator's analysis of effectiveness

of the policy could have limitations imposed by either the phenomenon of group-think or proximity. In either case, to the working of the Government, the price of error could be heavy.

(3) *Distance between the decision-maker and the people who are affected by the decision*: The decision-makers at senior levels in the administrative hierarchy are far removed from those who are affected by the decision. The recruitment and promotion policies generally place administrators in significant policy roles toward the tail-end of their careers when they have been long removed from direct contact with the public. The supportive organisation for policy formulation must maintain contact with several levels of administration; and certain policy matters should systematically involve officers who are in close touch with the public. Perhaps a hierarchy of decision-roles is necessary in the Government system given the vast areas of its operation. Systematic data on ecology of the society is not easily available to decision-makers. In most cases, therefore, the perceptions of reality are at best obtained through secondary sources and often escape the present realities of the social situation. The closer one moves towards the top of the administrative hierarchy, the more responsible one is for basic policy formulation, and all the more distant from the people and the situations that are affected by the decision-choice.

In large and complex organizational systems such as the Government, or the public sector enterprises, the remoteness of the top personnel from base-line activity is a serious difficulty in evaluating policy alternatives. Organisational patterns have to consciously develop the inherence of providing valid data to men at the top.

The Administrative Situation

The intelligence and design activities require invention, innovation, analysis of data and the evaluation of alternatives open to the decision-maker. Research suggests that innovative activity[4] often requires perspectives, attitudes and organisational relationships different from routine and repetitive activities. The innovation would be possible when the analyst has a flexible perspective which is often different from that of the decision-maker. The analyst has to question his assumptions, the organisational realities and traditions in order to achieve new perspectives. If the analyst does not employ new perspectives for the same data, his contribution to analysis, and to seeking innovative solutions in policy situations would have marginal utility. The design activity thus poses a challenging question for designing an organization, viz., how the decision process could strive to be optimum in its innovativeness. The nature of the bureaucratic system and the emphasis on precedents and rules too often inhibit people within the organisation from employing perspectives that may be different from those borne out by history. These factors reflect not so much on the quality of the men in public service as on the system's inability to induce innovation and change.

The *choice* activity in decision-making requires experience, maturity and administrative judgement. Simon[5] has suggested that in administration we are concerned with satisfactory and not optimum decisions. A satisfactory decision implies a decision that is acceptable to the largest number of people who are concerned with it. Though it may not be an optimising decision, it is likely to work out better because it is accepted by a greater number. Through the administrator's concern for arriving at satisfying decisions the Government could maintain continuing public confidence in itself and be able to exercise its legitimised authority.[6]

The organisational implications of a satisfactory decision as against an optimising decision is that the administrator's maturity and judgement in the *choice* activity are crucial factors in decision-making.

Requirements of the Decision-Situation

This discussion of the *intelligence*, *design* and *choice* activities suggests that support systems in an organisation are necessary to improve policy formulation and have to be explicitly recognised in order to aid decision-making in administration.

The support systems must provide data, analysis, interpretation and innovative solutions to recurring as well as new issues in public administration. Some of the systems needed for policy formulation are discussed below :

(1) *Data base*: Social, political and economic data are necessary for decision-making. More reliable our data, greater the probability of predicting the consequences of the policy-decision.

For top level decision-making in India, the information available is fragmentary. Each ministry interprets and deals with the information in its own way and for its own purposes. To take an example: an organisation of great significance to India's economy has four divisions. Each of the divisions functions as an autonomous unit. Each obtains, stores and processes data separately. There is little interchange between them, even when the decisions of one division impinge upon the tasks of the others. The cost of operating this system is high, but more importantly, the expertise in other divisions is seldom used in decision-making by any of the four divisions and is wasteful.

Effective analysis of data at design stages of decision activity requires a holistic perspective of the data, i.e., recognition of both the parts and the totality of the interacting situation. Without this holistic perspective in basic policy decisions, the evaluation of the choice activity in decision-making would be largely ineffective.

There is less apparent concern than necessary for evaluating public response to policy except at the political level through the advisory committees attached to Ministries and through the party system. The administrative organisation seldom has a reliable built-in system for obtaining feed-back of public response. An independent mechanism to evaluate public response to Government policy is a very important factor in satisfactory policy-making.

In this connection, the work of Cantril is noteworthy.[7] During the War years, Cantril had developed a survey technique by which he was in a position to obtain the response of representative population and through this he was in a position to determine how the country, or a community, would react to a particular Government policy. These data helped the U.S. Government to decide on many sensitive policy matters involving war strategy on certain crucial issues.

(2) *Personnel and organizational requirements*: Experiments in organizational change and innovation suggest that innovative tasks require an open system and a certain kind of work environment.[8] The significant features of the environment are the following: (a) facility for interaction between peers and with reference groups within and outside the organisation, (b) freedom for experimentation, and (c) trust between the superior and the subordinates. These conditions for innovative tasks rarely exist in a Government office.

In recent years, leaders in Government have been relying on advisers from the academic environment and other professions. This is perhaps due to the recognition that a new perspective could be contributed by qualified persons who have not been conditioned by the system. The Indian conception of an independent Planning Commission is also consistent with the requirements of the planning task, viz., an independent and professional perspective to the planning of growth and development.

Thus the *intelligence* and *design* activities in the decision process need an organizational environment that is designed to support innovative work towards policy formulation.

(3) *Familiarity with context and people*: Another condition necessary for effective formulation is the recognition of, and familiarity with, the special characteristics and culture of the administrative system. The search for consequences and prediction of results required both understanding of the system from within and knowledge of the environment. Far from being a mechanical exercise, the analysis of the available data is the backdrop that the analyst and the decision-maker must keep in mind while deciding.

What is suggested by this discussion of the process and conditions of decision-making is that complex organisations must design their own apparatus for effective decision-making. It is often said that the influence of political parties is all-pervasive in any policy decision in Government. Such influence is legitimate and necessary in the democratic system of Government.[9]

In recent months in India we have observed the dominance of the political system in many situations. Trade unions settle their differences with Cabinet Ministers. Recommendations by appointed Commissions of Enquiry or Committees are further negotiated at the highest levels of the ministerial command. These measures may be necessary, and perhaps justified, but they reduce the authority (decision-making capacity) of the administrator. The balance which is required to be established between the administrator and the legitimised representatives of the people is lacking. This lack introduces bias into the entire process of decision-making.

The creation of effective balance among the forces playing upon the decision-situation is important for administrative effectiveness. The essence of an effective decisions-situation is balance, avoiding bias.

Organisational Implications

I have briefly examined the activities involved in decision-making and the conditions necessary for optimising policy decisions. What is the nature of supportive systems required for policy-making functions of the Government?

Policy-making requires two inter-related aspects: one having to do with *intelligence, design* and *choice* activities in decision-making; and the other, with the personnel and the organizational environment needed for decision-making.

Data Analysis Task

Intelligence and design activities in the policy function at the top level in public administration are far from easy because the influences (discussed earlier) on Government administration are complex. It is difficult for the Administration to control the variables. The ideological differences among political parties often result in support or denouncement of the administration causing, among other things, serious morale problems for senior levels of administration. For example, constant criticism of relief operations in Bihar by political parties during famine in 1967 had created severe morale problems for the higher levels of administrators. They had to deal not only with the conditions created by drought but with this problem as well.

Policy level tasks consist of three related areas: (a) review of the effectiveness of policy, (b) design activity for new policy decisions, and (c) anticipatory policy. Design activity in decision-making requires data for on-going review and analysis of earlier policy decisions because through such analyses alone, improvements in the design and choice activities become possible. Anticipatory policy tasks involve forecasts of policy needs and action that renders the administrative organisation ready for contingent changes within the system and in the environment. In Government there is a dire lack of anticipatory policy functions.[10] In the areas of economic, international and domestic policy a lack of systemic analysis and contingency planning of action is both costly and contrary to national interests.

Thus, the need for basic policy formulation arises at the level of each ministry and the Government as a whole. Notionally all major decisions are Cabinet decisions; and therefore, they are seen to be decisions taken by the Government as a whole. Constitutionally this position is tenable. Administratively, the ministry and the cabinet each must have an organization to design decision-choices.

The supportive systems for policy formulation at the differentiated level (ministries) and the integrative level (Government as a whole) rarely exist. In public administration there is emphasis on creating differentiated systems and de-emphasis on integrative systems. For this the rationale lies in the underlying assumptions of the bureaucratic system: principles that govern functional specialization, the hierarchy of technical authority, the legitimisation of rules for work and behaviour. The rational-legal system tends to create rigid task boundaries.

Interactions across these boundaries exist mainly through formal committees set up for the purpose.

At the top levels in public administration, there is no recognisable integrative system. This function again is often performed by committees. The Cabinet and Chief Secretaries in the Centre and State governments perform distinct functions assigned to their positions which include responsibility for integration of inter-ministerial issues.

The integrating role, however, is not specific. The Cabinet Secretary obtains his sanctions indirectly by virtue of his position as Secretary to the Cabinet and its committees, and as chairman of the committees of secretaries. The same holds for Chief Secretaries at States level. These roles have no supervising function over the Secretaries, because each is responsible to his Minister. The relationship is delicate and the effectiveness of the role depends more upon the personal skill of the individual than on the design of the position.

Given the system, no single position is vested with, nor indeed can be assigned, the authority to perform the integrative task in the administrative organization. Industrial policy, licensing, banking, company law affairs, all relating to economic development, are interdependent and policy in one area would directly influence the performance of other areas. Yet different ministries deal with them without enough coordination, except through the Cabinet committee and Secretaries committee meant for this purpose. It is still an open question whether committees can perform the task of integration. They do not have an adequate information and analysis base.

Health, agriculture, community development have many common areas if integrated rural development is to be achieved; these aspects are separated at policy levels. Due to lack of integrative systems in Government organisation, the thrust of policy on, for instance, rural growth and development is too often lacking. This is supra-ministry level.

In field administration, integrative systems notionally exist at the block and the district levels. In most cases, the integrative role of the Block Development Officer and the District Collector is negated by strong functional links of the field functionaries with the state level departments. As a result, the activities at the field level become fragmented except in times of war or natural disaster when these extra links get submerged.

The absence of the integrative function in the organisations of the Government make it very difficult to design satisfactory machinery for decision-making. This factor will have to be taken into account in designing the organisational support for policy-formulation in Government.

The choice aspect of decision-making is clear. Familiarity with the administrative situation, maturity and responsibility for the task, are important requirements for the decision-maker. This task must be performed by those who have the responsibility for the consequences of their choice, i.e., the administrator, the minister or the cabinet, as the case may be.

The intelligence and design activities require a supportive system which can perform the task of collecting relevant data, collating, analysis and interpreting the data for policy purposes. The data are necessary for both formulation and review of public policy, and for policy planning.

The support systems for the intelligence and design activities in decision-making are necessary at the top and at the critical levels of administration such as the district. The type of decisions taken may differ at different levels of administration. The decision-processes are, however, similar. The support systems for the intelligence and design activities would be required at top and at key levels. Its composition, expertise and involvement may differ from one level to another, depending upon the nature of decisions taken at different levels.

The supportive system at the top level of administrative organisation must have the capability of building a base for relevant data, analysis and design activities in decision-making. Such an organisation would be engaged on data retrieval, analysis of the effectiveness of public policies and advising on new policy. The task is innovative. It requires application of rigorous analytical methodologies and familiarity with the operating tasks of the Government.

This kind of support organisation would be needed at the level of the cabinet, some of the ministries and the district administration. There would have to be sharing of data because in many cases the basic data would be the same.

Personnel Organisation

This task requires research expertise and also familiarity with the administrative system. It will have to be a team consisting of people drawn from sources outside the Government and from within. It would also seem that such an organisation would have to encourage a system of self-renewal as a philosophy, or as an accepted practice. It may require changing by rotation of personnel from outside and from within because a prolonged sense of routine and conditioning in such a system can be self-defeating.

If such an organisation has to be created, the Government would have to establish closer contacts with academic and non-Government personnel to utilise their talent for improving decision-making in the Government. I am persuaded that support systems of the kind suggested here are essential for the ever-increasing tasks that Government has assumed in India.

Notes

* From *Indian Journal of Public Administration*, Vol. XIX, No.4, 1973. pp. 429-440.

^ I am obliged to Mr. R.N. Haldipur for his valuable comments on an earlier draft of this paper.

1. Interesting research is now being undertaken in the emerging subject of policy science which is the study of that aspect of administration that focuses attention primarily on factors relevant to public policy on the processes through which decision is made. Briefly policy science is concerned with the process of decision-making in the task of formulating public policy.
2. H.A. Simon, *The New Science of Management Decisions*, 1960, New York, Harper, p. 2.
3. Otto, Klineberg, "Tensions Affecting International Understanding", 1950, *Social Science Research Council, Bulletin* 62, New York.
4. Donald C. Pelz, and H.M. Andrews, *Scientists in Organizations*, Wiley, 1966; G. Dalton and P.R. Lawrence, *Organisational Change and Development*, Irwin, Homewood, 1970.
5. H.A. Simon, *Administrative Behaviour*, London, Macmillan, 1961.
6. C.I. Barnard, *The Functions of the Executive*, Cambridge (Mass.), Harvard University Press, 1938.
7. H. Cantril, *The Human Dimension: Experience in Public Research*, New Brunswick, Rutgers University Press, 1967.
8. Donald C. Pelz, and H.M. Andrews, *op.cit.*; D.M. McGregor, "New Concepts of Management", *The Technology Review*, Vol. 63, No.4, February 1961.
9. An important basis of the election of a party to power is its programme and the confidence of the masses in its leadership. There is, however, need to see the distinction between a statement of intent and a statement of policy. Most often the election manifesto is an expression

of the end results to be sought and of a broad approach to their achievement. It is a statement of intent. It is not a policy as defined here. Administrative policy is specific, definitive and action-based. In the determination of public policy, it would be unrealistic to identify the significance of only the political or only the administrative system. The relative influence of these would vary according to the power each has in a given situation. It is a dynamic situation. In another context, Wilfred Brown (*Exploration in Management*, Heinemann, London, 1960) has suggested that in any organization several forces operate simultaneously and a balance among them has to be achieved for maintaining the viability of a system. In a business organization shareholders, customers and employees independently influence the activities and the decisions of a corporation. In public administration the political system, the public, the employees, all influence the activities of the Government. If the political system dominates in routine administrative matters, the administrator's authority (decision-making capacity) is seriously curtailed and the political system is likely to dominate over the administrative. If the political system is weak, the reverse happens: the administrator could dominate the political system.

10. V.A. Pai Panandikar, *Bureaucracy and Policy Making (cyclostyled)*, paper presented at the Seminar on Public Services and Social Responsibility held at the Indian Institute of Advanced Study, Simla, October 6-11, 1973.

9

Administrative Culture Desiderata*

YEHEZKEL DROR

'Administrative Culture' is not easy to define and circumscribe, dealing as it does with overall values, orientations, propensities, cognitive maps, symbols, rituals, perceptions, self-identity, language-games and similar features of organisations and organisational networks. The concept is fuzzy in many respects, overtly aggregate in ignoring diversity and pluralism, and open to divergent descriptions and interpretations.

Still, administrative culture is an essential concept for understanding administrative behaviour and its evolution and for reforming it, as recognized by growing attention being devoted to the subject in literature and professional practice alike.[1] Changes in administrative culture should accompany all administrative reforms and can clear the way for them, while also being important by themselves.

But reshaping of administrative culture is a difficult task, lip service and exhortations characterising it more than successful action. Two main reasons explain frequent failures of administrative culture change efforts: first, this is inherently a difficult task, administrative culture being grounded in history and broad societal features and shaped by multiple factors, most of which are immune to available policy instruments. Also, directed change of administrative culture takes long 'social' rather than short 'human' or 'political' time,[2] 10-20 years being often a minimum for achieving significant impacts on administrative culture in the absence of draconian revolutionary measures, which too frequently fail in the short-run (though crash programmes to change some pivotal features of administrative culture are possible).

A second main reason for failure of attempts to change administrative culture is lack of adequate specification of desired features. Efforts to change administrative culture often pick inappropriate goals which are selected more according to prevailing fashions and fads or dogmatic beliefs than being carefully designed to fit particular needs. In addition, Third World countries frequently suffer from administrative culture conceptions copied from the First World and pushed by experts coming from there, even though not fitting local needs. The fact that administrative cultures in the First World are obsolete and do not fit any more the needs of their countries of origin, as increasingly recognised there, makes reliance on them as models for other types of societies all the more counter-productive.

My studies lead to the conclusion that absence of public administration models, including administrative culture conceptions, fitting the needs of high-aspiration Third World countries is a main source of governance difficulties in the latter, frustrating many reforms efforts. This is all the more the case because theories and professional conceptions, which necessarily influence public administration practices in the Third World, continue to be unduly Western-based.

Administrative culture needs of Third World countries, as well as broader issues of capacities to govern, must be studied within a broad historic, comparative and theoretic frame which fits real conditions and contexts and which is partly detached from Western administrative thinking domination. Only with the help of such studies can one hope for deep understanding and comprehensive theories fitting real needs, which can serve as reliable bases for improvement. But urgent needs for radical upgrading of capacities to govern require short-cuts.

This article is such a short-cut, presenting some "bold conjectures"[3] on desiderata for the administrative culture of the higher levels of Indian national public administration. It is based on my general approaches to upgrading of the capacity to govern,[4] my experiences as a doctor to governments in a variety of countries, and diligent, though inadequate, readings on Indian public administration. Presentation of a desideratum does not imply that Indian administrative culture necessarily lacks the recommended features. Rather, the desiderata also serve as a concept package for empiric evaluation of actual Indian administrative culture, as a step towards improvement attempts. This article is submitted without presumption to do more than hopefully provide some stimuli, with the proposals to be put to severe tests by professionals who really know India.

Subject to these caveats, let me proceed to preliminary presentation and exploration of nine main desiderata for Indian high-level national public administration culture is pluralistic and in part contradictory. This fits the nature of cultures and needs alike, not homogeneity but rather better a mix of heterogeneity being aimed at.

Avant-Garde Self-Identity and High Energy Mission Commitment

A country like India, which aspires to far-going self-transformation, while facing demanding predicaments, needs an administrative culture with avant-garde self-identity and high energy mission commitment. The higher civil service culture is not, cannot be and should not be, a true reflection of societal cultures at large, but rather must fit the special needs of the societal guidance cluster and be in nature 'elitistic', though based on achievement criteria, open, and strongly committed to democracy.

The administrative culture should accordingly sustain an avant-garde self-identity aware of playing an important role in shaping the history trajectory of India, subject to the values and instructions of elected politicians. This will also strengthen a sense of cohesiveness, reinforcing the role of public administration as a centripetal national institution.

Related is the need for a high-energy administrative culture. This does not imply a 'meddling' or 'dirigentist' culture, which tends to be over-active and indiscriminately intervention-prone, with inadequate self-restraint in large domains where grassroot autonomy, market mechanisms and other societal processes perform much better. But, to fulfil essential functions of the state in reshaping and accelerating the historic trajectory of India, high energy must be a cultural norm of public administration.

These features converge in a sense of mission, up to a connotation of 'calling'. Administrative culture in India must be committed' demanding total devotion to tasks and identifying personal self-realisation with a job well done.

Value Permeated

The value dimensions of administrative culture should both reinforce and contain the sense of commitment, strengthening its positive functions while serving as safeguard against its inherent dangers. Untempered, a strong sense of commitment may lead to disparaging of procedural rules and extraneous norms, such as strict observance of the law, which seem to hinder achievement of main goals.

The point well illustrates that the desiderata are not absolute imperatives displacing all other considerations, with the more being always the better. Rather, a balance among the desiderata and between them and other norms and requirements is needed. Thus while absence of strong commitment to main missions may result in unproductive substitution of procedures, legalism, etc., for substantive goals, monodimensional 'true believer' cultures, can easily become malignant, undermining political supremacy and social values. Therefore, my emphasis on the importance of the value dimensions of administrative culture, as against visions of public administration as 'value free' and 'value neutral', which while being in part unrealistic in all countries, are in India incorrect normatively and prescriptively.

Most, though not all, of the values should be provided by the political order and by societal norms. But some needed values are specific to administrative culture. In addition to professional ones to be considered later, administrative culture should be characterised by long-term time preferences; and by regarding the national public interest, however hard to specify, as the dominant value principle, as opposed to sectoral and particularistic values. Also, under prevailing and expected conditions, I think that readiness to take risks and positive evaluation of innovation should be integral to administrative culture values.

It is not for me to postulate the more substantive values to be included in Indian administrative culture, all the more so as they are more a product of tacit social and political dynamics than of explicit and deliberate norm-setting. Let me, therefore, limit myself to underlining the need to anchor administrative culture in main social and political values embraced by India. Still, the matter is more complicated. As already hinted at, administrative culture should not fully reflect societal culture, but be somewhat differentiated so as to fulfil avant-garde functions. This also applies to values, with soulcraft,[5] in the sense of deliberate efforts to change societal values, being one of the task of societal guidance in India. In a country with so rich a culture as India, this raises the fundamental question how far to follow prevailing global *Zeitgeist*, dominated as it is by Western culture, or how far to deviate from dominant ideologies,[6] and strive for value autonomy. This is not a matter for slogans, but rather for complex societal and cultural processes, involving many dilemmas – which should stand in the centre of Indian administrative culture as a subject of shared perplexity and soul-searching. Therefore, the values permeating administrative culture should be pluralistic, in part contradictory, and search-directed, reflecting value futures choice as an existential concern of India.

Strategic Orientation

Administrative cultures can be more tactics oriented or more strategy and even grand-strategy oriented, in emphasising handling of details and issues as they come along or in putting main weight on critical choices, policy paradigms, and overall national directions. A mix between these polar orientations is needed to handle multiple realities and fulfil diverse tasks. Still, administrative culture can lay more emphasis on disparate tactical handling of issues or coherent strategic steering of national pathways.

Preferable administrative cultures depend in this matter on national situations and on preferred policy philosophies. Under some conditions and according to some policy philosophies, disparate tactical handling is better. Thus, when countries are on ascending curves and established policies work well, then incremental improvement on a tactical level are adequate. But, when countries face fundamental difficulties, are on unsatisfactory curves and aspire to transform themselves – then strategic orientations should dominate administrative culture.

I may be wrong, but my estimation of the Indian situation leads me to the conclusion that administrative culture should tend more towards a strategic than a tactical orientation.

Deep Professionalism and Multi-Disciplinarity

Without transgressing into the subject of political institutions, it should be noted that the avant-garde self-identity and high-energy mission commitment and value permeation desiderata should, in the main, be shared by political culture and administrative culture, though in political culture the avant-garde element should be diluted by more pronounced public representation features and the value contents will be different in some respect. In contrast, deep professionalism distinguished administrative culture from political culture, even if the latter should be required to be more knowledge-demanding than is at present the case. In the division of labour in governance, the main unique contribution of public administration is professionalism and the legitimation for an important and autonomous, though subordinate, role for senior officials in societal guidance is in their professionalism. Therefore, professionalism should be a main feature of administrative culture.

To elucidate this desiderata, both deconstruction and reconstruction are called for. It is necessary to get rid of the 'generalist' versus 'expert' bogus controversy; and the concept of 'professionalism' as proposed for administrative culture needs elucidation. Briefly put, the glorification of 'common sense' of 'muddling through' and of the educated gentleman as helper to the Rulers as against the disparagement of 'experts' as narrow[7] and "to be kept on tap and not on top", as formulated by Harold Laski, who should have known better, is one of the main barriers to upgrading administrative performance still over-shadowing British administrative cultures and those of countries influenced by it, though rejected for the UK by the Fulton Committee.[8] But there is more than a grain of truth in the clinging of British and some other administrative cultures to an ideology of superiority of cultivated generalists, if the alternative is narrow specialisation. What is needed, instead of both of these inadequate options, is an administrative culture of professionalism but not constricted expertise. Deep professionalism in policy making and management as broad domains of knowledge and practice should be in the centre of administrative culture injunctions.

This leads us to the concept of professionalism. Its essence consists in a capacity to build bridges between abstract theory and concrete concerns, in striving to go beyond surface phenomena into underlying deep-seated processes and, to use a formulation of Schoon[9] to "think in action". Scepticism about 'common sense' when confronting uncommon problems, readiness to search for counter-conventional solutions, capacity and willingness to reflect abstractly about concrete predicaments, ability to adopt a stance of 'clinical concern' and to think coldly on white hot issues, and constant search for new knowledge which may be relevant – these are core features of professionalism as a core content of administrative culture.

I add the qualification 'deep' to professionalism in order to emphasise that administrative culture in the higher national echelons should be anti-pragmatic, demanding instead penetration beyond manifest phenomena into underlying realities and grounding of judgment and action on consideration of fundamental processes rather than on looking at visible realities alone. This view of mine may be anathema to many practitioners, but I am convinced that popular conceptions of 'pragmatism' (which have little to do with pragmatism as a philosophy developed by Charles Peirce, William James, John Dewey and others) constitute a main obstacle to correct comprehension and effectively handling of fundamental problems facing a country like India. Therefore, my recommendation is that administrative culture should postulate as a main norm 'deep' professionalism predicated on application of abstract knowledge to concrete issues.

An additional specification is needed here, namely inter-disciplinarity. No single disciplinary approach must dominate administrative culture. Instead, it should be multi-disciplinary and inter-disciplinary in cognitive maps and modes of problem handling.

I do not want in this article to go too far with abstract ideas, howsoever essential for better practice they may be. Still, let me hint at a more advanced formulation of the desideratum: administrative culture should reflect and express a highly developed philosophy of judgment and action, instead of 'generalism' and 'pragmatism' slogans. When discussing policy sophistication below, some elements for a philosophy of judgment and action, fitting the needs of administrative culture in a country like India, are illustrated. Further than that I cannot go in this article.

Cost Consciousness

Harsh resources scarcity makes it imperative for administrative culture to include cost consciousness. It should be emphasized that various techniques to increase cost accountability of senior public executives are quite inadequate in the absence of a cost conscious administrative culture and that the main aim of introducing such techniques is to influence administrative culture, rather than nominally holding one or another executive financially responsible. The proclivity of a strong sense of mission as well as of some professional values to belittle cost considerations as secondary to achieving believed-in goals make it all the more necessary to counter-balance those recommended features of administrative culture with cost consciousness (illustrating the pluralistic and in part contradictory nature of required administrative culture). The difficulties in all countries of containing medical costs and the dependence of success in doing so largely on making medical professionals more cost conscious well illustrate the problematic nature of making administrative culture cost conscious.

Cost consciousness is not only a matter of being aware of costs, trying to estimate them correctly and applying cost-benefit frames of thinking, even though qualitatively, to main issues, but also requires broad consideration of options in terms of opportunity costs. Even more important, cost consciousness sharpens the need for tough priorities and tragic choices, where important values and goals must be given up for even more important ones. Therefore, cost consciousness is not a mundane matter but a fundamental orientation absolutely essential in the administrative culture of countries where resources are very scarce in comparison to aspirations, as in India.

Science and Technology Friendly

However hard to realise, there will probably be little disagreement with my suggestion that administrative culture should be cost conscious. Quite a different reception may await my stipulation that administrative culture must be science and technology friendly. Let me first explain what I mean and what I do not mean and then give my reasons for this imperative.

I do not mean that administrative culture should only or mainly be science and technology directed. If this were the reality, I would, on the contrary, require literati-friendliness as a main administrative culture requisite. But Indian public administration culture, as that of nearly all countries, seems to have a strong literati-orientation, which may need betterment but is already highly developed. However, what is sorely missing is science and technology friendliness.

Science and technology friendliness means that administrative culture regards background in science and technology (including engineering) as a good path to top level positions; that all senior staff is expected to be science and technology literate, in the sense of regularly reading and understanding a periodical of the type of *Scientific American*; and that science and technology ways of thinking and substantive inputs are regarded as integral to all of policy making and management.

My reasons for this proposal are multiple: to be advanced in science and technology is the most important factor in shaping reality, with immense potentials for all aspects of India. Also, the methods and modes of reasoning of science and technology are in part applicable to many other types of problems, though this must be done in a sophisticated way. And, to move on to a more conjectural proposition, it may well be that one main trajectory for India should be to move rapidly, though by phases and in a modular way, towards becoming a high-technology, high-culture multi-society. Ergo, administration culture must be science and technology friendly.

Let me further operationalise and prompt this proposition by posing two sub-specifications for administrative culture: It should be human-machine congenial and it should be numeracy-congenial.

Transformation of all of public administration into a human-machine system is the main road to mutation it on to a qualitatively higher level of effectiveness and efficiency (and also an essential early step on the road to a high-technology, high-culture society). Albeit, it is less a matter of introducing data processing systems and supplying low and medium level staff with computerised work stations. Rather, required is an administrative culture which pushes towards human-machine systems and which looks upon a senior public executive, who does personally use ardently advanced computerised work stations as passé.

Let me add here a word on interaction between administrative culture and transformation of public administration into a human-machine system. A supportive administrative culture is very helpful in moving to a human-machine system. But, an alternative approach is to forcefully transmute public administration into a human-machine system – which, in turn, will shock much of administrative culture and permit introduction of various changes into it, in addition to pushing it towards acceptance and, with time, liking of human-machine systems. This illustrates potentials for reshaping administrative cultures by various intervention modes, demonstrating that changing administrative culture may be feasible, though in this article I do not delve on ways for doing so.

More unconventional is my proposition that administrative culture must be numeracy-congenial, in addition to being literati and in conjunction with being science and technology friendly. Numeracy does not imply a belief that everything can and should be quantified, nor does it demand advanced mathematical skills. But it implies rejection of innumeracy[10] as intolerable ignorance, looking for a maximum of quantitative data, and – most important and most demanding of all – favouring numerical thinking as one of the main modalities of reasoning.

Open-Mind and Self-Doubt

Open-mind and self-doubt are regarded as obvious desiderata, but are very problematic. They contradict commitment to mission, which necessarily involves intense belief in what one stands for. Furthermore, they stand in opposition to widespread and in part useful administrative culture features, such as shared cognitive maps, common assumptions and widely accepted policy orthodoxies. Also, too much self-doubt may result in Hamlet's syndrome, with intellectual indecision displacing choice and implementation determination.

Still, rapidly changing situations put a premium on open mind,[11] with active search for new inputs and abundant readiness to change one's mind. Such an open-mind administrative culture must be accompanied by much self-doubts, with strong awareness of motivated irrationalities (in the sense of Pears)[12], blind stops and other administrative culture, 'cognitive caves' and also 'psychic prisons'[13] – reinforcing, in turn, readiness to revise one's position.

Iconoclasm Encouraging, Learning Supportive and Innovation Happy

Closely related to the above desideratum is the present cluster of iconoclasm encouragement, learning support, and innovation happiness. Encouragement of iconoclasm is a *sine qua non* for preventing public administration from constituting a ballast on societal dynamics and a heavy part of decline-causing tyrannies of the *status quo*[14]. In my view, societal self-transformation capacities are essential for avoiding decline[15] and realising national aspirations in a rapidly changing world. It follows that public administration, because of its avant-grade and strategic functions, must be a pacesetter in self-transformation. And this requires, *inter alia*, an administrative culture with strong iconoclasm tolerance and encouragement, also on policy paradigms and policy orthodoxies, however painful this may be.

The idea of learning administrative cultures is fully accepted in professional literature[16]. But stubborn governmental zero-learning[17] testifies to the strength of intractable counter-learning barriers. Hence, the need to reinforce this dimension of administrative culture.

The need for innovativeness including creativity and public entrepreneurship, is also increasingly recognised,[18] in part thanks to growing business management interests in venture encouragement[19]. But how to imbue administrative culture with innovativeness in the face of often strong intertia tendencies is an open question, all the more so as competitiveness, as a main force pushing innovation in successful industries,[20] is hard to apply to the core of public administration.

But, however difficult to realise, making administrative culture iconoclasm encouraging, learning supportive and innovation-happy is essential in a country like India – justifying, if essential, rather radical reforms in some main features of senior civil service policy and of administrative macro-structure.

Policy Sophistication

The last substantive desideratum to be proposed in this article returns us to the deep professionalism specification, applying it in a way as policy development. Rather than provide abstract formulations, which will not help to convey my intent without a shared base in advanced policy thinking, let me epitomise the idea of 'policy sophistication' with the help of three illustrations:

1. Policy making should be viewed, analysed, sensed, intuited and 'felt' as a process of fuzzy gambling, up to gambling with history when fateful choices are faced. This is an unavoidable, though bitter, inference from the prevalence of irreducible uncertainties in all major policy issues. Therefore, essential in administrative culture are tolerance of uncertainty, risk-taking readiness, willingness to subordinate misleading intuitions to disciplined decision protocols, and many other features of 'uncertainty sophistication'[21] as a main facet of policy sophistication.
2. Thinking-in history (going far beyond Neustadt and May)[22], within a broad perspective or rise and decline of nations and success and failure of large national enterprises, is essential for strategic choice in a country like India. This involves absorption of much historic and social change knowledge, careful consideration of appropriate policy scale,[23] struggle with alternative development strategies and much more. Deep thinking-in-history on critical national choices requires special policy R&D organisations of the "Think-Tank" type. But all of administrative culture must be receptive to such ways of policy thinking and understand the need for them, in short be policy sophisticated.
3. The very notions of 'rationality', as a main grounding of administrative choice and underlying much of administrative culture, needs upgrading – within the frame of organisational

potentials and their upgrading,[24] and more important and more demanding, in terms of moving up to advanced philosophic notions of rationality.[25]

These illustrations of policy sophistication as a desideratum of administrative culture may be too simple for those who know the subject and too enigmatic for those who do not know. But this is the best I can do in this article, hoping to have at least given some inkling of the idea of policy sophistication as an urgent necessity of administrative culture.

Administrative Culture Change Possibilities

If and in so far as the proposed list of desiderata is accepted, at least in part, the question is reached what can and should be done to move reality in the direction of the preferable model. Experiences indicate that administrative cultures can be changed, though with great difficulties, by deliberate action, ranging from imposing political resolution (e.g., England under Thatcher)[26] to modifying senior civil service policy, intense retraining, shock effects of organisational reshuffling, novel incentive systems and more (such as already mentioned transition to human-machine systems). It is a difficult process, but administrative cultures can be changed if a need to do so is recognised and a will to do so is formed.

But, in order to evaluate needs to change administrative culture and provide a compass for doing so, a realistic vision of a preferable administrative culture is necessary. To provide some elements of such a realistic vision in the form of a set of desiderata was the mission of this article. It is up to the readers to judge whether the proposed administrative culture desiderata fit Indian needs and what action may be appropriate to advance in desired directions.

Notes

* From *Indian Journal of Public Administration*, Vol. XXXVI, No. 3, 1990. pp. 374-383.

1. Edgar Schein, *Organisational Culture and Leadership: A Dynamic View*, San Francisco, Jossey Bass, 1985; and Les Metcalfe and Sue Richards, "Evolving Public Management Culture": in Kjell Eliassen and Jan Kooinsan (eds), *Morajing Pubic Organisations*, Beverly Hills, CA, Sage, 1987.
2. Femand Braudel, *On History*, Chicago, University of Chicago Press, 1980.
3. Karl Popper, *Conjectures and Refutations: The Growth of Scientific Knowledge*, London, Routledge and Kegan Paul, 4th edn., 1972.

4. Yehezkel Dror, *Public Policy making Reexamined*, New Brunswick, NJ, Transaction, updated edition, 1983; and *Policy making Under Adversity*, New Brunswick, NJ, Transaction, 1980 (paper back 1988).
5. George F. Will, *Statecraft as Soulcraft: What Government Does*, New York, Simon and Schuster, 1983.
6. Nicholas Abercrombie, Stephen Hill and Bryan S. Tumer, *The Dominant Ideology Thesis*, London Allen and Unwin, 1980.
7. For fuller examination, see Yehezkel Dror, *Ventures in Policy Sciences*, New York, American Elsevier, 1971, pp. 235-39.
8. *Report of the Committee on the Civil Service*, Fulton Report, London, HMSO, Cmnd. 3638, Vol. I, 1968, p. 11.
9. Donald A. Schon, *The Reflective Practitioner: How Professionals Think in Action*, New York, Basic Books, 1983.
10. John Allen Paulus, *Innumeracy: Mathematical Illiteracy and its Consequences*, New York, Hill and Wang, 1988.
11. Milton Rokeach, *Open and Closed Mind*, New York, Basic Books, 1960.
12. David Pears, *Motivated Irrationality*, Oxford, Clarendon Press, 1984.
13. Gareth Morgan, *Images of Organization*, Beverly Hills, CA, Sage, 1986, pp. 199-231.
14. Mancur Olson, *The Rise and Decline of Nations: Economic Growth, Stagflation, and Social Rigidities*, New Haven, CT, Yale University Press, 1982.
15. Roberto Managabeira Unger, *Variations on Themes of Politics, A Work in Constructive Social Theory: Plasticity into Power – Comparative-Historical Studies on the Institutional Conditions of Economic and Military Success*, Cambridge, Cambridge University Press, 1987.
16. N. Donald Michael, *On learning to Plan - and Planning to Learn: The Social Psychology of Changing Toward Future – Responsive Societal Learning*, San Francisco, Jossey-Bass, 1973; and Kenyou B. De. Greene, *The Adaptive Organisation: Anticipation and Management of Crisis*, New York, Wiley, 1982.
17. Lloyd S. Etheredge, *Can Governments Learn? American Foreign Policy and Central American Revolutions*, New York, Pergamon, 1985.
18. Gunther F. Schaefer and Eamon McInemey (eds.), *Strengthening Innovativeness in Public Sector Management*, Maastricht, European Institute of Public Administration, 1988.
19. Thomas J. Peters and Robert H. Waterman, Jr., *In Search of Excellence: Lessons from America's Best Run Companies*, New York, Harper & Row, 1983.
20. Michael E. Porter, *The Competitive Advantage of Nations*, New York, Free Press, 1990.

21. Yehezkel Dror, "Uncertainty: Coping with it and with Political Feasibility", in Hugh J. Miser and Edward S. Quade (eds.), *Handbook of Systems Analysis: Craft Issues and Procedural Choices*, New York, North-Holland, 1988, pp. 247-281.
22. Richard E. Neustadt and Emest R. May, *Thinking in Time: The Uses of History for Decision Makers*. New York, Free Press, 1986.
23. Paul R. Schulman, *Large-Scale Policy Making*, New York, Elsevier, 1980.
24. James G. March, *Decisions and Organizations*, Oxford, Blackwell, 1988.
25. For example, see Jon Elster, *Ulysses and the Sirens: Studies in Rationality and Irrationality*, Cambridge, Cambridge University Press, 1979; and Thomas C. Schelling, *Choice and Consequence: Perspectives of an Errant Economist*, Cambridge MA, Harvard University Press, 1984.
26. Peter Hennessy, *Whitehall*, London, Secker and Warburg, 1989.

10

The Policy of Preventive Detention, 1950-1963*

DAVID H. BAYLEY**

I

In the early afternoon of December 19, 1963, the Lok Sabha extended the life of Preventive Detention Act, 1950, by a vote of 236-68. Thus, for the eighth time in the short history of independent India the policy of preventive detention was examined and confirmed. So regular have become these requests for an extension of the Preventive Detention Act that the debate has by now become a set-piece of Parliamentary tactics and oratory. The Home Minister, speaking for the Government, presents the case with regret and apology; the Opposition, speaking with discordant voices, thunders its denunciation, utilizing such well worn phrases as "lawless law" and "black act"; Congress backbenchers dutifully fill in the middle portions of the debate with rambling expressions of support for the measure; the Government majority is marshaled and overwhelmingly extends the life of the Act; and, finally, the opposition reflexively walks out in protest.

The wooden predictability of the debate should not, however, be allowed to obscure the significance of the matter involved. The Preventive Detention Act provides for the arrest and detention of persons who, in the opinion of Government, represent a threat to the social stability of the country. The courts are expressly forbidden

---

**For several points, particularly those having to do with unchanged legal implications of the Preventive Detention Act, I have drawn on an earlier study I made of preventive detention for the Journal *Pacific Affairs* (Summer, 1962, pp. 99-115), I refer the reader also to my *Preventive Detention in India*, Calcutta : Firms K.L. Mukhopadhyay, 1962.

to question the necessity for any detention orders issued by Government; subjective satisfaction of the detaining authorities is determining in every case. Here, clearly and unambiguously, is an exception to the canons of legitimacy commonly accepted in liberal-democratic theory.

The Preventive Detention Act represents one answer to the most puzzling questions confronting statesmen in the newly independent nations, namely, to what extent may Government arrogate to itself in the name of democratic tutelage the power to regulate the rules of political interaction without, by that very action, jeopardizing the long-run development of democracy? If rules and guidelines are left inchoate, so the argument runs, it will be difficult to mould the behaviour of individuals and groups to the requirements of democratic tutelage. Left uninstructed, political behaviour may cleave to the habitual patterns of traditional society. On the other hand, leaders of Government may in their zeal to teach and shape restrict too tightly the manner of political interaction, producing a stability based not on trust but on repression and fear. The builders of democratic nations must thus try to balance requisite tutelage in the ways of democracy with the permissiveness in action which is the hallmark of democracy. They face the danger of social anarchy on the one hand and rigid authoritarianism on the other.

Since the life of the Act has been extended on so many occasions in the past fourteen years, Indians have had ample opportunity to reassess the wisdom of maintaining this instrument of social regulation. The Preventive Detention Act can no longer be called a temporary expedient, but must be acknowledged a permanent part of India's democratic experiment. In an effort to explore the general issue of the often opposing requirements of tutelage and liberty, this article will examine the experience of modern India with preventive detention from 1950 through 1963.

II

The Preventive Detention Act was originally passed in February, 1950, one month after the promulgation of India's first self-governing constitution. It has been submitted to Parliament for rejection or re-approval eight times between February 1950 and December, 1963. On three of those occasions and once-mid-way in one term of the Act, Parliament amended its substantive provisions. As passed in 1950 the Act was to run for a period of one year. This practice continued until October, 1952, when the Act was extended for a two-year period. In 1954 the term was increased to three years, and there it has remained. Since 1954 there have been no substantive alterations in the Preventive Detention Act; it has simply been re-extended at three-year intervals.

The Preventive Detention Act provides that upon order of the Central or State Governments persons may be detained in jail for periods ranging up to one year if the Government "is satisfied" that they are likely to engage in behaviour which would be "prejudicial" to any of the following interests: the defence of India, the relations of India with foreign powers, the security of India, the security of the State, the maintenance of public order, or the maintenance of supplies and services essential to the community.[1] At no time during the life of the Act has any attempt been made to define more specifically these interests the defence of which provides the *raison d'etre* for this grant of authority. The phrases are vague and general and will probably remain so.

In order to understand the legal status of preventive detention it is not enough to study the Preventive Detention Act itself. Legislative enactments acquire meaning through being placed by the courts within the boundaries supplied by the Constitution. Article 22 of Part III (Fundamental Rights) of the Constitution explicitly provides for preventive detention. In this manner the statesmen of Independence ensured the constitutionality of a resort to preventive detention and thereby frustrated a headlong conflict between fundamental rights and this form of governmental control. Article 22 stipulates that a person imprisoned under powers granted in a Preventive Detention Act need not be afforded the protection of the following rights which are normally guaranteed to "all citizens",[2] (1) the right to be represented and assisted by legal counsel; (2) the right to be publicly informed of all ground pertinent to the decision to issue a detention order; (3) the right to be produced before the nearest magistrate within 24 hours after arrest; and (4) the right to be held for a period not in excess of 24 hours except upon the express order of a magistrate.

The most important effect of these provisions is to deprive persons who have been preventively detained from having recourse to the courts. The decision to detain cannot be subjected to judicial scrutiny, but belongs exclusively to the executive. Detenus are thus expressly singled out by the Constitution and placed in a special category to which the fundamental rights do not apply. As one critic has said: "..... this Article confers on every Indian citizen the right, the fundamental right, of being detained without trial."[3]

The Constitution allows leverage upon the operations of the

Preventive Detention Act through the agency of the courts at only one point.[4] Clause 5 of Article 22 specifies that the detaining authorities shall be required to communicate to the detenu "as soon as may be" the grounds upon which the order has been made and that they "shall afford him the earliest opportunity of making a representation against the order". The Supreme Court has ruled[5] that this allows the courts to examine the question whether the grounds furnished are sufficient to enable the detenu to make a representation. This point alone is justiciable. The courts can inquire only into the form of government's presentation; they cannot question the truth or falsity of the facts adduced.[6] As a result, it is possible for the courts to find in a particular case that the detenu's right to make a representation has not been infringed, because the grounds specified are sufficiently specific, although the grounds may in fact be entirely fictitious.

Detaining authorities cannot, however, simply assert that a detenu has acted in a manner which indicates he is likely to be a threat to the interests enumerated in the Act. The authorities must cite particulars about the previous conduct of the detenu so that he can understand which of his activities have raised suspicion against him. Although the detenu may disagree with the Government's evaluation of his activities, as long as Government's statement gives him a clear idea about the factual basis for their evaluation the authorities have fulfilled their legal obligation. Information as specific as this will usually allow the detenu to challenge the factual accuracy of the Government's case against him. He will be able to respond "No, I was not there", or "No, I could not have done as you charge and for the following reasons". Vagueness of grounds, then, can be the cause of the invalidation of detention orders by the courts.[7] This, however, is a far cry from allowing the courts to challenge either the accuracy of the government's report or the opinion of the Government as to the harmfulness of the detenu's activities upon the interests to be safeguarded.

The fact of these rulings has been to set some limits upon the kind of information which government must have in its possession (or appear to have in its possession) in order to found a detention order. Government is nct entirely free to act upon impulse and without a minimum of study. To this extent, therefore, the courts have restricted the manner in which the executive may arrest and detain. Even this modest judicial check may be frustrated, however, by the invocation of clause (6) of Article 22, which stipulates that detaining authority shall not be required to divulge any facts which they consider to be "against the public interest to disclose". The sole hold permitted the courts by the Constitution upon the operation of the Preventive Detention Act is, ultimately, subject to the discretion of the executive. To the great credit of the Central and State Governments, they have rarely invoked this stultifying claim of privilege.[8]

The provision made for preventive detention in the Constitution of India, although undoubtedly a farsighted act on the part of members of the Constituent Assembly in that it provided for contingencies actually developing later, has had one constraining effect that warrants commentary. There has been a tendency in recent years to treat Article 22 not simply as *permission* to do but as a *directive* to do. The Home Minister, Mr. Nanda, in the recent debate referred to the Articles in the Constitution, specifically Article 22, as the "source" and "origin" of the Preventive Detention Act.[9] The authority of the statesmen of the Constituent Assembly thus becomes a justification for subsequent policy-making. This is an instructive example of the way in which an element of latitude embodied in a written constitution becomes a justification for government action.

III

There is another side to the picture, however. The Government and Parliament have not been content with the minimal guarantees provided to the detenus by the Constitution. Rather than allowing the Constitution to stipulate the sum total of rights to which a detenu could lay claim, they sought to devise additional safeguards without at the same time rendering nugatory the advantages to the maintenance of law and order which are the justification for preventive detention in the first place. Preventive detention is valuable, after all, exactly because it sets aside many elements in ordinary judicial procedure. It becomes clear, therefore, that no set of procedures designed to protect the detenu can quite substitute for the guarantees of judicial procedure.

What are the safeguards which have been provided in the Act? First, a person preventively detained must be informed of the grounds for his detention within five days from the day of detention.[10] This amounts to a definition of the phrase "as soon as may be" in Article 22 of the Constitution. Second, when a detention order is issued by a State Government, the Central Government must be notified of it "as soon as may be". Furthermore, State Governments must be notified of detentions ordered by their own subordinate officers within 12 days of the date of detention.[11] Failure to comply with these stipulations will invalidate a detention order. Third, and most important, all detention orders must be examined by a quasi-judicial body, known as an Advisory Board, within 30 days to 10 weeks of the date of detention.

Advisory Boards are appointed by both the Central and State Governments, and must be composed of three members who are, have been or are qualified to be appointed as judges of a High Court.[12] The Boards are empowered to collect any information relevant to determining the necessity for an order[13]subject to the restriction that information may be withheld which Government considers not in the public interest to disclose. The detenu himself has the right to appear in person before the Board. He is expressly denied, however, the right to be assisted by legal counsel.[14] The Advisory Boards have power to reverse the decisions of Government.[15] An order not positively confirmed by an Advisory Board within 10 weeks after the date of detention becomes void.

The Advisory Board procedure brings to bear upon the operations of the Act the acumen and concern of trained legal minds, while retaining the informality and speed of an administrative tribunal. The Advisory Boards are not prevented from examining the sufficiency of the grounds cited by Government for issuing an order; indeed, they are enjoined to question the judgment of Government as to the finding whether particular actions are, in fact, prejudicial to the interests enumerated in the Act.

On balance, then, although a detenu does not enjoy many of the judicial safeguards which are the right of the ordinary criminal, he is not left entirely bereft. The courts may declare a detention order void in three circumstances: (1) when the grounds submitted to the prisoner are so vague that he cannot make a representation against the order; (2) when the authorities act in a manner which is *ultra vires* of the Preventive Detention Act itself, as, for instance, when a State Government is not notified within twelve days of detention that an order has been put into effect; and (3) when the action of the detaining authorities is *mala fide*, that is, when the authorities employ the powers of the Act for purposes for which it was not designed.[16] Furthermore, standing between the detenu and the executive authorities is a quasi-judicial board, composed of men of High Court rank and talent, which is empowered to consider the case on its merits and to re-appraise all detention orders.

These protections notwithstanding, the conclusion is inescapable that the Preventive Detention Act, taken in conjunction with Article

22 of the Constitution, places in the hands of Government an instrument of tremendous power. The interests in defence of which Government may issue detention orders are singularly vague. Phrases like "maintenance of public order", "relations of India with foreign powers", "the security of the State", could be interpreted by the unscrupulous, as well as by the over zealous or the merely timorous, so broadly as to cover almost any kind of public Act. Two basic and extremely difficult judgments on the part of the authorities are not subject to the scrutiny of any judicial tribunal: (1) that an action will in fact have a harmful effect upon the interests enumerated in the Preventive Detention Act; and (2) that an action constitutes a threat so grave that it cannot be allowed to occur, even though the cost of prevention is incarceration. Only the Advisory Boards can challenge these judgements. Although the Advisory Boards are manned by men of high caliber, the position of this personnel on Advisory Boards is not as independent of the executive as it is when sitting upon Supreme or High Courts. Judges of the Supreme Court and the High Courts cannot be removed except upon the recommendation of the Government and by the vote of an absolute majority of the members of Parliament.[17] Members of Advisory Boards, on the other hand, serve upon the approval of the Executive; they may be removed at will.

Finally, in the event that a Government was determined upon unrestricted use of the power of preventive detention and found itself embarrassed by criticism or procrastination of courts or Advisory Boards, it could resort to a claim of security in the public interest, citing Article 22 of the Constitution, and thereby withhold all information from these bodies. There would be no recourse in the law; political solutions alone would avail. In the balance between private rights and governmental power, with respect to preventive detention, the preponderance is clearly on the side of Government. This is not to say that as a matter of factual record in the past fourteen years private rights have been wantonly trampled under foot. But it is to say that legal instrument exists for the ready accomplishment of this end. Laws harsh in their formal terms may be administered in a lenient and understanding fashion while laws innocuous on their face may be used to drive humanity to despair. In order to determine, then, how the Preventive Detention Act has borne upon the people of India, we must turn to a study of its operation during the past decade and a half.

IV

With the exception of 1957 the number of persons detained each year has declined steadily between 1950 and 1958. The Act was extensively employed at first, a total of 10,962 persons being detained in 1950. [18] Detentions fell by 80 per cent in 1951, to 2,316.[19] There were two primary reasons for this decline: first, the ending of the uprising in Telengana; second, the abandonment by the Communist Party of the tactics of violent revolution. For example, of the 10,962 arrested in 1950 approximately 6,000 of them had been from Telengana,[20] while in 1951 out of 2,316 only 727 were from Telengana.[21] By 1954 the number of detentions had been reduced to 325[22] and by 1958 to 177.[23] From 1958 through 1961 a plateau was established at about 175 detentions per year. In 1962, however, the figure once again rose to 219.[24] And in 1963 the number of detentions reached 288.[25]

All the States have not been equally or consistently represented as far as number of detentions is concerned. It is not unusual for fully one-half the States not to have anyone in detention at any given moment. As one would expect, variability in the distribution of detenus among the States correlates with the occurrence of violent agitation and protest. The statistics on detentions in Telengana provide one example of this; another is the arrest in 1955 of 101 persons in the Punjab where the Punjab *Hindi Raksha Samiti* had been conducting a prolonged "Save Hindi" campaign.[26] The total number of persons detained in all India in 1955 was only 292. The only States which have consistently accounted for a high proportion of detentions have been Bombay and West Bengal.[27]

It is important to avoid reading into these statistics more than is warranted. They show only, although quite unambiguously, that there has been a steady decrease in the number of detentions during the first eight years of the Preventive Detention Act. They do not reveal, as some have argued, that the Act is either necessary or unnecessary. As the Indian Civil Liberties Bulletin has pointed out: "If the detentions increase, then obviously the situation has become so bad as to be uncontrollable, except by the use of the Act; if on the contrary, they decline, then again, equally obviously, the Act has served its purpose of restraining the evil-doers and must therefore be kept. [28] The Government has capitalized on this point to get the best of both worlds. By the same token, the conclusion that Indian social and political life has become more pacific also cannot be drawn from these figures. In lieu of other information, one could as well contend that the Government has learned to live with instability and no longer regards the same events as requiring detention. Conclusions about the conditions of Indian life must be drawn from other sources than statistics about preventive detention.

A similar inconclusiveness affects arguments utilizing statistics in order to demonstrate the usefulness of the Advisory Boards or the courts in providing relief to detenus. For instance, from 1952 to 1957 the Advisory Boards confirmed 72 per cent of the orders sent to them, while reversing 28 per cent.[29] One can argue with equal justice that these figures show, first, that the safeguards provided by the Advisory Boards are not illusory or, second, that the detaining authorities are acting in a clearly slap-dash way and that although the Advisory Boards have been partially successful in mitigating this condition, the duly constituted courts would have been more effective. We are on firm ground at only one point: the Advisory Boards have not been unwilling to challenge the judgement of Government as to the potential threat posed by the activities of detenus.

V

The primary agency of relief to the detenu is the Advisory Board. The Advisory Board provides the only opportunity of *ex-parte* judgment to be brought to bear upon the reasoning of the executive authorities. In 1956 and 1957 the Advisory Boards quashed 33 per cent and 30 per cent, respectively, of the orders submitted to them.[30] In 1958 they rejected 44 per cent, an astonishing number of dismissals and a record for the 14 years' history of the Act.[31] Since then the percentage of dismissals has gone down sharply, being 16 per cent in 1959, 19 per cent in 1960, 20 per cent in 1961, and only 9 per cent in 1962. Generally, the States with the greatest number of detentions each year also account for the largest number of dismissals by Advisory Boards. Maharashtra (Bombay) and West Bengal consistently lead the list in both categories, although there has been a tendency in the past three or four years for West Bengal Advisory Boards to reject fewer orders proportionately than they had during the 1950's. But the figures do not show that particular inhibitory factors are at work upon the Advisory Boards of particular States. There could still be marked constraint in the operation of the Boards, but the figures create the presumption that constraint, if it exists, is to be found uniformly throughout India.

One curious feature in the operation of the Board is the reluctance of the Advisory Boards to go beyond the information submitted to them by Government and the detenu. The Advisory

Boards are empowered[32] to request additional information from the Government or from outside witnesses. Maharashtra (Bombay) is the only State in which other persons are consistently summoned to appear, and almost always people seem to be called in pairs, one in support of the case for detention and one in support of the detenu's plea for dismissal. For example, in 1957 and 1958 only Bombay State summoned other persons to present evidence. While in 1956, 1959, 1960, 1961 and 1962 Bombay State (Maharashtra) and only one other State summoned outside witnesses. Although the qualifications of Advisory Board personnel are the same in all the States, it certainly seems clear that it is possible for panels of Advisory Boards to develop their own special ways of doing business. And Maharashtra would seem to have evolved a really unique procedure.[33] At the same time, since Maharashtra does not account for a disproportionate number of dismissals of orders by Advisory Boards, one cannot conclude that Maharashtra's concern has produced a large measure of justice. Either that, or Maharashtra's executive officials have learned to be comparatively more careful.

In Parliamentary debates a great point has been made of the provision in the Preventive Detention Act that detenus have the right to appear in person before the Advisory Boards.[34] Through the years approximately 70 per cent of all detenus have had their cases considered by an Advisory Board. In the remainder of cases the State Governments have withdrawn the order *suo motu* or, in a very small number of instances, the courts have granted relief through writ petitions. In about three-fourths of the cases which came to Advisory Boards the detenus chose to appear personally before the Board. Just about half[35] of all people detained preventively have, then, appeared before an Advisory Board in the course of their detention. Although before arriving at a final judgment about the utility of this safeguard it would be important to find out why in about one quarter of the cases the detenus do not choose to appear, it is at least safe to say that the right of personal appearance seems to be an important option which the greater portion of detenus seeks to exercise.

Notwithstanding all the information provided about the working of the Advisory Boards, the critical questions still remain unanswered, namely, how independent of executive persuasion are the Advisory Boards? In order to make this determination one would need a great deal of information not ordinarily available: for instance, what have been the primary reasons for failure to sustain detention orders? How much importance has Government attached to the cases overturned by the Advisory Boards as opposed to those which they have sustained? What levels of Government have been instrumental in the decision to orders which Boards have either rejected or sustained? And what has been the turnover in personnel on the Advisory Boards? All of these matters are privileged and have never been revealed to the public.[36]

VI

The powers of the Act may be employed in the defence of six interests – the defence of India, the relations of India with foreign powers, the security of India State, the maintenance of public order, and the maintenance of supplies and services essential to the community. In fact, the vast majority of the cases have been under only two of these heads, namely, the security of the State and the maintenance of public order.[37] During the three years 1960 to 1962, for instance, 87.1 per cent of all detentions fell into these categories.[38] This is not untypical, for, throughout the 14 years of the Act, these causes have always accounted for more than 80 per cent of all detentions. The type of actions which Government has proceeded against in defending the security of the State and the maintenance of public order are "violent activities", including the preaching of violence, goondaism, communal agitation, the harbouring of dacoits, and, from time to time, espionage, terrorism, being a bad character, and, more recently, Naga-hostile activity. For example, from October 1, 1953 to September 30, 1954, the activities for which persons were detained under clause 3(1)(a)(ii) were as follows: 104 violent activities, 43 harbouring dacoits, 40 goondaism; 28 criminal activities, 8 student agitation, 7 espionage, 45 terrorism, and one for being a bad character.[39] And in a more recent period, October 1, 1960 to September 30, 1961: 4 violent activities, 8 preaching violence, 90 goondaism, 24 harbouring dacoits, and 5 for Naga-hostile activity.[40]

It is almost impossible to determine exactly what the authorities consider either a "violent activity" or a "threat". Both are catch-all terms. The statements of grounds for detention, which are submitted to all detenus, are not made public. In order, therefore, to explore the operational definition of such phrases, one must resort to three imperfect secondary sources. First, written judgments given by the courts in cases involving preventive detention sometimes reproduce part of the statements of grounds given by detenus. Their usefulness is limited because statements of grounds, or parts of them, will only be cited as they are germane to the point at issue. There are very few instances of the

Government's statement being reproduced in its entirety. Second, in Parliamentary debates, Members may sometimes repeat grounds cited to persons of their knowledge in order to demonstrate the Government's perfidy or its integrity, depending upon the Speaker's political affiliation. The presence of a transparent motive renders these illustrations somewhat suspect from the point of view of gaining a representative picture. Lastly, newspapers from time to time are informed of the contents of such statements by lawyers, officials, or friends of detenus. Again, there is no way of checking the reliability of the sources, although for the most part the reputation of the newspaper may stand as surety. For all these reasons one can obtain only an impressionistic idea of the manner in which the Preventive Detention Act has been used in actual practice. The following cases are representative of the many examples given in these diverse sources.

In 1950, Mr. Asutosh Lahire was arrested in New Delhi and the following reasons were furnished to him by the Government:

"You came to Delhi on March 27, 1950, and held a press conference in which you gave a highly exaggerated version of happenings in Bengal and East Bengal. It is understood that since after (sic) the press conference your activities have continued to be of a nature inciting communal passions. It has also come to notice that your activities during your stay in West Bengal had also been of a communal nature. Your activities in the present atmosphere in Delhi are likely to create hatred between different communities which may lead to disturbance of public peace and order".[41]

In 1956 four Kashmiris, all alleged to be members of the "End the Kashmir Dispute" Committee, were held in remand as suspects in the bomb explosions which had terrified Delhi on August 24 and 31. When the period of remand expired, three of the four were arrested under the Preventive Detention Act.[42] Evidently the Government felt that the evidence against them was strong enough to warrant forbidding them freedom of the city and an opportunity to engage in more terrorism.

In Calcutta in August, 1959, 35 prominent members of the "Price Increase and Famine Resistance Committee", including 7 members of the State Legislative Assembly, were taken into custody under the Preventive Detention Act and the West Bengal Security Act. It was charged that these persons had "threatened defiance of law", which was certainly true since the Committee had set August 20 as the occasion for a mass violation of laws for the purpose of compelling the "Government either to change its food policy or resign".[43] This is an example of the Act being used as a weapon to control situations of incipient lawlessness.

A revealing and controversial example of the use of preventive detention is found in Moradabad in November, 1955, Mr. Syed Halimuddin Rahat Maulvi, a pleader, was arrested under provisions of the Code of Criminal Procedure for making a speech supporting statements made in a local publication which were uncomplimentary to the Holy Prophet. The speech was inflammatory in nature and evidently designed to arouse the passions of listeners. The defendant was arraigned and released on bail. Upon leaving the gate of the jail, on November 28, he was apprehended by the police and held in detention. A petition was presented to the Allahabad High Court, but it was dismissed, the Court contending that if the District Magistrate felt the man was a threat to public order and security, the Court could not challenge the order. The Government's evaluation of the precariousness of a situation and of an individual's possible effect upon it could not be examined by the courts. This case illustrates one of the main advantages of the Preventive Detention Act: persons may be removed from a troubled scene quickly and surely; the authorities do not have to wait for judicial approval in the form of a verdict or tolerate the release of a defendant upon bail pending trial. Preventive detention is sure; conviction is uncertain and time-consuming.[44]

An illuminating recent example of the use of preventive detention was given by the Home Minister, Mr. G.B. Pant, in the Lok Sabha in August, 1960.[45] Mr. Prabhu Narain Singh, M.P., was detained on May 2, 1960, for acting in a manner prejudicial to the maintenance of public order. Specifically, he had held meetings exhorting the people of Varanasi District to contribute funds and enlist volunteers for a mass protest movement. This *satyagraha*, as it undoubtedly would have been called, was to involve cutting down of trees, occupation by force of public land, picketing of public offices, breaching of canals, and pulling of alarm chains on rail-road trains. The detenu submitted a petition of the Advisory Board, as was his right, and appeared himself before it, but his efforts were unavailing. The Board confirmed the order and he was ordered detained for a full year.

This was only one of a number of dramatic cases involving prominent political leaders. The most tragic of these concerned Mr. S.P. Mookerjee, M.P. from West Bengal and President of the Bharatiya Jana Sangh. In June, 1953, Mr. Mookerjee announced his intention of crossing from Punjab into the restless State of Jammu & Kashmir and there to campaign for militant Hindu policy for the State. Having been informed by Mr. Mookerjee in a telegram of his impending visit, the authorities in Jammu & Kashmir took out a preventive detention order against him. He was informed that should he implement his plan, the authorities would have no choice but to arrest him. Mr. Mookerjee disregarded the warning, crossed into the State on May 11, 1953, and was immediately jailed. On the morning of June 22, after a month of detention, Mr. Mookerjee suffered a heart attack and was removed from his cottage to a nursing home. The following day he suffered a second stroke, to which he succumbed. A prolonged, acrimonious, and anguished debate was held in the Lok Sabha, the result of which was a vote absolving the Government of all blame and a rejection of the motion of the Opposition that a Commission of inquiry be appointed.

Dr. Ram Manohar Lohia was detained in the State of Manipur on April 26, 1955. A few days earlier he had been arrested by the police and arraigned in court for violating an order, under Section 144 of the Code of Criminal Procedure, against the assembly of five or more persons. Appealing to the courts on a *habeas corpus* petition, he was released on April 26. He was met at the prison gates by officials bearing an order for his detention under the Preventive Detention Act. He was very shortly released, in fact within two weeks, which is a tribute either to the stabilizing of the local situation or to the protests raised by the opposition political parties against Dr. Lohia's detention.

Perhaps the most famous case involved Sheikh Abdullah, former Prime Minister of the troubled State of Jammu and Kashmir. Arrested in 1953, he was held in detention until January, 1958.[46] The Government released Sheikh Abdullah upon good behaviour. The experiment did not last long and he was re- arrested on April 30, having amply revealed in a number of public speeches and statements that his opinion about the political future of Jammu & Kashmir had changed not at all. His brief respite from detention had lasted just 96 days.*

*The statement made here is not factually correct. According to the Indian Constitution the subject Preventive Detention, so far as Jammu & Kashmir is concerned, lies entirely in the State sphere. Constitutionally the Central Government have no *locus standi* in the matter. Therefore, the arrest of Sheikh Abdullah in 1953 or his release in 1958 or his subsequent arrest in the same year could only be acts of the State Government. The State Government have legislated a separate Preventive Detention Act which is substantially different from the Preventive Detention Act in force in the rest of India. These constitutional and legal issues have been dealt with in D.D. Basu's" Commentary on the *Constitution of India*", p. 292, Vol. 1. – Ed.

Although the Government of India, and the Government of the States, have not been above using the powers of the Preventive Detention Act against political figures, as the previous examples show, it cannot be proved that the Act has been used deliberately and frequently as an instrument of political repression. Time and again, this charge has been leveled against Congress Ministries, but always it has fallen to the ground. In the Lok Sabha, so often the scene of nearly violent debates on preventive detention, Opposition members have been continually challenged to prove their assertions, but have been notoriously incapable of doing so. There is an irony here. The best that the Communist Members of Parliament have been able to do in proving the charge of political advantage in the operation of the Act has been to cite figures of the political affiliation of detenus. The Communists have shown, and the Government has admitted, that more Communists have been detained than members of any other political group. However, humourless to the end, the Communist Members of Parliament have failed to see that this argument cuts in more than one direction. In defending itself from these charges, the Government has noted with pride, and justly so, that before the general elections of 1951-52 and 1957, as well as in various State elections, detenus desiring to run for political office have been released for this purpose before their prison terms expired.

When one undertakes to assess the impact of the Preventive Detention Act upon individuals and political life in India and considers the comparatively small number of persons detained each year, the vigour of Advisory Board intervention, the lack of political opportunism in the implementation of the Act, and the close correlation between employment of the Act and the existence of aggravated threats to law and order, it is difficult to escape the conclusion that the Act has been administered in a generally careful and circumspect manner, by both Central and State Governments. Though the temptation to less restrained use of the Act may often have been present, and though the Government undoubtedly has occasionally succumbed to it, over all it has been scrupulously resisted.

VII

The very restraint which Government has shown leads to the important question: Why has the Government been so insistent about keeping the Preventive Detention Act on the books over the years? Except in 1950-51, very few people have been affected by it. Can its direct contribution to the maintenance of law and order have been so large? Indeed, the Act has been employed continually against ordinary criminal types....goondas, the harbourers of dacoits, and bad characters. For instance, in 1953-54, the proportion of people detained for these reasons was 43 per cent,[47] in 1958, 50.5 per cent,[48] in 1961, 64.4 per cent;[49] and in 1962, 84.9 per cent.[50] The Government has even said at one point: "(the bulk)....of the detenus has been detained for entirely non-political reasons and it was mainly in order to curb the activities of habitual goondas in the cites of Bombay and Calcutta".[51] Does the Government look upon the Preventive Detention Act, then, simply as an addition to the ordinary criminal law of the land? Are its purposes the same as the Indian Penal Code, for instance, or the Code of Criminal Procedure? Or is one to conclude that goondas and harbourers of dacoits constitute so serious a threat to the security of the State or the maintenance of public order that they have to be proceeded against so summarily? In short, considering the way in which the Act has been employed, both as to types of persons apprehended and total numbers, what justification can the Government give for its attachment to an Act so patently open to abuse?

From the moment of the Act's introduction in Parliament, the Government of India has argued that the country has been faced with a pervasive and recurrent threat to the existence of the rule of law and the maintenance of public order. Indian society, it has been pointed out, is extremely volatile, given to spontaneous explosions of human passion, often assuming the form of violent riot and agitation. There are, moreover, individuals and groups in the country all too willing to exploit these lurking passions, ready to push to the very brink of civil strife, and even beyond. No Government can allow the rule of law to collapse; if life and property are not secure, any Government's credentials become suspect. No Government can stand idly by and allow the interests of the society as a whole to be jeopardized by the self-centered activities of a minority. In the words of a Home Minister, "The endeavour here is to preserve freedom, restore freedom, safeguard the security of the country, at a cost of one year's detention."[52] The Government goes on to stress that the defence of the rule of law is even more imperative and demanding in India because respect for procedures of orderly interaction has yet to be developed widely. In the interests of inculcating democratic habits of mind, so argues the Government, law and order cannot be permitted to become a political football, to be challenged at will by every group with a grievance, while the agencies of law enforcement are castigated as callous oppressors. Respect for law, the only sure defence of any constitution, cannot be built upon a quixotic disregard for peaceful processes of redress.

The Preventive Detention Act contributes to all these purposes, the Government maintains, by deterring would-be male-factors and by providing the Government with an instrument, ready to hand and sure and swift in its operation, which can be used to prevent the exploitation of unstable inter-group relations for the benefit of parochial interests. Even though the Act is sparingly used, the Government cannot afford to have its immense powers lapse. Until Indian society heals its multiple divisions and learns to affect compromise among them by means of democratic institutions, the Government is loath to indulge in the luxury of stacking arms. Thus the core of the Government's argument is, first, a two-fold appeal to the needs of an "infant democracy" and to the fundamental duty of any Government towards the maintenance of law and order and, second, its own assessment of the character of social relations in India, the popularity of violent protests, and the prevalence of groups eager to fish in troubled waters.

Basic to the soundness of the Government's argument is the correctness of its empirical judgment about social conditions. One would, therefore, have expected the Government to dwell at some length upon the precise nature and magnitude of the threat facing Indian society and Government. Curiously, this case has never been carefully presented by the Government. In fact, in all the debates on preventive detention there has been a total failure to produce empirical data to validate the premise that social conditions have in fact, and at any given moment, attained critical gravity. The need for preventive detention has been based upon an *assertion* and not upon a *demonstration* that conditions were threatening.

The best that the Government has been able to do is allude to particular instances of riots and public violence, with the presumption that these exemplify a general situation. It has consistently cited communalism, communism, or terrorism[53] but has never disclosed the size of these threats. The attitude implicit in these many ad *hominem* references has been that surely the brutal happenings which are a commonplace in India amply prove the imperative need for preventive action. Only the blind or the deliberately hypocritical, the Government seems to be saying, could have failed to be aware of the prevalence of violence in Indian society and of the massed human forces at work exacerbating latent frustrations. At other times the Government has seemed to recognize the limitations of mere assertion, but it has then retreated to arguing on the ground of special knowledge, as if it were in possession of compelling information not available to the general public.[54]

In the recent debate the Home Minister, Mr. Nanda, repeatedly challenged by the Opposition to be specific in his citations of social danger, ventured to give a comparative assessment of the need for the Act. Asked whether the situation was as threatening as three years ago (1960), he said that it was at least as bad, particularly with regard to communalism; while with regard to spies, it was much worse.[55] Yet within a very few moments he noted, looking back over the history of the Act and the causes of detention each year, that about the same number of persons were being detained for harbouring dacoits as in the past, more for goondaism, but fewer for communal tension. But Mr. Nanda left no room for doubt as to the kinds of elements in the country against which the Government would use the Act: "....people who take up violent activities, terrorising their neighbours and others, spies, goondas, people engaging in anti-national activities, those who harbour dacoits, etc..."[56]

The existence in force of the Defence of India Rules, also authorizing preventive detention, produced one salutary effect in the recent debate on the Preventive Detention Act. It compelled the Government to distinguish between the purposes of each, thus eliciting for the first time a precise statement of the place of preventive detention in non-emergency situations. The Opposition contended vigorously that if the Preventive Detention Act and the Defence of India Rules were not directed at different situations, then their operation together was redundant and one of them should be retired. The Home Minister argued forthrightly that they were both needed because there is an "intermediate state" between normalcy and emergency, and it is to this non-normal or quasi-emergency situation that the Preventive Detention Act is directed:

> There is an emergency, but short of this, there may be abnormal conditions, and this may be an intermediate stage. Now, if the conditions are not normal, if there are disturbances, if there are those elements, which there are in the country unfortunately, people whose emotions are aroused, exploited, for various purposes, the communal hatred is inflamed and fanned and then there is the question of linguism, regionalism, provincialism, all these various passions and emotions, we have not yet been able to fully

integrate the nation on the basis of complete, full, democratic values. (sic)[57]

From the point of view of making an argument sufficiently convincing to gain the support of Parliament for preventive detention, the Government has probably been quite right in not presenting more particulars. Many, if not most, Members of Parliament have had vivid first-hand experience with the instability of modern India and do not need to be shown factual reports and statistical summaries. Moreover, there are vast intellectual problems involved in constructing an empirical test which can demonstrate, even to "an averge reasonable man", the degree of danger implicit in a human situation. The Government's failure to strive for this kind of demonstration does not necessarily indicate moral insensitivity or a cynical disregard for facts; it may only indicate an understandable tailoring of argument to political need.

VIII

The purpose in pointing out the logical limitations in the Government's argument for preventive detention is not to cast doubt upon the sincerity of the conviction that preventive detention is desperately needed or to imply that the conviction is not well founded. Few observers who have studied the Indian scene since Independence would seriously dispute the proposition that political and social life have been very unstable from time to time and that in these situations the future of the rule of law has often been in doubt. But there are a number of reasons why the Government's failure to make an empirical case may have important and harmful effects upon the future history of the Act, and the Government has shown little indication of having considered them.

First: without specification of the circumstances which necessitate recourse of preventive detention, lawmakers and the general public will be unable to determine when the Act is performing its job successfully. Unless one has a clear idea of the need for a law, it is difficult or impossible to estimate the balance between benefits and liabilities in making use of the law. Preventive detention has many unsavoury features; its defects cannot be condoned as necessary evils unless one makes a judgment about need.

Second: Without a clear idea of when the Act is needed the chances of the Act being voluntarily abandoned are reduced. For, as Mr. Nanda himself noted, won't there always be stray incidents of goodaism, of spying, and of communal passion? Moreover, there is an unfinished revolution going on in India which occasions great social stress; this revolution will not be finished for many years to come.[58] Is the Preventive Detention Act to be kept until India has achieved full prosperity and social peace?

Third: the ability to avoid general grants of power and to specify with precision the manner in which the Act is to be administered depends directly upon the exactness with which the purposes of the legislation are formulated. The far-reaching power of preventive detention will not be limited either by making its operation contingent upon specified circumstances or by limiting the scope of its application, unless the threats to which it shall apply are defined carefully. Imprecision in the demonstration of need leads to vagueness in the statement of scope of the Act.

For example, goondas and dacoits certainly constitute very difficult criminal elements for the police to cope with, but are their activities so disturbing that they create a situation which can be fairly characterized as an intermediate stage between normalcy and emergency? The authorities have only to say so and the preventive Detention Act becomes a tool for general use against quite ordinary malefactors. If the purposes of the Act were spelled out with great precision, such extensions in practice would be more easily restrained by the courts.

Fourth: the larger the proportion of empirical fact to subjective evaluation the fewer are the dangers that the fearful and panicky in league with the dedicated and opportunistic may successfully use the Act to undermine the whole gamut of democratic rights in India. One of the best defences in the future against the precedents of the past is an explicit statement of the circumstances of need.

Mr. P.K. Tripathi in an excellent article in the *American Journal of Comparative Law*[59] has shown that as a result of two Supreme Court rulings[60] the courts can examine a sedition law which infringes freedom of speech, but they cannot examine a detention order which prevents the making of seditious speeches:

"Supreme court has taken the view that where a person is detained under a law of preventive detention avowedly with the object of preventing him from, say, making a speech, the court will not consider it within its province to examine whether the prevented speech was entitled to constitutional protection,"[61]

The Preventive Detention Act therefore becomes the vehicle for the wholesale restriction of the rights supposedly guaranteed in Article 19, and particularly of the right of freedom of speech and expression.

Fifth: probably the greatest danger for the future is that the manipulators of governmental practice will themselves become insensitive to departures from principle. However necessary the Act may be, however moderately it has been administered, the fact remains that it is an invitation to compulsion. A precedent has been established by Mr. Nehru himself that recourse may be had to forms of control outside the ambit of democratic legitimacy. In the days of political jockeying, infighting, and striving which are sure to come with the death of Mr. Nehru, will his successors be able to resist his towering example? Has a precedent been set for the bypassing of the judiciary, the circumscription of fundamental rights, and the truncation of due process of law? It is possible that the Preventive Detention Act may become the thin end of the wedge for future acts of constriction all in the name of national unity, political stability, and economic development. An age of smaller men, more concerned with personal privilege than national destiny, could cultivate the history of preventive detention as assiduously as Mr. Nehru and his lieutenants have cultivated their legacy of fundamental rights.

The Preventive Detention Act of 1950 shows every indication of becoming a permanent part of the legal arsenal of Government for controlling incipient threats to law and order. Political leaders have gradually come to the realization that for them emergency is a way of life. In 1950, despite the horror of Partition and the bitterness of the struggle in Telengana, leaders could still dream of a brief transition during which India's independent millions would heal the divisions within their society, would learn to temper political behaviour with the sweet reasonableness of compromise, and would mobilize their energies to increase the physical well-being of the entire nation. These goals still inspire, but the time schedule for accomplishment has lengthened. Communalism, religious fanaticism, language rivalry, provincial separatism, and caste recrimination have not disappeared. They have shown an unlooked for hardihood and, as a consequence, the legal weapon which has been forged to cope with their harmful effects has been extended time and again. The Preventive Detention Act is a symbol of India's permanent emergency.

As to the future, the key lies in the ability of the Indian people to learn those habits and attitudes which are the necessary prerequisites of democratic interaction. If the control which presently restrains is not supplemented with the tutelage which changes, the future of preventive detention is bound to be melancholy and prolonged. Those who resort to preventive detention in the name of democracy must never forget that permissiveness can only be developed as the concomitant of discipline internalized.

Notes

* From *Indian Journal of Public Administration*, Vol. X, No. 2, 1964. pp. 235-256

1. Preventive Detention Act, Section 3(a). There is also a provision, rarely exercised, for the detention of foreigners within the meaning of the Foreigners Act, 1946 (XXI of 1946), with a view to regulating their continued presence in India or making arrangements for their expulsion from the country.
2. Preamble to the Constitution of India.
3. Government of India, *Parliamentary Debates*, Part II, Lok Sabha Debates, May 30, 1956, col. 10079.
4. In the test case of the constitutionality of the Preventive Dentention Act, A.K. Gopalan *vs.* State of Madras, 13 S.C.J. 174 (1950), the Supreme Court ruled that operations under the Act come within the purview of Article 22 alone. Counsel for Mr. Gopalan had argued that the Act was unconstitutional because it contravened Articles 19 and 21 too. One important effect of this decision will be discussed on page 255.
5. State of Bombay vs. A.R.S. Vaidya (1950), S.C.J. 208.
6. A.I.R., 1954, S.C. 179.
7. Dr. Ram Krishan Bharadwaj *vs.* the State of Delhi, A.I.R., 1953, S.C. 318; Prem Datta vs. Superintendent, Central Prison, A.I.R., 1954, All. 315.
8. See, for instance, Athan Razvi vs. State of Uttar Pradesh, A.I.R. (1951), All. 458. The reason for the Government's claiming "security" in this case was that the information about M.A. Razvi's activities had come from Government undercover agents in Uttar Pradesh and the Government was afraid that divulging the facts upon which the order was based would jeopardize the entire surveillance system.
9. *Lok Sabha Debates, op. cit.*, December 17, 1963, opening statement by the Home Minister.
10. Preventive Detention Act, Section 7.
11. Preventive Detention Act, Section 3 (3).
12. The Chairman of an Advisory Board must either be or have been a High Court Judge; potential candidacy is not enough. *Ibid.*, Section 8.
13. *ibid.*, Section 10.
14. *ibid.*, Section 10(3).
15. *ibid.*, Section 11.

16. *Mala fides* is extremely different to prove, hinging as it does upon a finding that the apparent motives of the authorities are not their real motives.
17. India, *Constitution of India*, New Delhi, Manager of Publications, Articles 124 and 127.
18. Home Minister, Lok Sabha Debates, *op. cit.*, May 29, 1956, cols. 9981-82.
19. *ibid.*
20. Deputy Minister for Home Affairs, Lok Sabha Debates, *op. cit.*, December 11, 1954, cols. 2603-04.
21. *ibid.*
22. *ibid.*
23. India, *Report of the Ministry of Home Affairs*, 1958-59, New Delhi, Government of India, 1952, p. 94.
24. Ministry of Home Affairs, *Statistical Information regarding the Working of the Preventive Detention Act*, 1950, during the period 30th September, 1961 to 30th September 1962.
25. Statistics concerning the working of the Preventive Detention Act usually cover a period from the 1st October of one year to the 30th September of the following year. The figures for 1963, therefore, are very nearly coincidental with the State of Emergency. Although I am not concerned with the subject of preventive detention under the Defence of India Rules, I should not that the number of detentions under the D.I.R. was given by the Home Minister as 1,269, covering presumably the period from the declaration of the Emergency until his statement in Parliament, from which I am quoting, December 19, 1963.
26. Home Minster, *Lok Sabha Debates, op. cit.*, December 9, 1957, col. 4229.
27. Through 1959 Punjab could also have been included. Detentions have fallen off markedly there in 1960-62.
28. *Indian Civil Liberties Bulletin, July*, 1956, p. 126.
29. Deputy Minister of Home Affairs, *Lok Sabha Debates*, December 9, 1957, col. 4328.
30. Ministry of Home Affairs, *Statistical Information regarding the Working of the Preventive Detention Act*, 1950, March 31 to October 31, 1956 and October 31, 1956 to September 30, 1957.
31. *ibid*, September 30, 1957 to December 31, 1958.
32. Preventive Detention Act, Section 10.
33. It should be noted in passing that Maharashtra's Advisory Boards summon witnesses in almost the same number of cases in which the detenu appears before the Board. For example, in 1960 detenus

appeared in 21 cases; the Advisory Board summoned withnesses, both for and against the detenu, in 20 cases. Again, in 1961, the detenu appeared in 25 cases; witnesses were summoned in 19. The point cannot be confirmed without further research, but it seems a reasonable hypothesis that Maharashtra's Advisory Boards are taking much greater pains in those cases in which the detenu makes an oral argument against the case presented by Government.

34. As originally enacted the Preventive Detention Act did not allow the detenu to appear before the Advisory Board. The Act was, however, amended on several occasions in the early 1950s, and by 1954 this important right was firmly established within the Act.

35. 53.3 per cent between 1956-62, for example.

36. Frank Anthony (Nominated, Anglo-Indian), in an unusually acerbic attack upon the independence of the Advisory Boards, declared that the whole procedure was "a mockery and a sham"; that the personal of the Boards were utterly subservient to Government, their first qualification "that of being political lickspittles". *Lok Sabha Debates, op. cit.*, December 18, 1963, cols. 5439-41.

37. That is, clause 3(1) (a) (ii).

38. Computed from *Statistical Information regarding the Working of the Preventive Dentention Act*, 1950.

39. Lok Sabha Debates, December 9, 1954, cols. 2365-66.

40. Statistical *Information regarding the Working of the Preventive Detention Act*, 1950, op. cit.

41. Asutosh Lahrie vs. State of Delhi, 1950, *Lok Sabha Debates, op. cit.*, July 21, 1952, col. 4221.

42. Overseas *Hindustan Times*, September 27, 1956, p. 2.

43. *Times of India,* August 18, 1959, p. 1. col. 3.

44. *Indian Civil Liberties Bulletin*, January, 1957, p. 221.

45. *Lok Sabha Debates, op. cit.*, August, 1950, cols. 2936-37.

46. By virtue of Article 370, Constitution of India, the Preventive Detention Act has been amended in its application to Jammu & Kashmir. Thus the Government of Jammu & Kashmir not required to release the Sheikh after one year.

47. Lok Sabha Debates, *op. cit.*, December 9, 1954, cols. 2365-66.

48. Computed from figures given in *Statistics regarding the Working of the Preventive Detention Act*, 1950-1958.

49. *ibid.*, 1961.

50. *ibid.*, 1962.

51. Minister of State for Home Affairs, Shri Datar, Lok Sabha Debates, *op. cit.*, December 1, 1960, col. 3410.

52. Home Minister, Lok Sabha Debates, August 6, 1953, col. 5713.

53. *See*, for example, Mr. Nehru, *Lok Sabha Debates, op. cit.*, August 2, 1952, col. 5192.

54. For instance, the Home Minister said in the Lok Sabha, August 1, 1952, col. 5001: ".... there are still very many black clouds in the horizon and very many danger signals to be seen. I am not in a position and it would not be proper for me to say what sort of information is received from time to time, almost every week by Government and we cannot possibly be complacent about it."

55. Lok Sabha Debates, *op. cit.*, December 17, 1964, cols. 5190-91.

56. *ibid.*, December 19, 1963, col. 5638.

57. *ibid.*, col. 5647.

58. Nanda, *Lok Sabha Debates, op. cit.*, December 19, 1963, col. 5650.

59. *Spring*, 1960, pp. 219-48.

60. A.K. Gopalan *vs.* The State of Madras, 13 S.C.J. 174 (1950) and Ram Singh *vs.* State of Delhi, A.I.R. 1951, S.C. 270.

61. Tripathi, 224.

11

Professional Policy-Making : The Case of Indian Population Policy*

UDAY C. DESAI

This is a paper about policy-making in India, not about population. As the title of the paper indicates, it deals with population policy-*making* in India. Thus, we are primarily concerned with the *process* of population policy-making, and not with either the desirability of a particular set of policies or the problems of management in population programme. Questions such as the following are addressed in this paper:

1. How is the population problem defined and by whom?
2. How and why has the definition of the 'problem' changed over the years?
3. Who participates and in what ways in defining and changing the definition of the programme or policy responses to the 'problem'?
4. What are their underlying assumptions and self-interests?
5. How are these policy-making groups (definers, formulators) tied to the implementation machinery? Or are they interested or involved in implementation?
6. How do the policy administrators participate in policy-making? What are the consequences?

In general, we are concerned with the question of: *Who* makes the policy, in response to what and to *whose* needs and perceptions? Who implements these policies and programmes, in response to *whose* needs and perceptions?

The paper attempts to identify the major actors, both individuals and institutions, in making, influencing and implementing population policy for India. Their self-interests, their perceptions of the public interest, and their ideology are identified and their impact on population policy is explored.

In all the voluminous literature produced on the population problems and policies of India, and it certainly is voluminous, we have been unable to find a single source that systematically deals with the process of *making* population (family planning) policy. Ours is an account of this policy-making process.

The Congress and Population Policy

It is commonly agreed that the Indian Government was one of the first in the world to recognise its population problem and to have a stated national position on it. However, concern with India's population problem had existed long before her independence. National leaders were drawing public attention to the problem. It is clear, for example, that the Congress Party leaders were concerned about the increasing population of India long before independence. In 1936, at the Haripura session of the Indian National Congress, Subhas Chandra Bose, in his presidential address, remarked: "With regard to the long period programme for a free India, the first problem to be tackled is that of our increasing population. I.... want to point out that where poverty, starvation and disease are stalking the land, we cannot afford to have our population mounting up by thirty million during a single decade..... It will, therefore, be desirable to restrict our population until we are able to feed, clothe and educate those who already exist. It is not necessary at this stage to prescribe the method that should be adopted to prevent a further increase in population, but I would urge that public attention be drawn to this question."[1]

Apparently the need for restricting population was clearly perceived and not too politically controversial. The appropriate method, on the other hand, was either not clearly perceived or was a politically sensitive issue at the time. The National Planning Committee, chaired by Nehru, in 1938 resolved that "It is desirable to lay stress on self-restraint as well as to spread knowledge of cheap and safe methods of birth control."[2] Gandhi, however was quite unambiguous in his views on both the need for population control and the proper methods. "There can be no two opinions about the necessity of birth control. But the only method handed down from ages past is self control or *Brahmacharya*. It is an infallible sovereign remedy, doing good to those who practise it. The union is meant not for pleasure but for bringing forth progeny."[3]

Other leaders, particularly civic and professionals in health, medicine and demography also publicly raised the 'population' problem. As early as 1931, the Census Commissioner for India had remarked: "The increase of population is from most points of view a cause of alarm rather than satisfadtion."[4] The All-India Women's Conference in 1933 passed a resolution that "birth control be included in all municipal public health servies."[5] In the year preceding India's independence, the Health Survey and Development Committee (The Bhore Committee)[6] published its 1200-page report. It unanimously recommended birth control and outlined measures that the Government should take. These governmental measures were to provide free contraceptives to women who need birth control, for health reasons, to regulate the sale and manufacture of contraceptives, to support financially research on effective methods of birth control, and to educate the masses on the desirability and methods of family planning.[7]

The National Planning Committee in its 1948 report on population called for vigorous propaganda via municipalities, district boards and panchayats advocating families of four children or less, spaced from two to four years apart.[8]

However, there seems to have been little awareness of the difficulties inherent in preventing births. The stress was on self-restraint; only a cautious mention was made of spreading knowledge of cheap and effective artificial methods of birth control. No national or Congress Party policy on the matter existed then. The problem was perceived. It was perceived, defined and debated by national leaders in the Congress Partly and by experts in the closely related fields. There was little sense of urgency about it. The urgent task was to gain political independence.

After independence, the primary task was seen as the removal of mass poverty and backwardness through economic growth and social transformation. A new body, the Planning Commission, was set up to prepare national development plans and to make recommendations for their implementation. From the beginning, the Planning Commission has articulated overall governmental population control policies. This Commission, under Nehru's chairmanship, accepted population growth as a problem, a hindrance, but not a major hindrance, to raising the standard of living of India's masses.

The draft outline of the First Five Year Plan noted that

"increasing pressure of population on natural resources retards economic progress and limits seriously the rates of extension of social services so essential to civilized existence", and pointed out that" frequent and ill-spaced child-births undermine the health of the mother. A high birth rate under conditions of poverty and malnutrition is inevitably connected with a high rate of infant mortality."[9] The Commission thus defined the population problem as follows: 'too many babies are born every year. This diluted economic progress and social services for the masses'. It was also defined as a cause of poor maternal health and high infant mortality. Thus the Commission followed in the same line of thinking as earlier by the National Congress Party leaders. It did not go any further.

The family planning programmes were included in the health section of the Plan. The family planning programmes to be effected during the First Plan period (1951-56) included providing medical advice on family planning in hospitals, maternity and child welfare clinics, to married women who needed it for the sake of their health, *collecting data* on people's reproductive patterns, attitudes, and motivations, developing methods of educating the people on family planning, *conducting* laboratory *research* on the physiology of human fertility, and *studying* the inter-relationships between economic, social and population changes.[10]

The Planning Commission provided Rs. 65 lakhs for family planning programmes in the First Plan. However, only about Rs. 15 lakhs were spent. The emphasis, in the First Plan, was on gathering basic information (demographic and attitudinal) and conducting research. There was little, if any, 'action', on making contraceptives available to the masses or on increasing 'awareness' of the masses. Rhythm and abstinence as birth control techniques were emphasized.[11]

Family Planning in the Plans

The treatment of the population problem in the First Plan reveals certain basic assumptions of the planners. It was assumed that the solution to the population problem is to increase family planning by married couples in reproductive years, and that family planning is rightly a part of maternal and child health care and welfare. Thus the solution was implicitly assumed to be found through health care. The Plan then emphasised programmes for collecting a wide range of pertinent demographic data and for research in human reproductive behaviour.

The population problem had thus been transformed into a family planning problem and that in turn into a health problem. Advice on birth control and contraceptives, it logically followed, was to be dispensed at hospitals and health clinics, especially maternity and child welfare clinics, by medical officers. The dominance of traditionalists and Gandhians on birth control policy was evident in two important policy choices made in the First Plan. One was the proviso that contraceptive advice be offered only to mothers and only for health reasons. And second, rhythm was advocated as the method. The then Health Minister, Rajkumari Amrit Kaur, was strongly opposed to any mechanical or chemical methods of contraception, both on religious and philosophical grounds. Her view prevailed, and rhythm became the method dispensed by the Government health clinics. The Health Ministry established a bureaucratic jurisdiction on the family planning policy and programme at this early stage.

One other significant event should be mentioned. The Government of India requested and received help, in the form of a visit by an expert, from an international organisation, WHO. This is significant, because by it, India gained an international reputation as a leader in the family planning field, and also because it established a pattern of reliance on international experts and advice that has continued since then.

To sum up, population was perceived and defined as a problem at a macro level, for its impact on economic growth. The national planners and some Congress Party leaders were responding to the perceived consequences of population growth on their aims of rapid aggregate economic progress. Theirs was an abstract, largely quantitative concern with aggregates. The problem was perceived quite differently by the health bureaucracy and professionals. They were responding to the need for enhancing maternal and child health and welfare through the provision of family planning and contraception services to mothers. The first group was dominated by economists and demographers; the second by medical doctors, public health experts and social work professionals.[12]

There was little, if any, public debate on the issue. The political leadership, particularly in the Health Ministry, with their traditional and Gandhian biases, kept the policy responses in line with the traditional and moralistic thinking. The masses did not see a national problem in having too many children. They did not expect or hope the Government to make it possible for them to have fewer children. It was a problem perceived and defined by the national elites, especially professional elites, with some support from "Western" minded political leadership.

Both the professional elites and the traditional political elites could agree to set up a large programme of data collection and research. For professionals this was both an essential prerequisite to the formulation of a rational policy and programme and also a source of future, political strength (since knowledge is, after all, the basic source of professional power). For traditional political leadership, it postponed the need for any clear policy regarding the population problem.

During the 1950's the concept that the population problem is essentially a family planning problem became deeply embedded in the thinking of the national elites concerned with the problem. The Ministry of Health at the Centre and the health bureaucracy in the States and the field were strengthened administratively with regard to their family planning capabilities. A substantial network of urban and rural family planning clinics was set up under the health bureaucracy. The Second Five Year Plan (1956-61) envisioned the setting up of about 500 urban clinics and 2,000 rural clinics (to be opened in association with primary health units). The establishment of institutes for training family planning personnel and of centres for contraceptive testing and evaluation, and bio-medical and demographic research was also envisioned. The Plan allocated nearly Rs. 5 crores for family planning programmes. However, at the end of the Plan period, less then half of the monies allocated to family planning was spent. The emphasis in the Second Plan was on clinico-based provision of birth control services to the people.[13] The Plan also made provision for extended research in demography, physiology of human reproduction and means of communications. In the last year of the Plan male and female sterilization as a contraceptive method was officially sanctioned.[14] Research on reproductive biology and demography was emphasized. The medical and health professionals established themselves as the group solely responsible for the administrative machinery through which policy was implemented. The demographers established their place in this policy process as experts in collecting, refining and interpreting the basic information on population necessary for any rational policy formulation. A number of demographic and medical research and training centres were set up to provide an institutional base for these professionals and to train new members. The power of the traditional, moralistic, political elite over the family planning policies disappeared in the latter part of the decade. A clear break came when male and female sterilization was officially sanctioned and Central assistance for sterilization was made available in 1960-61. Rajkumari Amrit Kaur and the traditionalists she represented had lost their influence in this policy area by the end of the decade.

International Agencies Support

International agencies, particularly private American foundations, became more active in family planning policy and programmes, primarily through their monetary support for research and for inviting western experts to advise Indian agencies. The Ford Foundation and the Population Council were most active. The U.N. also provided some support for research and training.

By the beginning of the 1960's, the policy process had become institutionalised. The major participants were: the Health Ministry, especially the family planning bureaucracy, at the Centre; the Planning Commission, especially the officials in charge of health; professional elites in the fields of health, medicine and demography, including academic and private practitioners as well as governmental and research and training centre personnel; the international donor agencies, and the international consultants (mostly Americans).

The (economic) planners and demographers provided continuous articulation of the population problem, with arguments based on more thorough and accurate demographic data.

The Health Ministry at the Centre consolidated and expanded its jurisdiction on the family planning programmes. The family planning programme had become synonymous with the population policy, the response to the population problem. It stressed close integration of family planning services with the basic health service network. The medical profession had established its jurisdiction on the research and approval of methods of contraception. For example, it cleared the IUD's for mass use in 1965. Thus the health professionals and bureaucracy had established their primacy over implementation of family planning/population policy.

No other Ministry was substantially involved. This was true at the Centre, State and the periphery levels. The political **executives** and the legislature at the State level were almost totally ignored and were, in turn, indifferent to the whole thing.[15] The political parties and leadership generally showed similar indifference to the whole issue. The populace, of course, was still in no way involved in the policy processes. The masses were still unaware of the existence of the problem, let alone a response to the problem.

Outside the relevant professional circles, little or no public or political debate took place. It became a bureaucratic, 'professional' policy, to be discussed and agreed upon by 'experts' in and outside the Government. Issues related to implementation mechanisms (administrative and organisational arrangements and re-arrangements) came to claim the most energy and concern, since the professional experts readily agreed upon or respected the basic assumptions, needs and self-interests of their fellow professionals, even outside their own professions.

By the mid-1960's, there was one important addition to this policy process which had become institutionalised, the increasing influence of western, particularly American, donors and advisors. In 1964, some eminent Indian gynecologists and family planning experts were invited to New York to take part in an international conference on the IUD. The IUD was introduced in India with wildly exaggerated claims and fanfare soon afterwards.

In 1965, the then Secretary-General of the International Planned Parenthood Federation, Sir Colvile Deverell, led a UN Evaluation Mission to India. It commended the Indian Government for its family planning services and made recommendations to strengthen the administrative and organisational machinery of family planning.

The international agencies and experts conferred increased status to the policy formulated and implemented by the professionals and also provided personal opportunities for travel and research. Whether the international experts and consultants contributed anything useful is not readily agreed upon.[16]

In the second half of the 1960's, the pattern of policy-making established earlier continued with some shifts in emphasis. Concern with the administrative mechanism, natural to bureaucrats, continued, and various administrative and organisational changes were made. A department of family planning was established in 1966 within the Ministry of Health, renamed as the Ministry of Health and Family Planning. This was to give 'fillip' to the family planning programme - a typical bureaucratic response to the shortcomings of the programme. At the political level, a new Cabinet level committee of five Union Ministers, headed initially by the Prime Minister and later by the Finance Minister, was set up to provide policy guidance. The other four members of this committee for the Ministers of Health and Family Planning and Works, Housing and Urban Development and the Ministers of State for Finance, Social Welfare and Health and Family Planning.

Also created was a Central Family Planning Council. Advisory in nature, it included all the State Ministers for Health and Family Planning, representatives of voluntary organisations, institutions and some distinguished individuals. The Union Minister for Health and Family Planning serves as chairman, the Minister of State for Health and Family Planning as vice-chairman.

In 1967, Dr. S. Chandrasekhar, a well known demographer and crusader for birth control, was appointed Minster of State for Health and Family Planning. The influence of foreign experts and consultants then reached its peak. Dr. Chandrasekhar publicly (proudly) acknowledged the role of foreign experts when he commented that his "predecessor was opposed to including the pill in the official family planning programme, but *after discussions with experts in the World Health Organisation and the* USAID, I have approved its use".[17] He further claimed that there was no need to worry about expenditure of hard currency to buy the pill, because he had received a promise of generous American dollar aid for this, from President Johnson and AID officials, during his visit to Washington, D.C.[18] A more detailed and lucid example of the great influence of foreign experts in population policy-making is supplied by Marcus Franda in his short journalistic description of the Nirodh programme in India.[19] The idea of marketing condoms on a mass scale was first discussed in 1963 by a small group at the Indian Institute of Management in Calcutta (IIMC). Peter S. King from MIT, who provided the leadership for the group, and Dr. Donald Bogue of the University of Chicago formulated many of the original ideas. The group also included two family planning consultants from the Ford Foundation. The original idea, as Mr. King put it, was simply "*to secure the co-operation of Government* and private business to *adopt what might be termed a 'brute force' promotional strategy*".[20] The IIMC group decided, apparently without much difficulty, that condoms were the thing to be marketed.

This group apparently made a major policy decision, almost entirely without public debate or participation by elected or appointed public servants. The decision of this small group, dominated by American experts, it appears, became the policy of the Government of India, i.e., of the family planning bureaucracy. More American and western experts and consultants were called in.[21] One American consulting firm honestly admitted total ignorance in this area. It wrote in its report to the Ministry of Health and Family Planning that "it must be said that this project is being launched into largely uncharted seas.... and that there is no historical precedent anywhere in the world's history for this."[22] The experts did not need to worry about most of the programme. Most of the initial cost of the advertising was paid by USAID, through a grant to the family planning bureaucracy. USAID also provided hundreds of millions of condoms.

A major policy decision was made by a few foreigners and high level (usually western educated and rich or upper middle class) Indians, in and out of Government, to launch a nationwide promotional campaign and marketing scheme without any necessary basic knowledge at their disposal. The wholesale distributors and local retailers were the key to the success of the programme, but played no role in formulating it. It should, therefore, come as no surprise that their continued participation in the Nirodh programme depended on Central Government support and not on a perception of self-interest by the retailers or wholesalers, since the profit margin was negligible. It should also not be surprising that the condom promoters were greatly immersed in the discussion of issues such as whether the Nirodh condom was too large for Indian males, since its size is based on the physique of the western male, or whether the latex presently used to make the condoms is a nonconductor of heat. Such technical problems are always preferred by experts (is it not why they are called experts?) over the broader question of whether the whole approach may be irrelevant under present Indian conditions.

What has been achieved, so far, by the massive expenditure in money and manpower on family planning programmes? Absolute numbers on achievement measures are impressive. By the end of March 1971, about seven million sterilizations were performed, three million IUDs were inserted, and by 1968-69 over 325 million condoms distributed.[23] In terms of health infrastructure also, numbers are impressive. In 1970 there were 3,687 urban family planning clinics, 41,151 centres and 862 mobile units.[24]

However, compared to the magnitude of the task, the achievements fall far short of expectations and needs. At the end of 1971, a full 21 years after the Government officially embraced population control as a national goal, the Ministry of Health and Family Planning estimated that 13.33 million couples were protected by various methods, representing only 13.3 per cent of all Indian couples in the reproducing years.[25] This 13.3 per cent is a far cry from the target of more than 90 per cent users.[26] What has been the effect of this massive effort to 'protect' couples, in the reproductive years, on the rate of population growth in India?

None, a glance at the population growth rate figures would suggest. "The population increase of 24.7 per cent between 1961 and 1971 was the highest ever, the earlier increase by census decades were 11.00 per cent in 1931, 14.23 per cent in 1941, 13.31 per cent in 1951, 21.6 per cent in 1961.[27] Thus the rate of population growth has gone up over the years, not down. Everything considered, we may conclude with Ogale[28] that some progress has been made, but the problem is far from under control and farther still from being solved.

The population policy-making process has not, as far as we can determine, greatly altered in the first half of the 1970's. However, a number of critical voices, mostly from among the ranks of professionals and experts, have been raised.[29] A little more attention is given to it by the Indian press and a few more political leaders and parties are showing signs of a little less than total indifference to the population problem. Not all of them or even most of them agree either with the basic assumptions of the policy elites or with their definition of the problem. However, it may be the beginning of genuine public debate and of the involvement of political leadership of all parties and at all levels of the Government and society.[30] The general coolness of the relationship between the U.S. and India and the departure of Dr. S. Chandrasekhar from the Government must certainly mean a decrease in the influence of American experts in the policy-making. There are rumblings that the population problem is too important to be left to the health and family planning bureaucracies and experts. It is being increasingly pointed out, in professional and academic circles at least, that population policy is not synonymous with family planning. Educational and social security policies may have more to do with solutions to the population problem than family planning programmes. Government may not be capable, by bureaucratic apparatus alone, of making any impact on the problem, but instead all institutions in the society – voluntary, business, industry, labour and social institutions such as tribal and caste organisations – must be made active participants if the problem is to be linked at all. However, these are only rumblings. The policy process is still dominated by professional experts and bureaucrats, most in health and demography. The top level political leadership agrees that there is a population problem, but still has no clearer idea than in the early 1950's as to what policy and programme responses are called for to solve it. Consequently, it has left the specific policy and programme responses to the professional experts and bureaucrats as in earlier periods.*

Summing Up: Need For Empirical Studies

The family planning policy process in India for the period covered in this paper may well be summarised as follows:

The Ministry of Health and Family Planning provides guidelines to the Secretary (or Commissioner) of Family Planning who produces a plan. This plan is reviewed by the Planning Commission's family planning section, which may request outside evaluation The key actors in the process are bureaucrats and technicians (experts). There is little interest and virtually no participation on the part of the public or local institutions. Policy is created in a vacuum of public and political apathy, overlaid with interna bureaucratic competition and meddling by foreign experts. There are no public demands for family planning services. The fertility reduction targets that have been established and missed so regularly are largely the creation of imaginative bureaucratic mind responding to donor agency pressures.[31]

We have attempted in this paper to outline the population policy-making process in India over the last 25 years. We believe that a better understanding of past failures, present difficulties

---

* In the last six months or so, there has been a great increase in public debat and involvement of political leadership in the 'population' area. A recen conference on population of political leaders from the States and the Centre and the Centre's 'population policy' resolution, are some concrete indication of increased interest and participation by the Central and State politica leadership. Many State Governments and politicians have taken a ver aggressive position on population control, and have suggested or even introduce legislation at the State level calling for compulsory sterilization after two o three children. Newspapers and weekly magazines have been full of featu stories, editorials, and letters to editors, on this issue. In all, there has bee widespread public debate on the issue of population control and politicians hav been in the forefront of it. This is indeed in stark contrast to the period covere by this paper. It is quite likely, if this political leadership persists and broa based public discussions continue, that a more successful population contr programme will be formulated and *implemented*. There are already indicatio that a much broader conception of 'population policy' is emerging, instead the narrow, health-orinted approach of the past decades. Labour union industries, Government agencies, educational institutions and many oth social and economic institutions are being brought into the gambit implementing 'population' programmes. In short, a much more comprehensiv grassroot approach seems to be evolving. It is indeed too early to say wheth this trend will continue and become institutionalised or whether the ne policies and programmes will be more effective in reducing population grow than the old policies and programmes.

and future responses may be gained by understanding the process of policy-making. There are inherent biases and limitations in any process depending upon who is making and implementing the policy, in response to what pressures, and in response to whose needs. In this paper we have shown not only these elements of the population policy process in India, but also their links to the outcome of the process itself.

There is a need for more detailed and extensive empirical studies of the policy-making process in India in general and the population policy process in particular.

Notes

* From *Indian Journal of Public Administration*, Vol. XXII, No. 4, 1976, pp. 692-704.

1. Census of India for 1951, Vol. I, Pt. I, quoted in C.B. Mamoria, *Population and Family Planning in India*, Allahabad, Kitab Mahal, 1959, pp. 76-77.
2. *ibid.*
3. *ibid.*, p. 82.
4. Census of India for 1951, *op. cit.*, p. 76.
5. *ibid*, p. 77.
6. *ibid.*, p. 78. It was made up of "top-ranking" medical men in the country.
7. GOI Health Survey and Development Committee, *Report*, Vol. II, Government Publications, quoted in Mamoria, op. cit., pp. 77-78.
8. National Planning Committee, *Report of Population*, 1948, p. 67, quoted in Mamoria, *op. cit.*, pp. 77-78.
9. Draft Outline of the Five Year Plan, 1951, p. 16, quoted in Mamoria, *op. cit.*, p. 80.
10. C. Chandrasekaran, "Population Policy in India", in S.N. Agarwala (ed.), *India's Population: Some Problems in Perspective Planning*, Bombay, Asia Publishing House, 1960, pp. 144-145.
11. B. Chatterjee and Navrekha Singh, *A Guide to Voluntary Action in Family Planning*, New Delhi, Population Council of India, 1972, p.11.
12. For a good brief history of the women's movements in India and their involvement in family planning work, see Kamla Mankekar, *Voluntary Efforts in Family Planning: A Brief History*, New Delhi, Abhinav Publications, 1974.
13. Chandrasekaran, *op. cit.* pp., 146-47
14. Chatterjee and Singh, *op. cit.*, p. 11.

15. Exceptions existed, of course; Madras State was one. For detailed treatment of this point, see J.D. Sethi, "Political Aspects of Family Planning," in V. Jagannadham, ed., *Family Planning in India: Policy and Administration,* New Delhi, IIPA, pp. 241-246.
16. For a critical view of international experts in the population policy and programmes of poor countries and of India respectively see: Aaron Segal, "The Rich, the Poor and Population," in *Demography: India*, II, 1 (June 1973), pp. 5-17. D. Banerji, *Family Planning in India: A Critique and a Perspective*, New Delhi Publishing House, 1971.
17. S. Chandrasekhar, "How India is Tackling her Population Problem", *Population Review*, 13, No. 1 and 2, January-December 1969, 31. Emphasis added.
18. *Ibid.*, for details on USAID assistance for Indian family planning programmes see AID Bureau for Technical Assistance, Office of *Population, Population Programme Assistance,* October 1970.
19. Marcus Franda, *Marketing Condoms in India: The Nirodh Programme* (Field Staff Report) Vol. XVI, No. 8, *American Universities Field Staff*, August 1972.
20. *Ibid.*, p. 2, Emphasis added.
21. Marcus Franda, *op. cit.*, p. 2.
22. Arthur D. Little Associates, quoted in Franda, *op. cit.*, p. 2.
23. *See*: GOI Planning Commission, *Fourth Plan: Mid-Term Appraisal*, Vol. II, December-1971, p. 222 and S.L. Ogale, *The Tragedy of Too Many*, New Delhi, Academy Books Limited, 1969, p. 24.
24. S. Chandrasekhar, *Abortion in a Crowded World*, George Allen and Unwin Ltd, 1971, p. 77.
25. David G. Mandelbaum, *Human Fertility in India*, Berkeley, University of California Press, 1974, p. 8.
26. *ibid.*
27. *ibid.*, pp. 8-9.
28 Ogale, *op. cit.* p. 30.
29. For example see various essays in V. Jagannadham, *op. cit.* Also see D. Banerji, *op. cit.*, and Aaron Segal, *op. cit.*
30. J.D. Sethi, *op. cit.*
31. National Academy of Sciences, *In Search of Population Policy*, Washington, D.C. 1974, pp. 19-20.

12

Policy Issues in Wildlife Conservation*

W.A. RODGERS

Wildlife is perhaps the most complex of all natural resources (forest, air, water, soil, minerals) for the administrator or manager to deal with. There are several reasons for this:

1. Everybody believes he has an important viewpoint on wildlife conservation matters, be the village, tourist, forester or decision maker.

2. People's perceptions to wildlife are often emotional and significantly affected by religious belief, culture and, nowadays, the advertising power of the media: television, papers, books, etc., which portray animals in an emotional way.

3. Different people have widely disparate views on the value of wildlife; from the villager whose crops, livestock and own life may be at stake, to the tourist who wants to see his country's natural heritage, to the conservationist interested in genetic resources. There is, of course, a polarisation between the rural poor and the richer urban elite on these issues.

4. Many of the perceived values of wildlife cannot be easily quantified or given economic price tags. Despite the essential role of clean air, water, terms. Still less can we assign value to the non-tangible aesthetic aspect of wildlife.

5. Each interet group perceives a shortage of their resource. Rural communities want more land, more grazing, more

fuel, etc., Conservationists want more and bigger sanctuaries. Resource users want more productive forest.

6. Wildlife is a complex entity, not just large mammals, but all plants and animals from the biggest to the smallest, within their natural communities and environment.

Finally, in this context, it must not be forgotten that whilst we see major problems today, the scale of problem will continue to increase as population pressure grows. Today we have just over 800 million people. By 2030 there will be at least 1.3 billion!

Aims of Wildlife Management

Management of any resource or system cannot take place in a vacuum. The very act of management suggests there is a goal or an objective to be obtained by that management. Goals may be simplistic: maximise yield, reduce inefficiencies, preserve a species, maintain stability, maintain *status quo*, etc., or they may be a complex balance between several possible conflicting end points. One problem with wildlife management is that all too often the overall goals are not stated; or if they are, they are so vague and generalised as to be non-definable. "To preserve nature", is such a non-reachable target. As 'nature' cannot be readily defined, and as 'preserve' is open to a wide variety of meaning, the manager cannot tell when or if he is reaching his goal.

Goal setting stems from the overall policies which are in vogue at that time. Policies do change; witness the complete alteration of official policies on wildlife hunting in the past 20 years. Present policy for wildlife in India at all but the most general level is hard to define. The *Constitution* specifically prescribes:

> The State shall endeavour to protect and improve the environment and to safeguard the forests and wildlife of the country. {Article 48. Constitution (Forty-second Amendment) Act 1977}
>
> It shall be the duty of every citizen of India....to... (g) protect and improve the natural environment including forests, lakes, rivers and wildlife, and to have compassion for living creatures. (Article 51A).

But these are difficult to interpret. How much should be protected?

How and where? are immediate questions.

In 1983, Government, through the National Wildlife Action Plan of the Ministry of Environment, laid down several sets of activity by which wildlife should and could be conserved. It is hard to construe this as a policy document. But the preamble to the plan takes guidance from the Prime Minister's statement to the Indian Board for Wildlife in 1982, which listed aims for wildlife conservation. These include:

- There should be a network of protected areas to cover representative samples of all major wildlife ecosystems and with adequate geographic distribution.
- Degraded habitats in these protected areas should be restored to their natural state.
- Rehabilitation of endangered species, including restoration to former habitat.
- Development of adequate corridors for genetic continuity in production forests and pastures.
- Development of appropriate management systems for protected areas. Long term conservation of wildlife based on the scientific principles of evolution and genetics.

None of these genralised aims relate to the different values we obtain from wildlife, or put wildlife into a larger community or national framework, or integrate wildlife into other resource management strategies.

In 1988, Government introduced a new "National Forest Policy" which includes a number of statements on wildlife and biodiversity:

- Conserving the natural heritage of the country by preserving the remaining natural forests with the vast variety of flora and fauna, which represent the remarkable biological diversity and genetic resources of the country.
- For the conservation of total biological diversity, the network of national parks, sanctuaries, biosphere reserves and other protected areas should be strengthened and extended adequately.

However, there has been considerable criticism of this forest policy document, especially as to the provision of long-term rights to tribal and rural communities dependent on forest resources. The document does make sweeping statements, many contradictory, with no guidelines on implementation.

Gaps in Present Policy and Policy Making Issues

Many management problems arise from inadequate policy statements, for example, problems relating to elephants. The last few years have seen many examples of elephant herds radically changing their home range. Elephants have moved from Tamil Nadu to south Andhra Pradesh and have killed many people. There is no protected area in south Andhra Pradesh. Elephants and have moved from Central Bihar to east Madhya Pradesh and have killed many people. There is no protected area in that part of Madhya Pradesh.

What should be done? The animals cannot be driven back. Some officials are talking about finding new protected areas in these states, specifically for elephants. But should this be done, and why? Who should make this decision?

Policy does not help, policy merely suggests we "ensure the conservation of elephant". Does Madhya Pradesh want or need an elephant population? Does it have the space to do so? Who should decide — the Chief Minster? The Legislative Assembly? The Chief Wildlife Warden?, or The people of the area where the elephant will be? There are no guidelines.

Even within elephant states, there are similar problems. West Bengal has some 150 elephants in the northern forests. Perhaps 100 are in two large sanctuaries, the others are in smaller fragmented forest patches from which they frequently emerge and raid crops, grain stores, local 'toddy' stores and kill people. How many elephants does West Bengal need and who should decide this? Elephants are to be protected in Buxa and Mahananda Sanctuaries. Fine. Do we then need to keep elephants in nonviable habitat for the foreseeable future? There is no conservation value in doing so.

My interpretation of conservation policy (for all countries) is that they have a duty to conserve the species present in that country and the genetic components of that species – the major populations. They do not have a duty to conserve each and every individual of the species. Attempts to conserve each individual and herd, when these individuals are in conflict with human populations, can have a serious backlash against the larger objectives of conservation. People become antagonistic towards conservation activities and will often take the law into their own hands and 'remove' problem animals. This is part of what happened around Dudhwa National Park, the poisoning of tigers being a backlash against slow official response to man-eating problems. What is government policy on man eating? There is no easy answer. Opinions of past expert committees set up to investigate the problems have not been ratified after many years.

Policy must address the question of animals **in** agricultural land. People must be involved in this policy making.

Much has been written about the Bishnoi community and their pro-conservation attitudes towards wildlife, usually blackbuck and gazelle on farmland. However, as human densities and irrigated dry season crops increase and fallow land decreases, the attitudes change. These changes are accentuated in drought years when there is a fodder scarcity. But blackbuck is a Schedule I specie under the law, how then can communities deal with crop raiding animals? Again policy is silent. Only now, in the past few months, have these issues begun to be debated in the national press.

Most major management issues arise from human-animal-protected area conflict. Wildlife authorities have developed adequate strategies to deal with under-abundance within protected areas. Wildlife policies to date have virtually all been developed to deal with inadequate conservation input. Yet we have now reached the stage where, in some places, there is localised overabundance of wildlife. We have not yet developed strategies to cope with this problem. Frequently, the law, as a result of past policies, does not permit rational strategies to be implemented. It is for these conflict issues that administrations need more explicit policy guidelines. These policies must involve local people as well as the wildlife authorities if they are to succeed.

Conflict in Wildlife Conservation

One form of conflict arises from the shortage or perceived shortage of land for people, for forest and for wildlife. It is accentuated by the intimate interspersion of people in forest land due to fragmentation of the forest resource and the creation of forest villages. Even today, most of our national parks and sanctuaries have villages within their boundaries, most wildlife populations are in close proximity to villages. There is little really "remote jungle" left ! The land, the money or the will to relocate villages within protected areas, or to replan protected area boundaries, seemingly, does not exist.

This conflict will continue to grow as human populations increase and land hunger and resource requirements become more acute. It will also grow as conservation succeeds and animal populations increase. An example of this latter problem is apparent in Gujarat as size of lion population increases in Gir National Park. Lions naturally attempt to regulate population size by dispersal, by moving out to the edge as they cannot find territory space elsewhere. At the edge, they come in conflict with people and livestock. More lions, more people, means more conflict. There have been over 100 incidents, including ten fatalities in the last 18 months, all outside the park.

What can be done? At present, lions are caught and released back into the forest centre; from where evidence shows they will again disperse back to the edge. Obviously this is no long-term solution. People should be taught how to cope with lions (i.e. do not approach, etc.) but this is not a real solution; it is crisis management. People cannot tolerate, and government should not permit, dangerous animals within land zoned for human occupation. If individual animals are excess to conservation needs and causing conflict, then they must be culled. Only limited numbers of dangerous animals can be taken to zoos, safari parks, or for elephant, domesticated. Policy does not easily provide for such a pragmatic solution. Sentiment and the cultural ethos of people, who make policy frequently, may not permit such a solution. They are not the ones who live close to lions or elephant !

A list of conservation conflict issues is given in the Annexure. This is of interest in that it shows a third category of conflict in addition to that between people and animals. There is/are conflict(s) between resource managers and the administration, and the resource users, and the environmentalists. Many of these conflicts again reflect gaps in policy, mainly land-use policies. Environmental debate over Silent Valley is a well publicised example, but there are many such issues. Government sheep farms within Dachigam National Park, Army firing ranges in many sanctuaries, salt mining in the Wild Ass Sanctuary, proposed dams in Parambikulam and Kalakad in the Western Ghats, proposed railway line through part of Kaziranga are further examples. Nearly always there are alternatives for communications, industry and power. There are no alternative sites for wildlife.

Many conflicts arise from the narrow points of view held by protagonists. Wildlife is but a single component of a land-use system. It cannot be debated in isolation from other legitimate demands on land and resources. There is a real need for an effective and national level land use planning forum to coordinate such issues.

Wildlife as a Part Environmental Conservation

It can be argued that wildlife conservation is a luxury compared to the conservation of essential resources, such as water, clean air and soils. But wildlife conservation is not incompatible with these resources, rather it enhances them. Wildlife areas are the best protected natural areas (with potentially the strictest legal safeguards) and so they will have the greatest catchment capabilities. Natural forest has a greater catchment capability than exploited forest, than plantation forest, or plantation agriculture, such as tea. If wildlifers were to stress these material advantages instead of highlighting "tiger" or "elephant" or "orchid" values, then wildlife conservation may have greater acceptance in rural areas.

The benefits of wildlife conservation are not easy to explain to many segments of society. The potential values of genetic resources, scientific understanding and ecological reference centres are difficult to grasp. The intangible values of culture, heritage, aesthetics, and God-given rights of all creatures to exist cannot be used for people suffering resource loss. The real values of water, tourism, soil, environmental buffering may be appreciated, but often elicit a "not in my back yard" (NIMBY) response, "Please go and conserve these resources elsewhere". We need to find ways to show the long-term benefit of conservation to rural people. Government's emphasis on rainfed agricultural areas in the coming Eighth Five Year Plan can help. Agricultural development is dependent on maintenance of local watersheds and local rainfall. Adequate forests are the best way to maintain water inputs.

Rationalisation of Wildlife Conservation

In brief, what wildlife conservation needs is a long term and pragmatic development and management policy, which is appreciative of the needs of other land-use agencies. Plans should be able to cope with the situation today and with the long term future.

Policy requires us to ensure a network of protected areas covering the full range of India's biodiversity. Conservationists must set priorities and decide on the implementation of this network now. Protected areas to be viable have to be large, conservation science now has capability to determine just how big. But there are limits. Planning must be a rational compromise between biological needs and people's requirements. Conservation cannot successfully be imposed on people, there must be some degree of acceptance if conservation is to work.

The scale of legitimate demand on forest lands—for timber, for fuel, for minor produce, such as tendu leaf and fodder—means that resources have to be shared. This can be catered for in wildlife conservation planning by the core and buffer concept, and the regulation of buffer zone use. Natural production is finite, and over-use does destroy the resource capital —the soil, the rootstock, and the growing regeneration. Long-term conservation must ensure against such overuse. This is best done through rural society, not perpetually via the policing actions of government agencies. Involving rural people will need extension and education schemes, which are not in use today. Buffer zones permit a sharing of resources between people and wildlife. Ideally buffer zones should not have permanent settlement, but be forest areas where people can go in day time to collect resources. Buffers provide an edge habitat where man and lion for example could co-exist.

Finally, we must accept that people living near wildlife areas will have lost access to many forest resources. There should be adequate complementary development to reduce this forest dependence, and provide sustainable agricultural production on village land. This can be referred to as "ecodevelopment," an idea often talked about, but rarely implemented. Micro-dams, agro-forestry, tree farming, improved husbandry, sericulture, poultry, cottage industry, pisciculture, etc., are all potential components of ecodevelopment.

This will cost money and it will need expertise. If we are to achieve long-term conservation, then it is going to cost initially a great deal of investment finance. In the long run, however, the returns from this investment will be overwhelming in terms of water, forest cover and genetic resources. To recreate water production mechanisms or arable soil cover after forest loss would be prohibitively expensive. But now, to achieve environmental stability, investment must be greatly increased, more staff, more extension, more subsidy, more planting, more rehabilitation, more ecodevelopment, more knowledge and more planning.

Who should pay? Simply, those who will extract benefit. At present, the rural communities surrounding protected areas have paid, indirectly, by resource loss, usually not compensated for. The urban communities who either enjoy wildlife by actual or television based tourism pay very little. Their water is almost free, their fuelwood and their power is greatly subsidised. Government, via reduced subsidy and increased taxation, must invest more heavily in conservation. Administrations must ensure that conservation becomes a priority for investment. Administrations, resource managers and the people must determine policies and strategies to allow conservation to succeed.

As wildlife does not have a large set of written material to address their issues, there is a need for all those involved in wildlife conservation to contribute ideas, experience and knowledge to the literature ! Only then can more definitive and workable policies evolve.

Annexure

An Illustation of the Type of Wildlife Conflict Situations in Indian Wildlife Mangement

Situations where wildlife conservation adversely affects people:

- Man killing by elephant, by predators.
- Stock lifting by predators.
- Crop damage by large herbivores, monkeys, porcupines.
- Loss of traditional forest resources when conservation is enforced.

Situations where people affect wildlife:

- Poaching or "retaliation killing" of animals.
- Illegal and overuse of forest resources in wildlife habitat including livestock grazing.
- Encroachment on wildlife land.

Conflict between land managers, administrators and public:

- Dual control (!) of wildlife land between wild-lifers and commercial foresters.
- Loss of wildlife land for irrigation, communication, etc.
- Antagonism between conservationists (NGOs, researchers) and wildlife authorities.
- Antagonism between tourists, their developers and wildlife authorities.
- Antagonism between people's organisations and wildlifers, e.g., tribal development
- Antagonism between the administration (finance, legal procedures, etc.) and wildlife authorities.

Note

* From *Indian Journal of Public Administration*, Vol. XXXV, No. 3, 1989. pp. 461-468.

Select Readings

The National Wildlife Action Plan, Ministry of Environment and Forest, 1983.

The National Forest Policy of 1988, Ministry of Environment and Forests.

Eliciting Public Support for Wildlife Conservation, Task Force of the Indian Board for Wildlife, 1984.

W.A. Rodgers and H.S. Panwar, *Planning a Wildlife Protected Area Network in India*, The Wildlife Institute of India, 1988.

Wildlife and People, The Proceedings of a Workshop at the Wildlife Institute of India, April 1989. (in press).

A Kothari, P. Pande, S. Singh, D. Variave, *Management of National Parks and Sanctuaries in India: A Status Report*, New Delhi, IIPA, 1989.

PART II
Some Selected Writings of B. Venkatappiah

13

Light and Shade*

B. VENKATAPPIAH

In considering India's administration we may borrow a feature from the modern techniques of project evaluation. We may first attempt a dark view and then a bright view of the situation. Both views would be based on agreed facts. Only emphasis and interpretation would differ. Some where in between would lie a reasonably objective assessment of the data. I propose to devote roughly twice as much space to the pessimistic as to the optimistic presentation.

The pessimistic view starts by questioning whether there is as much room as one in three for optimism. In 1950, yes. But now? Some fifteen years ago there was a sense of achievement based on achievement – witness the integration of States – and a feeling of exhilaration *based*, let us say, on new-won independence. But at what point of time, in more recent years, have promises been redeemed or all the brave new talk translated from words into deeds? Have not slogans taken the place of policies; and poor performance ever sought to be compensated by still higher targets? A nation may be drunk with independence, but should the hang-over persist after nearly twenty years?

For such little as has been performed, the technician has contributed more than the bureaucrat, and the bureaucrat more than the politician. The words are used advisedly: politician, not statesman; bureaucrat, not administrator; technician, not scientist. There are still a few of these latter; but on the whole we seem to have run short of scientists, administrators, and statesmen.

We have been more successful in dealing with machines than with men, and with men than with policies. We have been able, though after long delay, to set up a Bhakra Nangal there, a Koyna here and a Rourkela somewhere else. We have brought together, *en masse*, steel and water and electricity. We have taken water to the farmer but not succeeded in helping him to use it. There is electricity – quite often not enough of it – for the bigger industrial complexes, but none in the village for small industry. There is steel for gigantic structures in Bombay and New Delhi, but little or no pig iron for the small entrepreneur in Howrah and Batala.

Alice Again

Where men are concerned – and most men are small men, some in cities but a great many more in villages – we have been unable either to help them or to organize them to help themselves. There is, of course, a great deal of schematic assistance. This is where the bureaucrat comes in. But the trouble is that he does not move any farther. He has beautiful plans on paper and rigid rules to thwart them. It is Alice in Wonderland all over again:

> 'But I was thinking of a plan
> To dye one's whiskers green,
> And always use so large a fan
> That they could not be seen.'

While the bureaucrat is laying foundations of files for schemes that do not see the light, the politician is busy building images of his party and himself. Each new image is one more step removed from reality. Our secretariats have become forward exchanges of paper plans and toy targets. They are like certain forward markets which deal so much in 'futures' that the turn-over has no relation to the actual commodity. In either case there is that distance from reality which lends enchantment to the speculation. It needs statesmen to bring the promises back to the level of practicability and raise performance to the level of possibility. And it needs administrators to dissociate the schemes from the slogans.

Our greatest failure has been in the villages. Why is this so? Perhaps it is because we have achieved a democracy which is describable as a government of the people by the townspeople for the townspeople. Our bureaucrats and our politicians indeed punctuate their notes and their pronouncements with pious references to the rural masses much as a Hindu may say, '*Ram Ram*', or a Catholic cross himself. Nevertheless, the water in the government canal is not channeled to the ultimate field; and seed and fertilizer and credit do not reach the small farmer.

The prices are often tilted against the producer. Cooperatives, alternatively exalted and denigrated by a government that is unable to make up its mind about them, reel under the changing policies. And almost the only development which panchayats have activated is that of local power politics. In the higher echelons of government there is lack of understanding of rural needs and lack of responsiveness to rural demands.

Camouflage

There is no lack, however, of orders, circulars and the whole paraphernalia of district and village administration. The bulk of the village remains unaffected by these in any significant way. It is affected of course in the sense that it interprets these new orders as yet another form assumed by older tyrannies and adapts itself to their existence in the well-known ways of a little corruption here, a little acquiescence there, and a great deal of camouflage everywhere.

The net result is that, at some cost to itself, the village as a whole resumes once more its former mode of life unmindful of plans and targets. It has immense confidence in the village officials. They can be trusted to dish up the right-seeming data for the benefit of visiting dignitaries. Appearance is all important, and reality once more respectfully makes way. Records are fudged, not results achieved.

Turning to Delhi, the visitor is naturally puzzled and bewildered after knocking his head on a few of its blank walls and closed doors. He begins to wonder whether responsibility is not some high-bred specimen of the canine species, well-kept and well-kennelled, but hardly taken out and exercised. For, experience has shown the bureaucrat that there are many dangers in exercising responsibility. But occasionally there is a spurt of activity. And then one wonders whether it is any one's job at all to ensure that the different ministries are bestirring themselves to a common purpose.

Diffusion

In a State Government, such a function would be discharged by the Chief Secretary. Delhi has nothing corresponding. It has an administrative plateau, not apex, at the top. Neither the Cabinet Secretary nor the Home Secretary, able and senior though they may be, possesses a writ that runs through all ministries. And in the name of coordination, departments are set up which make the general flabbiness still flabbier. There is diffusion, not devolution of responsibility.

One observes something even more disturbing. Ministries are constantly engaged in carving out for themselves an almost self-sufficient autonomy, an empire within an empire which through attached and allied officers, extends in sub-regal ramification throughout the country. Union ministers, when they are not abroad, love traversing the length and breadth of their own special jurisdiction. Strictly speaking, it is a functional jurisdiction, weak maybe in many respects, but strong in the will to become stronger.

The beginning of the end of the Mughal Empire was its territorial vice-royalties which would not hang together and therefore fell apart both from one another and the Centre. Today we seem to see the rise of functional vice-royalties. We cannot afford these.

The Prime Minister's will – if you like, the Cabinet's will – must be known, respected and observed by all ministries and throughout each ministry, even as, in all appropriate matters, the Union's writ must run in all States and throughout each State. There is double danger to be faced: that of Union ministers becoming functional viceroys, and chief ministers becoming territorial satraps.

Special mention must be made of the Finance Ministry. It has a difficult task, but a task which can be made needlessly more difficult, for it as for every one else, if it behaves as if it were the sole repository of the country's good governance. Nothing could be more important for a developing country than an understanding and constructive Finance Ministry; nothing so fatal as an interfering and imperialist one. And what Finance finishes, Audit buries with appropriate texts read over the dead body.

Corporations

When ministries expand upto a point they begin to think that a change of name would lend respectability to any more extension. The fashion nowadays is to call each such further accretion a corporation. Now, a corporation is an excellent idea provided it is not merely an idea. There are certain essential requisites for the successful working of a corporation. First, there must be a need for it in the sense that there is something to be done which it can do better than a department. Second, it must have much more autonomy, financial and other, than a department, as also much more flexibility in procedure and operation. Third, the right person or persons - chairman and directors – must be chosen to head it, and then left to run the corporation with the minimum of interference. Fourth, while the essence of accountability is secured, the threat should be eliminated of minor, meticulous and widely publicized post mortems at every suitable and unsuitable opportunity. Initiative and inquisition do not go together.

The actual position today would be extremely comic if it was not so depressing. Most of the corporations we have – and more are springing up every month – are a duplication of audit orthodoxy, governmental control and departmental rigidity. Corporations are created; then everything possible is done to stifle them, if not out of existence, certainly out of usefulness; and thereafter fresh corporations are sought to be set up. The enthusiasm for more and more corporations is worthy of a better cause.

One is reminded of the minor Victorian poet who waxes eloquent about joint stock companies. He has an original and rather awesome thought. The universe itself, he concludes, is in conception and design of a joint stock company. And God is its Managing Director!

Delay, inefficiency and corruption, all these continue to make the citizen's life more and more irksome. To these need not have been added lack of common consideration and common courtesy. But it is. The Indian bureaucrat, along with whom may be classed the Indian minister, has little use for public relations except as a section in one of his departments. There is great emphasis on production; but how are farmers, small entrepreneurs or even some of the bigger manufacturers treated when they go to the secretariats in State capitals or New Delhi? Well, they are dealt with in a manner which makes it most ironical that official or minister should describe himself in formal communications as the citizen's 'most obedient servant'.

One is reminded of 'A.C.G'S' verse which appeared in a newspaper shortly after Independence:

'Why Oh Why
Do you call yourself my
Obedient Servant. Oh Why?
When you very well know
Had you ever been so,
I'd have fired you long ago!'

The Optimistic Version

On this note, then, let us turn to the optimistic version of the situation.

A nation, like an individual, has every right to be impatient that transformation takes so long. There is another side to the picture not often seen. By the same token the transition is often made easier. The British had sought to impress on India the inevitability of gradualness. And now India in her own right is experiencing the gradualness of inevitability.

Economic and social development, hailed as certain, is meanwhile seen to be slow. Far from being traumatic, such change as has so far taken place requires econometricians to measure and social anthropologists to discover by micro-surveys. But there is virtue in gradualness. We may be in a sorry mess, but misfortunes have not come to us in an avalanche.

Value in Transition

Above all, there was one feature of administration which cushioned inevitability even if in the same process it retarded it. The nucleus of trained administrators left behind after Independence was of inestimable value in the prolonged transition. Not all the civil servants of the previous regime may have risen to the occasion, but the fact remains that a number of them did. They are now disappearing from the scene, but before doing so they have at least partially succeeded in transmitting what was good in their background to the younger people they have been called upon to train.

There is little doubt that the new material is excellent. This is not to say that the younger civil servants, whether engaged at home on administrative jobs or abroad on diplomatic assignments, are not often frustrated. So long as the core is sound there is no harm if they have to adapt themselves the hard way to a new or difficult environment.

The variety of jobs which the younger officers have to undertake is even wider than in the past. They are to be found in charge of schemes of economic development or manning industrial concerns in the public sector or occupying important positions in municipal bodies or other organizations of local self-government. They are also, of course, assistant collectors and collectors, under-secretaries, deputy secretaries and secretaries. In all these instances as also in the jobs allocated to the managerial and economic services, they show themselves to be keen and able officers on whom training and background have conferred special advantages.

Even today, few countries of the world have general, specialized and technical services of the content and caliber which India has. The right use of these cadres as efficient administrative instruments of socio-economic development is obviously a matter for the politicians, that is to say, for the ministers at the head of the governmental organization.

There are many States in which the right relationship between minister and civil servant is yet to be developed. The old gulf between the two, while indeed not disappearing, has narrowed down in more than one State. Just by working together both minister and civil servant have had, and day by day are having, a type of training that is all important. Moreover, for the minister there is a perspective no longer conditioned by the novelty of power.

Authority is good, but alas it is brief. Its uncertain graph has to be plotted in a dis-continuum of elections. A factor of some importance, though political accident is most important of all, is that the minister should if possible show results. And it is here that uses are discovered once again for the civil servant. Coordination between politicians and administrator is inevitable if only because of ministerial ambitions.

New Realism

In addition, a new spirit of realism may be discerned, not indeed in all regions, but in an isthmus here and an island there of planning and development. It may be premature to be optimistic, but what is optimism if not premature? With that general reservation, one may venture to see promise in the new programme of agricultural production. What is now sought is not to dissipate effort and resources, but to concentrate them where results are likely to be maximum.

High-yielding varieties of seeds are to be used in selected areas. Fertilizer is to be obtained and supplied in adequate quantities. So too pesticides and the other requirements of an intensive agricultural programme. On the food front at least the lesson seems to have been learnt. It is not enough to cultivate Americans. We must cultivate our fields as well.

No one welcomes military aggression, certainly not against oneself. One may not have lovable neighbours but that does not mean one is spoiling for a fight with them. But when, without provocation from oneself such fighting has come to pass, one must see the silver lining no less than the cloud. The aggression of Pakistan has had some beneficial effects. There sprang into being, readily, national cohesion and, more tardily, administrative purposiveness. And not least there came to be demonstrated with almost Euclidean conclusiveness the efficiency of the armed forces.

Would it be too much to say that at least for the time being, but nevertheless deeply and genuinely, this military incident induced a new sense of national realism.

Cut to Size

If necessary, we said to ourselves, set the sights lower, but hit the targets. Let aspirations be cut to the size of resources, but ensure that the effort itself is fruitful. There are signs that planning today is more sober and earnest, and the side-shows less flamboyant than at any time in the past.

If then, though this is a big if, earnestness and realism permeate all ranks – politician and legislator, minister and civil servant – there is hope that India may yet show that democracy and economic development are not mutually in-consistent. There may not be spectacular transformation. But there can still be substantial progress. Such an achievement would be made possible by completely ordinary means, namely proper planning and clean and efficient administration.

In summing up we may seek answers for a certain number of questions. First, what are our immediate objectives as distinct from far-off goals? Second, do we have the political conditions needed for the administrative pursuit of those objectives? Third, is the administrative organization adequate for the attainment of the objectives? Last, is the administrative personnel geared to the effort involved in gaining the objectives?

Basic Tasks

In concrete reply to the first question: we have to grow enough food for ourselves in the not too distant future, we have to check the growth of population, and we have to improve the condition of the poorest in villages and towns by providing employment through better agriculture and more industry. We have to do a number of other things, but these are the most basic. When spelt out, they cover between themselves most of the detailed aspects of immediate planning.

Second, the most important political requisite is an effective Centre. Effectiveness is not the same as power to dictate. It is the capacity to secure compliance. The Centre's will is of course not made up in a vacuum. It is made up in a context in which the States are very much present. So formulated, the Centre's will must be accepted by the States; and the acceptance must be genuine. In the absence of real conformity of will between the Centre and States there is already considerable difficulty in the implementation of policies. This is so even though the same party is in power in virtually all the States. The position might be much more difficult if that happens not to be the case in future. No administrative effort can bring about planned economic development if there is no agreement on at least the more essential features.

Third, the organizational structure of administration at the Centre and in the States undoubtedly needs looking into from the point of view of promptness and efficiency so far as execution is concerned; and integrity, courtesy and responsiveness so far as individuals and groups of citizens are concerned. Today it is difficult in Delhi to locate where the administrative conscience of government resides. It must be searched for and given a habitation. The structure of administration should be cut to size and vasectomy performed on those departments which are most prone to be prolific. Devolution of authority must no longer adorn manuals but step down to reality. Corporations must be autonomous and departments decisive, even though the former may break ministers' hearts and the latter the secretaries'. Accountability must express itself as a desire to assess the use of responsibility not stifle its exercise. In all these matters, among others, considerable reorganization and reform are undoubtedly necessary.

Fourth, the administrative personnel is by and large excellent so far as the material is concerned. Much however has to be done to remove frustration from its ranks. Consider the ill paid among them. They must have enough to feed, clothe and house themselves and their families and educate their children with. At all levels the pay must be such as to remove reasonable discontent. Enthusiasm must be infused and that will happen only if responsibility is given and conditions are created for discharging it.

That all these still remain to be done nearly twenty years after Independence makes for pessimism. But it is not unduly optimistic to believe that, late as it is, it is not too late to eliminate these drawbacks and ensure for India an administration that will serve it well and ably and honestly.

We are no longer in the mood when miracles seem within reach. But there is still time to turn the jungle into an orchard. And the fruits then within our grasp will be the fruits of our own labour.

Note

* From Seminar No. 85, 1966.

14

Some Thoughts*

B. VENKATAPPIAH

Rural poverty, far from being new, is one of our oldest realities, ante-dating in this respect Sankara's philosophy of Maya. If the Theory of Cosmic Illusion is twelve hundred years old, the Reality of Rural Poverty is of two thousand, perhaps three thousand years' duration. This is especially true of the chronic poverty of those down-trodden castes and tribes who have been with us through all history.

Nor is rural development, as an organised effort, notably new. If I may cite another Sankara – Sankaradeva of Assam – this saint-leader of the late fifteenth and early sixteenth centuries laid in the Brahmaputra Valley a three-fold foundation for rural reorganization which still stands, though the superstructure which he reared has long ago toppled down. The base which he established in each fairly big village consisted of a Village Council, a Village School and – since he was both a religious and a managerial sort of person – a Village Prayer-hall.

So far as the rural situation is concerned, therefore, neither the content of the problem nor the nature of the task can be said to be particularly recent. Indeed as I have hinted, we have managed to live with rural poverty, almost casually and carelessly, as with some historic habit that has been second nature, for centuries. One is reminded, somewhat inconsequentially, of the aspiring bridegroom in Oscar Wilde's play who, cross-examined by the prospective mother-in-law, admits he has lost both his parents. "Young Man", says she "to lose one parent may be a misfortune. But to lose both sounds like carelessness." Rural poverty throughout one millennium is bad enough; but rural poverty over two or more millennia seems to be national carelessness – if not callousness –

on a stupendous scale. The callousness is redeemed only partially, in India's long history, by the recurrent efforts of saints who were men of action and statesmen who were men of vision.

This topic may be succinctly described, in terms of concrete illustration, as "Farmer and Fertilizer" and in terms of managerial implications as "Policy-making and Decision-taking in Agriculture". In this latter aspect, the subject is a very broad and general one. At the same time, in my opinion, it lies at the very root of the managerial problem in rural development. It is connected with the fact that policy-makers in agriculture and decision-makers in farming are quite distinct. The policy-makers may be governmental or private and be concerned, for example, with either agricultural development or sales promotion of fertilizers. In either case, assuming that they are operating in a big way over large areas, how can it be ensured that they are adequately in touch with what is happening in the minds and fields of individual farmers? Here, obviously, is a common area of interest for those who want to sell policy and those who want to sell fertilizer. In either case, they have to deal with large groups of those millions of people who in different parts of the country are traditionally pictured as practicing agriculture as a given way of life rather than as a chosen means of earning a livelihood.

A complication arises because this picture was never quite an accurate one in the past and in any case is rapidly changing in the present. The Indian cultivator was always responsive to prices. He was also receptive to entirely new things to grow – as witness, cotton and tobacco – provided he found from experience, or better still from the experience of his neighbour, that they paid better. He knows his soil and he knows his skies. And in some agronomic part of his brain, of which he cannot explain the conscious working, he has a fairly reliable computer which correlates the constancy of the soil with the inconstancy of the skies. Indeed, he is more accustomed to the vagaries of the local skies than to the vagaries of the local administration. For, over the years, he has adapted himself competently to the defaults of the monsoon, but not yet completely to the delays of Government.

It is in this many sided context that high-yielding seed, fertilizer and pesticide make their entry into his world. His responses therefore vary from crop to crop, season to season, district to district. If better seed has earned him, not better income, but bacterial blight, he is understandably discouraged; and he will not go in for fertilizer until he is confident of Government's ability next time to supply pesticide as well, and to supply it in time. Or, in another part of the country, both fertilizer and pesticide may be available early enough, but if early fertilizer and late rains conspire to multiply the leaf and not the grain, and he can only gather where he had hoped to reap, he is understandably suspicious of the utility of agricultural programmes.

His responses are different according as he is a wet farmer or a dry farmer; is in an ex-zamindari district or a traditional rayatwari district; is tenant or owner; grows rice, wheat or millets or one of the commercial crops; deals with a wooden local administration or one which is reasonably alive; is literate and perhaps even educated up to the primary stage or is not; and so on. The responses of the farmer, then, are different for different groups and contexts and for different parts of the country. It is these responses, in an adequately representative manner, that must be ascertained, studied and influenced towards development in a sufficiently large number of regions. At one end, what is called for is a sociological-cum-economic enquiry of the most sophisticated kind; at the other, the job involved is extension-cum-sales promotion of a most complicated character.

What I have given above is no more than a broad picture, in one particular context, of the interaction between farmers' needs and farmers' responses. Management is deeply concerned with both the needs and the responses. More especially, two issues arise, not in the context of fertilizer alone – for that is merely illustrative – but of the total integrated programme of rural development. These relate to the means by which policy-makers and policy-promoters, public and private, whether at the Centre or in different parts of the country, keep in touch with millions of farmers with a view to ensuring (a) that the relevant responses are known in time so as to enable alteration in policy, procedure or method of implementation, and (b) that the responses themselves are informed, educated and modified in the direction of the total programme of agricultural development.

We have many rural projects which are country-wide in coverage, such as high yielding seed, multi-cropping, minor irrigation, small farmers and drought-prone areas. For the success of these national programmes nothing is so important as systematized data, prompt feed-back and periodical evaluation. In all these, both management and the management institutes can be of much assistance. Above all, there must be strict monitoring and efficient inspection of all on-going programmes of importance. In the absence of inspection, promise remains on paper and performance in the air. I came across, while in the Planning

Commission, a printer's mistake which seemed to me to concentrate within itself the accumulated lessons of three Five Year Plans succeeded by three Annual Plans. The mistake converted "national targets" into "notional targets".

It is my conviction that the lack of an inbuilt system of speedy feed-back and periodical evaluation led to some of the errors – though this could not, of course, have prevented any of the misfortunes – which beset the uneven history of community development.

* * * *

Nationalization of banks is a political decision. Rationalisation of the banking structure is a managerial operation. The issue I would pose is this: Banks have been nationalized; but have they been rationalized? I suggest that it is urgently necessary to rationalize the banking system with a view, on the one hand, to achieving economy and efficiency and on the other, to fulfilling a whole series of social and economic objectives.

The reviews which have hitherto been made of the banking system, such as the one conducted by the Banking Commission, either pre-date nationalization or over-lap it or overlook it. What is more important, they overlook not merely the event of nationalization but the eventual implications of nationalization.

Nationalized banking continues to be unnecessarily competitive and, in that very process, avoidably costly. Further, neither within the structure (that is to say as between bank and bank), nor outside the structure (that is to say, between banks on the one hand and different institutions, including governments, on the other) has there been adequate coordination with reference to areas of operation, types of lending (e.g. short-term and long-term), objectives and purposes. Need this lack of co-ordination continue? Need the cost be as high as at present? Cost is not merely a function of the wage structure of bank employees. If, for example, three or four branches of different banks co-exist in the same locality and do work which only one branch could very well do, the system is costly in a wholly exorbitant manner. I suggest that in an appreciable number of instances the new branches which today are springing up and have in the recent past sprung up in towns and cities are demonstrably supererogatory. These banks compete with one another. It is common knowledge that, in metropolitan and other big cities, both new and existing branches, often of the same bank, compete for the same deposits, especially those of Public Undertakings. Can we afford the luxury of such avoidable and infructuous competition at a time when the real need is for the extension of cheap and effective banking facilities to the rural areas, to the more vulnerable classes of people and to productive purposes of rural development including agriculture and rural industries?

What is overdue in the banking system is not so much its 'overdues'. What is really overdue is a managerial evaluation of the total structure of nationalized banks. The object of this much-needed reappraisal would be to ascertain how nationalized banks can fulfil at less cost and greater efficiency objectives such as those the Prime Minister has adumbrated in her programme.

I would particularly emphasise the aspect of inter-facing or coordination. The small farmers' and marginal farmers' agencies, the programme for making available inputs such as water and electricity to the agricultural community, the schemes for extension of rural industries: all these need much more detailed co-ordination and effort than exists today. It no longer suffices to say that the bank is in the same district, taluka or block as the one in which the other programmes are operating. Much more meticulous collaboration with the rest of the infrastructure is needed in order to ensure that the farmer who has dug the well can buy the pumpset and the one who has bought the pumpset gets the electricity.

In the rural context, the most important form of bank credit is supervised credit. Supervised credit implies something to supervise. What is supervised is, for example, an individual farm plan which in turn is part of a development programme. The programme is frequently a Government programme which aims, among other things, at distribution of inputs such as seed and fertilizer and water; it being left to the bank to supply the input of credit. It is a combination – and even more the synchronization – of these inputs that gives the programme its developmental character. In terms of the individual, the programme resolves itself into a plan for developing the farm and increasing the income. In terms of the farm, it is the incremental income which is the basis of credit, and the progress of the plan that is the basis of supervised credit. All this means that the bank has got banking officials who know what development is taking place and how it is related to the facilities which the bank can offer.

Note

* From Opinion, Vol. XVI, No. 35, 23rd December 1975, based on an address at Bombay on 20.12.1975.

15

Reflections on Rural Development*

B. VENKATAPPIAH

Rural development in India has engaged the attention of many people and many organizations over several decades. This has been especially so since Independence. In agriculture, there has been a two-fold endeavour: to reshape administration and to reform the infrastructure so as to be more in conformity with the objectives of development. The objectives themselves have often been stated to be growth on the one hand and social justice on the other: increase of production and reduction of areawise and classwise disparities.

We may take up in turn the two items I have mentioned, viz., administration and infrastructure, and examine them in relation to the total process and objectives of rural development.

I

Of the administrative aspects of rural development, some of the most interesting are those which pertain to organization. The structure of development organization has many levels. One may think principally of three: the primary or field level of implementation; the intermediate or district level of coordination; and the apex (State or all-India) level of policy formulation. I will here, for the most part, confine myself to the first two of these levels.

At a very early stage in post-Independence planning, Community Development and National Extension were jointly regarded as the most important factors in the determination of the development unit of organization at the primary level. The Community Development Block came into existence. Participation of those who would benefit from the local programmes, agricultural and other, was recognized to be imperative. It was, however, postulated that if, over two or three phases, initial outlays were provided for stimulating growth, full participation would follow to the extent of rendering unnecessary further assistance of a financial character. This would happen some-what earlier in advanced blocks than in the more backward ones.

Programmes were accordingly drawn up and fitted into what were called schematic patterns for different blocks in large areas of the country. A series of development officials for the block came to be created for activating development and extending to the farmers and others the latest know-how and inputs in agriculture and animal husbandry.

These arrangements were reviewed at a later stage because it was felt that enough progress had not been made under a set-up which was essentially administrative. Community Development and National Extension came under a cloud. Why did this happen? To answer this question we must ask another. What did Community Development do, or fail to do, to help the farmer to increase his production?

The focus here has to be on the all-important Village Level Worker. He was to stimulate the drawing-up of individual farm plans for each family in his charge. This he was to do with the help of the Cooperative Society or the Panchayat or the Village Council, as the case might be, choosing the most appropriate organization in the particular circumstances of his jurisdiction. In practice, the policy alternated between Co-operatives on the one hand and the Panchayats on the other. Where neither existed or both seemed unsuitable, there was even talk of entrusting the whole job to a village council, a notional body which has largely remained notional. The farm plans did not work.

The verdict of the years was inevitable. While Community Development had perhaps increased the farmer's social awareness, it had certainly failed to increase his farm production. This failure, it was confidently asserted, arose from the administrative orientation of the whole endeavour. It was not the lack of better seed that was bewailed (the high-yielding varieties were yet to come and capture the imagination of Government) but the lack of social dynamism. What was needed was the involvement of the popular will in the form of democratic management of rural development. The name given to the prescribed remedy was 'democratic decentralization'. In the three or four States where this was seriously tried, a series of development activities in the rural sphere were transferred to the Zilla Parishad: as for example in Maharashtra and Gujarat. Experiments of a similar nature were also adopted in Andhra Pradesh, Orissa and Rajasthan.

It happened, however, that the initiation and coordination of development activities at the district level by the Zilla Parishad did not fare well in some of the States in which it had been adopted. To what extent this phenomenon, or the psychology underlying it, could be traced to incipient discord between the elected representatives of the Zilla Parishad on the one hand and the local legislators (MLAs) on the other, or to clashes between other State-level politicians and district level leaders, would form an interesting study for the sociologist and the political scientist.

A number of organizational changes were initiated. By a process of atavism not unknown to Governments, the Collector came again to be regarded in many States as the prime coordinator of developmental activities at the district level. In Tamil Nadu, this has always been the case. In Andhra Pradesh, the concept of effective coordination by the Collector was given effect to with considerable thoroughness. In other States where the Zilla Parishad idea had not caught up, it is needless to say that in different degrees the function of coordinating development activities remained the task of the principal district authority.

Where Zilla Parishads were in fact functioning effectively and the idea of democratic decentralization was given a chance, much depended on the equation between the Chairman of the Zilla Parishad and the Chief Executive Officer or the District Panchayat Officer who was the principal executive of the Organization. Both in Maharashtra and Gujarat, where democratic decentralization has shown signs of significant success, this functionary has remained a senior administrative officer, generally of the rank of Collector.

Meanwhile, Indian agricultural scientists, with international help and collaboration, had successfully evolved a series of high-yielding and other varieties of seed, mostly of wheat, but also of other cereals and millets. The first results were impressive and it was thought that, if these were to be kept up, both know-how and extension would have to be organized at a very sophisticated level. Agricultural Universities came into their own and started practising extension, directly in some cases or indirectly and consultatively in other cases. Considerable experimentation was conducted with regard to the organization of extension and the division of the functions pertaining to it between the State Governments and the Agricultural Universities.

In retrospect it would seem not only unfair, but also unwise, to have minimized the importance of so basic a requirement in a village as Extension services and Community Development. True, it is no longer tenable to imagine that any one agency such as Community Development, operating on a countrywide scale and propagating what in effect are uniform moulds of schematic outlay, can sub-serve the real interests of either agricultural growth or rural development. In this mood of lost euphoria, however, there has been a tendency to throw away the baby along with the bath water, block-level extension personnel along with block-wise schemes of patterned expenditure. This seems a pity in so far as the basic organization at the village level is concerned. Whatever else it may or may not have done, surely the whole movement of Community Development and National Extension has given many parts of the country something which they had lacked before, namely, a focus on development administration at the level where it was most needed. The usefulness of this basic structure has been demonstrated again and again in the pursuit not only of agricultural improvement but of other objectives of rural development as well in the last two decades.

I will permit myself a brief digression to the subject of Cooperative organization. While this belongs essentially to the second part of my theme – namely, infrastructure – the cooperative is also interwoven with development administration at the primary level. It may have failed much and failed in many areas. It would nevertheless be most unwise to ignore its potentiality or adopt an attitude (not uncommon with Government) of boosting cooperatives unduly one quinquennium and studiedly cold-shouldering them the next according to the whimsicalities, passing for ideologies, of those in authority. The cooperative has at least the virtue of being part of the answer for parts of the country.

In a way the search (which had been initiated as long ago as the Second Plan) for a suitable village organization – village council, village panchayat or village cooperative – which could initiate farm plans and do a number of other things, is still on. It is a fruitless search if it is envisaged as having one uniform result for the whole of India. What works in one corner of the country may not work in another. In any case, so far as the cooperatives are concerned, the main failure of the last fifteen years has not been on the part of cooperators alone, but of all those responsible for top policy who thought that the whole superstructure of cooperative credit could be reared on a weak and misconceived infrastructure. Thus, deliberately turning away from the idea of viable cooperatives, that is to say of cooperatives which could -- at least after a period of four or five years – pay the trained staff they maintained, the policy-makers opted for what they regarded as the sociological village. Each village under this concept was a cohesive unit and each unit was to have a society. Since, however, many villages are no more than creations of the village maps of the Revenue Department, this has had the somewhat peculiar implication that social cohesion is a function of cartography. Many of these somewhat unfortunate decisions have been, or are now being, reversed along with the trends which emerged from them.

An important happening of the last few years – since it represents the first conscious all-India effort in development administration to provide a structural counterpart for the function of levelling down rural disparities – is nevertheless something which I can mention in passing. I refer to the establishment in a number of districts of Small Farmers Development Agencies (SFDA) and similar agencies for Marginal Farmers and Agricultural Labourers (MFAL). In setting up these institutions, care has been taken to avoid one of the pit-falls which, in the light of experience, may be said to have beset the path taken by Community Development. It consisted in the creation of a whole, large, countrywide machinery at the village and block levels, sometimes in duplication of, and almost always in addition to, the machinery which had already existed. This was one of the many ways in which Community Development suffered through being transformed into a countrywide programme, without first being tested out as a pilot experiment. In contrast, SFDA and MFAL are built into and remain part of a given structure. They are explicitly asked not to add to that structure through administrative proliferation of their own. Moreover, they are area-specific organizations with assigned resources and assigned tasks including, in particular, the identification of problems and testing out of solutions pertinent to the development of the weaker classes comprised within their charge. When the pilot stage is over – i.e., when, hopefully, local techniques have been evolved, local procedures refined and the local infrastructure of production and employment, marketing and credit made more responsive to the small farmer and the agricultural labourer – the normal institutions of the particular area would be much better equipped to assist in bringing about increased production along with reduced disparity. Another way of expressing this would be that SFDA and MFAL are in a sense an intensive effort on the part of the developmental agencies and those connected with the infrastructure to educate themselves for the task of helping the small farmer, the marginal farmer and the agricultural labourer in the normal course of their institutional functioning.

II

I turn now to the second of the two items I have listed as important preliminaries to rural development and employment. We have all been accustomed to hearing and using the word 'infrastructure'. It is a handy word because it seems to cover so many things. Nevertheless, it is a rather awkward and somewhat imprecise one which, in the rural context, is differently employed to mean rural 'institutions' – social, legislative and functional – agricultural inputs, and basic services and amenities. If we envisage the economy of the village as a structure, these, of course, are the foundation of the structure and everything that goes into it. In that sense, many distinct items such as seed and fertilizer, credit and marketing, roads and electricity, are part of the infrastructure.

The pattern of rights in land and the relationship between such rights and the pattern and fruits of production are undoubtedly part of this foundation of agricultural development. Hence land reforms are an important component of the infrastructure.

In the extended sense in which all social 'institutions' of the village which are significant for the villager as producer are themselves part of the rural infrastructure would be caste and corruption. But caste is a big subject by itself and corruption is far from being a purely rural phenomenon.

Important as the foregoing aspects are, I will confine myself here to four categories of services and inputs which may be described as part of the agricultural infrastructure. These are:

1. basic amenities, such as roads, irrigation and electricity;
2. service institutions such as credit cooperative societies, commercial banks and marketing societies;
3. tangible inputs, such as seed and fertilizer; and
4. intangible inputs, such as agricultural research.

What are the ways in which these important services and inputs could be further extended and strengthened in order to optimize the pace of rural development? Agricultural research has on the whole rendered a good account of itself. The new technology has found ready and fruitful response. But its impact has been confined to a few crops. Even where it has most succeeded, there is much scope for further progress. Wheat production, already augmented, can be substantially increased if genetic research is supported by good prices and a better market at home and abroad. In rice, the research is at a stage where promises seem about to transform themselves into results. Soil and other conditions, including pests, are much more diversified for rice than for wheat. The pattern of consumption is both varied and sophisticated. The problems of credit and marketing are more acute since the rice-grower, usually a small-holder, is dominated by the miller and moneylender. Then there is the dry farmer who has not hitherto benefited by the new technology. Nor has attention been sufficiently focused on the needs of specially undeveloped areas, such as those inhabited by tribes, or which are either arid or mountainous in character. In all these areas, as well as for the dry farmer and the small farmer, much needs to be done if larger production is to be accompanied by larger social justice. To this may be added the needs of the more vulnerable classes of the population, such as children and expectant mothers, who need not only more food but better nutrition.

Specifically, three purposes which will have to inform agricultural development hereafter may be summarized as follows:

1. Larger and more varied production, so as to meet the needs of the hungry and the ill-nourished;
2. More widely-distributed and more equitable production, so as to meet the needs of the dry farmer, the small farmer and the marginal farmer.
3. Market-sensitive production sub-serving the interests of progressive agriculture.

Let us now relate these purposes to the categories of infrastructure I have already mentioned.

For larger and more diversified production, the most important elements would be water, power and credit, the last-named covering the inputs it can command such as seed and fertilizer. As demonstrated by recurring years of drought, recent as well as past, the largest gap has occurred in regard to the biggest need, viz., water.

While all major works of irrigation now in progress will hopefully be completed during the next Plan (or the one after that?), it is most important that groundwater should be exploited to the fullest extent technically feasible and economically viable. This is all the more important as groundwater is found in areas where surface irrigation is often not available, and in its totality can cover production almost equal to that which surface irrigation now sustains. Moreover, groundwater enables a series of crops being raised throughout the year and in this manner can not only enlarge but diversify production.

Along with a programme of utilizing groundwater must go the accelerated promotion of electricity in rural areas. This should be done, not sporadically or on considerations irrelevant to development, but in a systematic manner which includes on the one hand a project approach, and on the other, that of integrated area development. It is an infrastructure of this kind that the Rural Electrification Corporation is attempting to foster through the State Electricity Boards and other agencies such as Rural Electric Cooperatives.

Lastly, credit through cooperative societies and commercial banks has to be increased in volume and streamlined in procedure for the financing of larger and more diversified production. The procedures have to be specifically tailored to the needs of the smaller people.

That takes me to the next direction in which the infrastructure has to be modified in the coming years. On the one hand, this concerns the interests of the small farmer, the dry farmer and other underprivileged classes of producers. It also concerns the economic imbalances between regions, States and even different areas of the same State. Nothing is more important in this context than the enlargement of the network of basic amenities, such as roads and electricity. One need only cite the examples of the more inaccessible valleys in Meghalaya or Himachal Pradesh or the vast territory covered by the U.P. Hills, to establish the validity of this point. Research too has much ground to cover in meeting the needs of these areas. The credit institutions would have to be geared to the special needs and disadvantages of the small farmer and the marginal farmer. Lessons must be learnt quickly from the pilot projects already established for this purpose and the requisite procedures incorporated in the infrastructure of the ensuing years.

What about those areas in which agriculture already shows signs of being progressive and near-commercialized? To ensure that the infrastructure adequately serves such areas will be an important part of the task which remains. Commercial banks would be a significant element in this context and so would specialized financial institutions including those which specifically serve the needs of agro-industrial and allied activities. The multi-agency system of credit would be particularly relevant. Most important of all would be the facilities provided by marketing and export organizations, including cooperative marketing societies and their federations.

Many studies have been carried on since Independence in regard to various socio-economic aspects of the development programmes of the country. In agriculture, this has necessarily implied an inquiry into the structure of rural society which in turn raised issues such as patterns of land ownership, effects of land reforms, operations of cooperative societies, beneficiaries under credit schemes, etc. One of the earliest of these studies, viz., the Rural Credit Survey (1954)[2] which, for field data, concerned itself with the year 1951-2, highlighted the total inadequacy of cooperative and governmental effort in the realm of credit as compared with the operations of the moneylender. The cooperatives did as little as 3 per cent of the total lending to the farmer.

The reason for this, according to the Committee, went deep into the structure itself. Cooperatives could not operate in conditions of very considerable disparity between the powerful and the not-so-powerful. In terms of the Indian village, this meant that the village official, the landlord, the moneylender, the educated person who had access to urban administration: all these were elements which, while in the village, were yet not of the village. By reason of their affiliation to powerful outside interests, they constituted part of the extraneous world of urban commerce, banking and bureaucracy which, in terms of collaboration, the village found it difficult to understand and, in terms of competition, impossible to withstand. It seemed that no village cooperative could, in the circumstances, flourish elsewhere than on the registers of the Registrar.

The remedy appeared to be that of rendering the cooperative as powerful as, say, a commercial bank, by enabling it to acquire requisite minimum capital and trained personnel. This, however, would not be easy without substantial help from the State. The Rural Credit Survey recommended, among other things, a comprehensive system of State partnership and State assistance as means to an end, the end being the attainment of a viable, effective and self-reliant cooperative structure. Another recommendation, also embodying the concept of State partnership, was that which resulted in the establishment of the State Bank of India on the foundations of the older Imperial Bank. A number of other institutions, such as the Central and State Warehousing Corporations and the National Cooperative Development Corporation – all of which have stood the test of time – also came to be created as a result of the recommendations made by the Committee of the Rural Credit Survey of 1954.

This however raises the whole question of institutionalization for the benefit of the rural masses. On the one hand, such institutionalization at national, State, district and other levels may seem inescapable because otherwise there will be no competition to a powerful, urban-oriented private sector which, at the farmers' level, includes the moneylender, the private trader and the individual vendor of fertilizer and other scarce inputs. On the other hand, to create an institution often means to create a bureaucracy along with it. In this sense, institutionalization is also bureaucratization. Can this be avoided? Is it possible, for example, to bring into being a large body of dedicated people who are as well-trained as they are well-meaning?

Institutionalization may be looked at from another point of view. In Sanskrit and in Telugu, and possibly in other Indian languages, there is an aphoristic verse which embodies sound wisdom when it says 'Live only in that village in which are present: one who lends money in time of need; a doctor who treats in illness; a spring which does not dry up in summer; and pandit who assists at lessons and worship'. These indeed are among the most basic needs which underlie rural welfare. But all the things which the old adage describes in terms of individuals have in modern conditions converted themselves into institutions. Instead of the individual moneylender, what the village needs to have is a cooperative credit society or the branch of a commercial bank. A dispensary is needed in place of a vaid. One looks for piped water supply rather than a running brook. The village pandit is replaced by a school. The very largeness of the canvas on which these services have to operate makes it necessary to substitute institutions for individuals.

To go back to the question I have posed: Is it possible to institutionalize and at the same time not bureaucratize? Eliminate the individual factor without losing the personal element?

This is one of those questions which it is not easy to answer. Or, to put it differently, it is one of those objectives which it is difficult to achieve.

Yet the issue itself is of fundamental importance to a developing country which seeks to ensure that development takes place along the lines of social justice.

There are two other issues which today are as important to us as the question whether we can effect institutionalization without bureaucratization. Both of them intimately concern the welfare of the rural masses.

One is whether we can operate democracy without corruption.

The other is whether we can bring about social justice without violence.

I like to think that these are still not entirely closed questions. That perhaps is an optimistic view. It may well be that the pessimistic view is nearer the facts.

June 1975

Note

* From Say Not the Struggle: Essays in Honour of A.D. Gorwala, OUP, Delhi 1976.

References

1. This contribution has, in the main, been condensed and adapted from two talks given by the author, one at Hyderabad and the other at Visakhapatnam. The former was at a Workshop-cum-Seminar (1971) organized by the National Institute of Community Development. The latter (1973) was in the form of an Endowment Lecture ('Metalapalem Penumatchavari') under the auspices of the Andhra University.
2. Mr. A.D. Gorwala was Chairman of the Committee of Direction of this Survey. Among the members were Prof. D.R. Gadgil and Mr. B. Venkatappiah.

Some Important Writings and Addresses of B. Venkatappiah

Burra Venkatappiah (Chairman), *Report of the Study Team on Financial Administration, Administrative Reforms Commission*, 1967.

Burra Venkatappiah (Chairman) *Report of the All Indian Rural Credit Review Committee Reserve Bank of India*, Bombay, 1969.

Burra Venkatappiah, *Small Farmers Development Agency: Outline of Programme for Action*–Address at 29th Annual Conference of the Indian Society of Agricultural Economics, Waltair, 30 September 1969.

Burra Venkatappiah, *Electricity and Rural India: A Development Approach*, Seventh Lal Bahadur Shastri Memorial Lecture, Indian Agriculture Research Institute, 30.1.1975, New Delhi.

Burra Venkatappiah, Some Thoughts, *Opinion*, Vol. 16(36), 1975.

Burra Venkatappiah Reflections on Rural Development in *Say Not The Struggle: Essays in Honour of A.D. Gorwala*, Oxford University Press, Delhi, 1976.

Burra Venkatappiah, Text of the Inaugural Address delivered at the National Seminar on *'Communication for Development'* at the India International Centre, New Delhi, February 1984.

Burra Venkatappiah, *Study of Feasibility of Forming Small Rural Electric Cooperatives* (and other forms of decentralized organizations) in Andhra Pradesh, 1985 (mimeo).

Index